CONTEMPORARY ISSUES IN SPECIAL EDUCATION

McGraw-Hill Series in Special Education

Robert M. Smith, *Consulting Editor*

CONTEMPORARY ISSUES IN SPECIAL EDUCATION

SECOND EDITION

Rex E. Schmid

Associate Professor of Special Education
University of Florida

Lynn M. Nagata

Graduate Assistant
University of Florida

McGraw-Hill Book Company

New York   St. Louis   San Francisco   Auckland   Bogotá
Hamburg   Johannesburg   London   Madrid   Mexico   Montreal   New Delhi
Panama   Paris   São Paulo   Singapore   Sydney   Tokyo   Toronto

This book was set in Times Roman by The Book Studio Inc.
The editor was Christina Mediate;
the production supervisor was Diane Renda.
Halliday Lithograph Corporation was printer and binder.

CONTEMPORARY ISSUES IN SPECIAL EDUCATION

1 2 3 4 5 6 7 8 9 0   HALHAL   8 9 8 7 6 5 4 3

ISBN 0-07-055331-9

Library of Congress Cataloging in Publication Data
Main entry under title:

Contemporary issues in special education.

    (McGraw-Hill series in special education)
    Includes bibliographies and index.
    1. Handicapped children—Education—United States.
2. Handicapped children—Education—Law and legislation
—United States.   I. Schmid, Rex E.   II. Nagata, Lynn M.
III. Series.
LC4031.C66   1983   371.9   82-18670
ISBN 0-07-055331-9

CONTENTS

PREFACE

As we revised *Contemporary Issues in Special Education,* we were motivated by the same factors that produced the first edition: "training programs for the student in special education are so stocked with general education requirements, management and method courses, and practicum experiences that many related controversies, techniques, and strategies are given, at best, a cursory examination. To the chagrin of the new teacher, however, these are often the very topics of discussion and study in the teachers' lounge, workshop and PTA meeting. This is not to imply that teacher educators feel the topics included in this volume are unimportant—only that under the time constraints of most teacher preparation programs, too much other subject matter must receive a higher priority. Consequently, it too often becomes the student's responsibility to examine independently these ancillary topics." Our goal was to improve the text's format so readers could review the issues more easily.

We elected to alter the format to include comprehensive review of each issue organized to include a definition, history, discussion of theories, and/or techniques and controversies. Supplemental readings from other authors with different viewpoints or opposing positions were also included. This permits the beginning student to gain an overview of the issue without spending the time to locate, review, and analyze all the separate opinions and research in the professional literature. The text also provides a starting point for the advanced student who wishes to research the issue in depth.

Each chapter begins with a list of objectives to focus the student's analysis of the chapter content. The objectives are followed by the overview material and related readings. A series of "enabling activities" provides a study guide and suggests the exploring activities needed by many students. These enabling activities are of three kinds: (1) the cognitive recall, paper and pencil type; (2) the activity, field-experience type; and (3) the demonstration-presentation type.

The issues selected for inclusion in this edition are those that have established themselves and generated controversy and research. We chose not to include issues so new that they might be an artifact of a particular time, social condition, or passing fad. Consequently, speculative issues such as the future of special education, specific treatments, or political issues were ignored. Four issues discussed in the first edition were eliminated: historical perspectives, sex education, the severe and profound child, and parents and families of exceptional children. They were replaced with: behavior modification, affective education, and teacher burnout.

The editors wish to express their appreciation to the authors of the articles reproduced here and their publishers. We also wish to thank our reviewers: Dr. Edward E. Gickling, Harriet Healy, and Dr. Robert Smith for their time and effort in reviewing the initial manuscript and for their excellent comments to improve it. Our special thanks to Christina Mediate, College Division Editor at McGraw-Hill, whose patience, perseverance, and sense of humor made this edition possible.

Rex E. Schmid
Lynn M. Nagata

1

MAINSTREAMING

After reading the selections presented in this chapter and completing the enabling activities, the student should be able to:

1 Prepare and defend a definition of mainstreaming.
2 Prepare a defense for the practice of mainstreaming in the public schools.
3 Briefly describe the historical events that provide the foundation for mainstreaming.
4 List and describe the elements necessary for a successful mainstreaming program.
5 Summarize the findings of the literature related to the efficacy of mainstreaming.
6 Accurately describe the mainstreaming procedures (or lack of) being used in the student's community schools.

Mainstreaming

Kathy Ruhl

Mainstreaming has been and continues to be one of the controversial issues in American education. A portion of the debate may be rooted in the profound implications of mainstreaming's success or failure. An element of emotionalism surrounds the issue, because it touches the lives of exceptional and nonexceptional students, their parents, and teachers. In a decade of financial belt-tightening, the question of mainstreaming's cost effectiveness remains unanswered. Additionally, professionals in education become, justifiably, thoughtful about the delineation of instructional responsibility. Basic teacher competencies become a concern for regular and special teachers, administrators, and teacher preparation personnel. Finally, the long-range impact is perhaps the overriding area of consequence.

The concept of mainstreaming, having been in evidence in one guise or another since 1810 (Gearheart & Weishahn, 1980), became widely popularized within the educational field through the implementation of PL 94-142, the Education for All Handicapped Children Act of 1975. Irrespective of the fact that mainstreaming and the related concepts of "least restrictive environment" and "normalization" have received legislative support, controversy remains. These terms have often been confused and used synonymously (Dybwad, 1980; Scholom, Schiff, Swerdlik, & Knight, 1981). Mention the word "mainstream" in a faculty lounge, at a Parent-Teacher Association Organization meeting, a school administrators' conference, or a seminar on the rights of the handicapped and virtually everyone present will have an emotion-laden opinion. It is questionable, however, whether these and other individuals share a common definition. A telephone interview of over fifty prominent individuals in special education was conducted as a portion of the Council for Exceptional Children's Bicentennial activities to gather a consensus on, among other topics, crucial issues confronting special educators in the mid-seventies. Rated among the top four critical issues in the field was the development of a lucid definition of "least restrictive alternative" and "mainstreaming" (Aiello, 1976).

Reynolds (1962) is possibly the first author to outline the hierarchy of special education services reflected in the numerous services extant today. To assist in arriving at an understanding of the hierarchy and subsequent constructs used in this chapter, portions of Reynolds's text are included.

The variety of programs which comprise special education may be summarized in a chart. At the first level, across the broad base of the chart, is represented the large number of exceptional children, mainly those with minor deviation, who are enrolled in regular classes in the schools. [the least restrictive alternative] . . . The gradual narrowing of the chart indicates the smaller numbers of children involved as programs become more specialized [more restrictive]. (p. 367)

The framework outlined above may be useful in stating a general attitude or policy toward these continuing problems of separation or segregation. The prevailing view is that normal home and school life should be preserved [normalization] if at all possible. When a special placement is necessary to provide suitable care or education, it should be no more "special" than necessary. In terms of the chart, this is to say that children should be moved upward only as far as necessary [kept in the least restrictive alternative that is necessary] and be returned [through the process of mainstreaming] downward [to a lesser restrictive alternative] as soon as feasible (pp. 368–369).

Without ever having used the terms "mainstreaming," "least restrictive alternative," or "normalization," Reynolds paved the way for the future conceptualization of these constructs into processes and outcomes. In the almost two decades since the publication of Reynolds's model, various definitions have evolved. However, certain characteristics remain fairly consistent across usages and thus common definitions may be extrapolated.

Normalization may be understood both in terms of a goal and a process. Normalization involves using methods as normal as possible in order to develop normal behavior and characteristics in those individuals usually exhibiting deviant behaviors. The basic underlying concept is that the experiences of handicapped individuals should be as similar to those of their nonhandicapped peers as is possible (Ysseldyke & Algozzine, 1982). It is a term most commonly used in conjunction with discussions of severe and profound populations.

Least restrictive environment is best thought of as a program placement. This concept, as expressed in PL 94-142, is not intended to mandate placement of every handicapped child in regular classroom settings. Rather, the educational placement of handicapped children should be determined on the basis of individual need in the least restrictive alternative. Placement should not hinder individual freedom any more than absolutely necessary for guaranteeing adequate educational services. In light of an individual child's needs relevant to the handicapping condition, the child should receive services in the setting which is *closest to normal* and *still meets the special needs*. For example, self-contained classes for severely handicapped individuals may be located in regular school settings (as opposed to institutions), where these students may use common facilities such as the cafeteria. The least restrictive environment (ideally) functions as the mechanism through which handicapped individuals experience the normal day-to-day happenings of their nonhandicapped peers (Ysseldyke & Algozzine, 1982).

Mainstreaming, like normalization, may be conceptualized both as a process and a goal. As a goal mainstreaming becomes synonymous with least restrictive alternative, being comprised of incremental steps toward regular classroom placement. Mainstreaming as a process is the act of combining the skills of regular and special educators to assure all children equal educational opportunity and to develop alternative strategies supportive of the provision of appropriate services in the least restrictive setting. Two key points to remember are that mainstreaming: (1) considers the individual educational needs of students rather than the child's label, and (2) is not the wholesale placement of every exceptional child in regular classes (Council for Exceptional Children, 1975). Mainstreaming is the placement of handicapped students in the educational setting which meets their unique needs and which is the closest approximation of the placement experienced by nonhandicapped students.

A BRIEF HISTORY

Mainstreaming was not born on November 19, 1975, when President Gerald Ford signed PL 94-142 into law. Rather mainstreaming was the next logical step in a series of events leading to public policies affirming the equal educational rights of all handicapped children. This educational movement is only part of a broader movement in the United States to end prejudice directed toward the handicapped, and the resultant isolation and neglect. It is a pervasive movement rooted in the fundamental, democratic ideas which are the foundation of this country (Reynolds, 1976).

Events directly associated with education and others separate from it contributed to mainstreaming's evolution. Economic affluence, world wars, litigation, legislation, and scientific advances are some of the factors that affected the mainstreaming movement in the past (Abeson & Zettel, 1977; Reynolds, 1976) and will, most likely, affect it in the future (Iannaccone, 1981).

From earliest history the treatment of handicapped persons has been moulded by prejudice and fear, with the result manifested largely through banishment, isolation, and even death (Gearheart & Weishahn, 1980). Concurrent with the expansion of Christianity during the Middle Ages, other attitudes developed. Depending upon the specific handicap, the era, and the location, exceptional individuals were viewed as less than human, fools, possessed by demons, or witches. It is of interest to note that within the last half of the eighteenth century educational programs for the deaf (1760), the blind (1784), and the retarded (1798) were initiated within the vicinity of Paris, France (Gearheart & Weishahn, 1980).

In the 1800s the trend in the United States, as in Europe, was to isolate handicapped persons in residential schools or asylums (Reynolds, 1976). These schools were not local facilities and served to "protect" the handicapped and nonhandicapped from one another. Near the close of the nineteenth century, Alexander Graham Bell began to urge educators to provide for "special education" annexes in the public schools. Eventually, in response to Bell's suggestions, the National Education Association formed a Department of Special Education just after the turn of the century (Gearheart & Weishahn, 1980).

The first half of the twentieth century was characterized by the growth of local community institutions and special classes. The majority of these programs were based upon the earlier residential schools (some of which continued to operate), due in part to the scarcity of teacher preparation programs. Teachers interested in special populations generally found it necessary to study at the larger, isolated facilities. It was only after the expansion of special services and the enactment and enforcement of compulsory school attendance laws that teachers with specialized skills became widely sought and growth in teacher preparation programs began to gain in momentum (Connor, 1976).

Public school programs during this period consisted primarily of self-contained classes for the retarded. Unrealistic goals and poor identification procedures led to failure and the classes were closed. Eventually, additional attempts were made at educating a variety of handicapped students in categorical, self-contained classes.

The Second World War and the conflict in Korea are generally recognized as landmark motivating forces in the expansion of the number and the quality of services for handicapped children. Veterans with visible and invisible handicaps were in the mainstream of society and these brave and honorable men deserved something better than isolation and abandonment. The public attitude became more sensitive and tolerant. Rehabilitation programs were initiated and research conducted to discover methods to enable these handicapped persons to lead normal lives. The developments and discoveries stemming from this research began to work their way into the schools. Public school programs began to expand. Reynolds (1976) stated that between 1945 and 1970 the number of students receiving public school exceptional children's services increased approximately 700 percent.

The fifties were marked by renewed, vigorous expansion of teacher preparation programs in colleges and universities. Also during this time, programs for special children began to function both in the public schools and universities under one department rather than as individual and independent groups: the departments of special education.

Parents of handicapped children joined together to form interest groups for support and to increase their lobbying power. The National Association for Retarded Children was formed in 1950. A "new" exceptionality was identified during the two decades following World War II and Korea. Learning disabilities was identified as an additional category requiring different specialized services or methods, a catch-all category for those children who did not fit into other categories.

During the first 70 years of the twentieth century the primary focus of services was in self-contained special classes. Then, in the late 1960s, activist parent groups and concerned citizens initiated litigation and began to assail state legislatures in the interest of exceptional children. The earlier school desegregation case (*Brown v. The Board of Education*, 1954) was a precursor to the flurry of legal activity and continues to be a viable force in the early eighties.

Litigation has been concerned with the right to education (*Pennsylvania Association for Retarded Children v. Commonwealth of Pennsylvania*, 1971; *Mills v. Board of Education of District of Columbia*, 1972), incorrect or inappropriate labeling (*Diana v. State Board of Education*, 1973; *Larry P. v. Riles*, 1972), and the extent of responsibility of public school systems (*Armstrong v. Kline,* 1979; *Mahoney v. Administrative School District No. 1,* 1979; *North v. D.C. Board of Education,* 1979). Reynolds (1976) noted that similar trends could be cited in criminology, social services, and mental health areas. The passage and implementation of PL 94-142 and mainstreaming were indeed the next logical step.

THE ISSUES: OUTCOMES AND EFFICACY

The controversy surrounding the concept of mainstreaming did not wane with the mandate of PL 94-142. Implementation only served to mark a concurrent shift in the professional literature from a seeming predominance of opinion articles to a greater number of data-based studies on the topic. Concern as to the effects on handicapped students of special class placement versus education in regular classes was not new. Expressions of concern were evident at least as early as 1905 by Binet and Simon (Bruninks & Rynders, in Meyen, Vergason, & Whelan, 1975). The issue was periodically evident to a minor extent up to Dunn's 1968 landmark article, which sparked heated discussion. The professional literature was filled with articles expressing philosophical opinions and occasionally presenting supportive research relevant to the issue. The inappropriateness of self-contained classes as the primary locus of special education services and accompanying support for mainstreaming was noted by a number of authors (Birch, 1974; Christopolos, 1973; Deno, 1970; Dunn, 1968, Johnson, 1962; Lilly, 1970; MacMillian, 1971; Rapier, Adelson, Carey, & Croke, 1972). Conversely, other educators and investigators continued to support the traditional self-contained special class, refusing to climb aboard the mainstreaming bandwagon (Kolstoe, 1972; McKinnon, 1970; Roos, 1970; Smith & Arkans, 1974; Vacc, 1968; Warner, Thrapp, & Walsh, 1973).

A brief review of the literature published in the early seventies indicates that the majority of the controversy centered around the projected results of mainstreaming and its effect on both handicapped and nonhandicapped students. The three positive outcomes of mainstreaming most commonly cited fall into two areas: cognitive and social-affective skills. The latter is relevant to anticipated outcomes for both handicapped and nonhandicapped students. The outcomes most frequently discussed were:

1 Mainstreamed handicapped children will perform *academically* at least as well as, and possibly better than, their handicapped peers in special classes. (Cognitive skills)

2 Mainstreamed handicapped children will perform in *social skills* and in *self-esteem*; and *adjust* better in adulthood than their self-contained peers. (Social-affective skills)

3 Nonhandicapped students will become *more accepting* and *tolerant* of mainstreamed handicapped individuals. (Social-affective skills)

These prospective outcomes of mainstreaming and the anticipated opposite results expounded by less optimistic individuals are still current today (Burton

& Hirshoren, 1979a and b; Clark, 1978; Cruickshank, 1977; Diamond, 1979; Ensher, 1980; Sontag, Certo, & Button, 1979; Vernon, 1981). The three major arguments for mainstreaming are:

1. *Mainstreamed handicapped children will perform academically at least as well, and possibly better than, their handicapped peers in special classes.* Early efficacy studies of regular versus special class placement resulted in academic achievement data which favored regular class placement. Gottlieb (1981) noted that the disenchantment with special class placement expressed by Dunn (1968) and other professionals was a result of the failure of early researchers to obtain results substantiating the superiority of special classes. Ten efficacy studies conducted between 1932 and 1965 were reviewed by Gottlieb (1981). He reports that five of these studies culminated in results indicating no significant achievement differences between students in special and regular classes. None of the remaining five studies resulted in data favorable to special, self-contained settings. This being the case, it would be difficult to justify the continuance of a mode of services that was apparently inferior to the regular classroom, particularly in view of the cost-effectiveness factor. Dunn's assumption was that education in the mainstream, at least for the mildly handicapped, would have academic results equal to or better than those obtained in special settings. Opponents of mainstreaming began to examine the early efficacy research critically and their findings (Guskin & Spicker, 1968; MacMillan, 1971) indicated the existence of numerous methodological flaws. Consequently, mainstreaming's opponents argued that the efficacy issue was as yet unresolved and special classes were still the educational locus of choice.

Dunn (1968) limited his comments to public elementary schools, which he believed to be progressively more capable of coping with individual differences than in the past. He attributed this new competence to numerous trends and developments in instructional practices, assessment, organizational patterns, and curricular innovations. Clark (1978), aware of Dunn's own self-imposed limitations, attempted to project the effects of mainstreaming to the secondary school. Recognizing the comparative rigidity of the secondary school and the gap in skills between handicapped and nonhandicapped adolescents, Clark emphasized the data being used to support mainstreaming was taken from elementary school populations and should not be generalized to the secondary school.

Academic skill development is the first objective of education. However, interest in the development of social-affective skills is also seen as valid even when not directly taught. Barclay & Kehle (1979) noted that results of research involving large numbers of students and classrooms clearly indicated a substantial portion of the variance attributed to academic achievement may be explained by social-interaction variables.

2. *Mainstreamed handicapped children will improve in social skills and in self-esteem; and adjust better in adulthood than their self-contained peers.* One of the underlying assumptions made by supporters of mainstreaming is that physical placement of exceptional children in regular classes will result in the development of more appropriate social skills as the result of the presence of

better models. It has been anticipated that the handicapped child will imitate the acceptable behaviors, social and academic, of nonhandicapped classmates (Gresham, 1982).

Another underlying assumption is that mainstreaming will result in delabeling. If this is true, an increase in self-esteem for the handicapped may be projected. Dunn (1968) saw a connection between labeling, stigmatization, and low self-esteem. He stated that specifically the EMR label, coupled with self-contained class placement, resulted in stigmatizing the handicapped student. If this were true, the delabeling (among other side-effects) accompanying mainstreaming would result in increased self-esteem for those affected. Unfortunately, special educators in the early 70s who shared Dunn's views did not yet have information compiled on the effects of stigma (MacMillan, Jones, & Aloia, 1974). Had this data been available, perhaps they would have arrived at the conclusion (McKinnon, 1970; Vacc, 1968) that the self-esteem of handicapped students educated in special classes was and would be higher than that of their mainstreamed counterparts.

Mainstreaming's supporters suggest that higher self-esteem and early confrontation with life's realities can only lead to better adjustment in adult life. If asked, they would probably reply that self-contained classes isolate but do not protect the handicapped from the ultimate confrontation with growing up and that it is ultimately better to learn to live in the nonhandicapped world at an early age. Opponents on the other hand, seem to be of the mind that the handicapped must first acquire the academic and social skills appropriate for use in the real world prior to being pushed out into the mainstream (Clark, 1978; Gresham, 1982), even if that means remaining in self-contained classes through the completion of high school.

It is difficult to separate the overall effects for the handicapped from the nonhandicapped social-affective area. Clearly, there is a relation between the handicapped students' perceptions of self and the manner in which they are treated by nonhandicapped peers. Consequently, the attitudes expressed by nonhandicapped students become an important outcome to consider.

3. *Nonhandicapped students will become more accepting and tolerant of handicapped individuals, especially those who are mainstreamed.* Christopolos and Renz (1969) expressed the hope that frequent interaction in the regular classroom between exceptional and regular students would result in increased social interaction and familiarity. Increased familiarity would in turn lead to improved social status for handicapped students among the entire school population. An increased social acceptance of handicapped students by their nonhandicapped classmates would result in the previously mentioned increased self-esteem.

That greater tolerance and acceptance of handicapped students will be an outcome has been questioned by Clark (1978) and Gottlieb (1981), both of whom cite earlier studies relevant to this issue. The conclusions drawn from studies

by Baldwin (1958) and Johnson (1950) indicate that negative observer perceptions of individuals or groups are the natural consequence of their socially deviant or unacceptable behavior. Educational labels, grouping, or placement have
little or no effect in this area. Contrary to the positive outcomes anticipated by
Christopolos and Renz (1969), Clark (1978) and Gottleib (1981) expressed concern that mainstreaming may have serious damaging repercussions in the form
of greater rejection by nonhandicapped peers and decreased self-esteem in the
handicapped. Clark (1978) observed that it was the original placement of EMRs
in regular school classes that resulted in this group's frustrations. These frustrations were manifested in inappropriate behavior, which in turn led to special
class placement in a setting more conducive to alleviating anxieties, fostering success, and supporting self-esteem. Now, the converse is considered by
some to be true. Special education has truly come full circle and what previously was identified as a root of the problem is seen by some as the basis for a
solution.

EFFICACY OF MAINSTREAMING

Research on the efficacy of mainstream versus special class placement can be
traced back as far as 1932 (see Table 1), when Bennett studied elementary EMR
students. Individuals unfamiliar with the demands of good research in general
and the difficulties of educational research in particular may not immediately
understand why 50 years of research into an issue's efficacy have not resulted
in definitive answers. However, this is the situation with the question of the
worthwhileness of mainstreaming. Conclusive statements as to actual efficacy
in any of the three areas of mainstreaming outcome are not currently possible
due to the contradictory results of the research (Barclay & Kehle, 1979;
Carlberg & Kavale, 1980; Gottlieb, 1981; Keogh & Levitt, 1976).

Contributing to this state of affairs are methodological weaknesses in numerous studies (Carlberg & Kavale, 1980). Jones, Gottlieb, Guskin, and Yoshida
(1978) cite many research-related difficulties. Among these difficulties are: (1)
the choice of models for research design; (2) issues particular to evaluation of
educational interventions; and (3) problems in measuring dependent variables.
Problems recognized as relevant to the selection of research designs included
large versus small group, experimental versus ex post facto, and a failure to
consider critical factors in the design consistently. Instructional time, integration within the regular class, unclear goals and objectives, teacher attitude, and
methods for monitoring individual student progress were areas of concern pertinent to evaluation of educational interventions. Finally, problems related to
the measurement of dependent variables such as attitudes, acceptance, adjustment, and cost effectiveness were included for discussion. Noting these and
other concerns (Carlberg & Kavale, 1980; MacMillan, 1971), it is easier to grasp
the difficulties surrounding efficacy studies on mainstreaming and the lack
of definitive evidence either in support of this concept or against it. The
lack of conclusive evidence is not for want of trying, however, as numerous

researchers have attempted to answer the mainstreaming efficacy question (see Table 1).

Anderson, Martinez, and Rich (1980) suggest that degree of handicap plays a role in whether or not mainstreaming is effective, while others believe that age (Clark, 1978; Scholom, Schiff, Swerdlik, & Knight, 1981) and category of exceptionality (Carlberg & Kavale, 1980) are significant. Each of these researchers and others have attempted, in spite of related difficulties, to make a conclusive statement on some area of the efficacy question.

Mainstreamed handicapped children will perform academically at least as well, and possibly better than, their handicapped peers in special classes. Only one efficacy study dealing with the academic issue and conducted between 1932 and 1958 (Blatt, 1958) reported research supportive of the academic superiority of the special class over the regular class. However, it could be argued that special education, having grown substantially (in numbers of students served, teacher preparation programs, new teaching strategies and materials), deserves another chance to prove itself at the hands of the researcher, and continual study of the question seems warranted. Of course, the methodological flaws of many of the earlier efficacy studies add support to continuation of research.

Research reported after 1958 up to the present has been reviewed extensively. Overall, research on EMR populations reveals minor differences on achievement test scores of mainstreamed and self-contained placements; EMR students read at a level lower than would be suggested by their mental age in either setting; and no mainstreaming studies to 1979 reported grade-equivalent mean scores higher than 3.8 for EMR children. If this data is indicative of education's (special or regular) appropriateness for EMR children, then the appropriate education has yet to be developed (Gottlieb, 1981). One could quite possibly say the same for other categories of exceptionality.

Mainstreamed handicapped children will improve in social skills and in self-esteem; and adjust better in adulthood than their self-contained peers. Again, conflicting data exist on this issue. Gresham (1982), while discussing social skills, makes the point that contrary to the opinion of some professionals, modeling is not a natural skill and mainstreaming efforts are doomed to failure unless social skills training is undertaken prior to placement in regular classes. He states that many handicapped students lack imitative skills. It is possible that a relationship exists between category of exceptionality, age of student, and social skill level so that Gresham's (1982) remarks must be interpreted with a consideration for this potential.

Self-esteem studies have reported conflicting results (Gottlieb, 1981). According to Gottlieb, consistent data is available, however, which indicate that handicapped students who receive instruction in both mainstreamed and segregated settings have significantly higher self-esteem scores than their self-contained peers. One possible explanation for this is that these partially integrated students have their mainstream peers as a reference group for "normalcy" and their other, special class peers as a reference group for capability (Gottlieb, 1981).

Adequate adjustment to adult life is a concern for all educators and one of the primary purposes of special education. Certainly one measure of the success of mainstreaming is how well former mainstreamed versus self-contained special education students function as independent adults. Only three studies have been reported in the literature. Again, conflicting results are presented. Two studies (Porter & Milazzo, 1958; Stephens & Peck, 1968) resulted in evidence suggesting that adjustment in adult life is enhanced by secondary special class programs. Contrary results were reported by Skodak (1970), who indicated that enrollment in mainstream programs appeared to benefit life adjustment significantly for former special education students. Obviously, this is an area demanding additional research. *CONC.*

Social skill acquisition, self-concept, and adjustment in later life cannot be completely severed from nonhandicapped peer acceptance and interaction. Several investigators have attempted, however, to measure these elements and resolve the controversy surrounding mainstreaming's third potential outcome.

Nonhandicapped students will become more accepting and tolerant of mainstreamed handicapped individuals. Christopolos & Renz's (1969) and Peterson and Haralick's (1977) suggestion that mainstreaming would, as a natural consequence, result in an increase in social interactions between nonhandicapped and handicapped students does not appear to be supported by research (Gresham, 1982). Gresham (1982) reports that research results do not warrant such optimism—social interactions decrease with mainstreaming. It is entirely possible that Gottlieb's (1981) and Clark's (1978) concern that increased exposure highlights the unusual and/or inappropriate behaviors of some handicapped individuals, serving only to lessen the number and quality of handicapped-nonhandicapped peer interactions, may have supportive evidence. However, Carlberg and Kavale (1980) again raise the consideration that contradictory results are available and just about any conclusion may be drawn. The sociometric status of handicapped students in regular and self-contained classrooms appears to be another unresolved issue.

Adding to the controversy are arguments pertaining to mainstreaming's efficacy for distinct handicapped populations (Burton & Hirshoren, 1979; Carlberg & Kavale, 1980; Sontag, Certo, & Button, 1979) considering factors such as age, category, and degree of handicap. For example, Anderson, Martinez, and Rich (1980) indicated their belief in the existence of two specific questions capable of being supported with theory and research results. One question is that of mainstreaming's effectiveness for severely handicapped individuals. The second is the question of efficacy of mainstreaming mild to moderately handicapped populations. It is their contention that the evidence suggests that severely handicapped children have not benefited from placement in regular class settings and, in fact, have performed less well. Conversely, mildly handicapped

TABLE 1
REPORTED RESULTS OF MAINSTREAMING EFFICACY STUDIES
(Comparing Performance of Mainstream vs. Special Class Placement)

Study	Supports (Mainstreaming)	Refutes	Category	Cognitive — Academic	Social Affective — Handicapped/Self-esteem & behavior	Social Affective — Nonhandicapped/attitudes	Other
†Bennett, 1932	X		EMR	Higher achievement in the mainstream.			
†Pertoch, 1936	X		EMR	Higher achievement in the mainstream.			
†Johnson, 1950		X	EMR			Totally mainstreamed EMRs rejected significantly more frequently than would be expected by chance.	
†Heber, 1956		X	EMR			Totally mainstreamed EMRs rejected significantly more frequently than would be expected by chance.	
*Carriker, 1957		X	EMR		Made greater gains in social and/or emotional adjustment in special classes.		
*Ellenbogen, 1957	X		EMR	Greater gains in mainstream.	Made greater gains in social and/or emotional adjustment in special classes.		
*Baldwin, 1958	X		EMR	Greater gains in mainstream.			
*Blatt, 1958		X	EMR	Greater gains in special class.			
*Porter & Milazzo, 1958		X	EMR		Made greater gains in social and/or emotional adjustment in special classes.		

Study			Category	Academic Finding	Social/Emotional Finding
*Ainsworth, 1959	X		EMR	Greater gains in mainstream class.	
*Cassidy & Stanton, 1959	X		EMR	Greater gains in mainstream class.	
*Jordan & DeCharms, 1959	X−	−	EMR	Greater gains in mainstream class.	No differences in sociometric dimensions between settings.
*Schell, 1959		X	EMR		Made greater gains in social and/or emotional adjustment in special classes.
*Thurstone, 1959	X	X	EMR	Greater gains in mainstream class.	Made greater gains in social and/or emotional adjustment in special classes.
*Wrightstone, Forlano, Lepkowski, Sontag, & Edelstein, 1959		X	EMR	Greater gains in special class.	
*Jordan, 1960	−	−	EMR		No differences in sociometric dimensions between settings.
*Mullen & Itkin, 1961	X		EMR	Higher achievement in mainstream.	
*Brown, 1962	X		EMR	Greater gains in mainstream class.	
*Kern & Pfaeffle, 1962	X	X	EMR	Greater gains in mainstream class.	Made greater gains in social and/or emotional adjustment in special classes.
*Bacher, 1965	X		EMR	Greater gains in mainstream class.	
*Goldstein, Moss, & Jordan, 1965	X		EMR	Greater gains in mainstream class.	Better behavioral adjustment in mainstream.
*Mayer, 1966	X−	−	EMR	Greater gains in mainstream class.	No differences in sociometric dimensions between settings.
*Rubin, Simson, & Betwee, 1966	−	−	BD/ED		No differences in academic, behavioral, or sociometric dimensions between settings.

TABLE 1 (continued)

Study	Supports Refutes (Mainstreaming)	Category	Cognitive Academic	Social Affective Handicapped/Self-esteem & behavior	Social Affective Nonhandicapped/ attitudes	Other
†Carroll, 1967	X	EMR		Partially mainstreamed subjects had significantly higher self-concepts than self-contained subjects.		
*Hoeltke, 1967	X	EMR	Greater gains in mainstream class.	Better behavioral adjustment in mainstream.		
†Knight, 1967	–	EMR		No differences between settings in self-concept.		
†Schurr & Brookover, 1967	X	EMR		Self-concepts higher in special classes.		
*Smith & Kennedy, 1967	X	EMR	Greater gains in mainstream class.			
*Budoff, Meskin, & Kemler, 1968	X	EMR	Greater gains in special class.			
*Vacc, 1968	X	BD/ED		Positive effects for special classes in general.		
*Cawley & Goodman, 1969	X	EMR	Greater gains in special class.			
†Skodak, 1970	X	EMR		Significantly better life adjustment for adults who were formally mainstreamed.		
*Strauch, 1970	–	EMR		No differences in sociometric dimensions between settings		

Study			Category	Finding 1	Finding 2
†Rodee, 1971	X	—	EMR	Higher scores on standardized reading test for mainstreamed subjects.	No difference between settings for standardized math test scores.
*Sabatino, 1971		—	LD	No differences between settings.	No differences in perceptual motor functioning.
*Spollen & Ballif, 1971		—	LD	No differences between settings.	No differences in perceptual motor functioning.
*Bersoff, Kabler, Fiscus, & Ankney, 1972		—	LD	No differences between settings	No differences in perceptual motor functioning.
‡Gampell, Harrison, & Budoff, 1972		X	EMR	Mainstreamed subjects interacted with classroom nonhandicapped peers and teachers less often than did self-contained subjects.	Low incidence of negative behavior by handicapped subjects across settings.
*Goodman, Gottlieb, & Harrison, 1972		X	EMR	Made greater gains in social and/or emotional adjustment in special classes.	
*Quay, Glavin, Annesley, & Werry, 1972	X		BD/ED	Positive effects for mainstreaming in general.	

TABLE 1 (continued)

Study	Supports Refutes (Mainstreaming)	Category	Cognitive Academic	Social Affective — Handicapped/Self-esteem & behavior	Social Affective — Nonhandicapped/attitudes	Other
†Shotel, Iano, & McGettigan, 1972	X				Fulltime special class placement resulted in higher sociometric standing among nonhandicapped students than that of partially mainstreamed students.	
*Vacc, 1972	–	BD/ED	No differences in academic, behavioral, or sociometric dimensions between settings.			
†Walker, 1972	X		Higher score on standardized reading test for mainstreamed subjects.			No differences between settings for standardized math test scores.
‡Gampel, Gottlieb, & Harrison, 1973	X	EMR		Mainstreamed EMR behaved similarly to non-EMR control groups, displaying fewer negative behaviors than the special class EMRs.		
*Gottlieb & Budoff, 1973	X	EMR		Made greater gains in social and/or emotional adjustment in special classes.		
*Flynn, 1974	–	EMR		No differences in sociometric dimensions between settings.		
*Gampel, Gottlieb, & Harrison, 1974	X	EMR		Better behavioral adjustment in mainstream.		

Study				Findings	
*Glavin, 1974	−		BD/ED	No differences in academic, behavioral, or sociometric dimensions between settings.	
*Guerin & Szatlocky, 1974	−		EMR	No difference in sociometric dimensions between settings.	
*Iano, Ayers, Heller, McGettigan, & Walker, 1974	−		EMR	No difference in sociometric dimensions between settings.	
*Lewis, 1974		X	EMR	Made greater gains in social and/or emotional adjustment in special classes.	
*Rouse, 1974	X		EMR	Greater gains in mainstream class.	
§Sheare, 1974	X		EMR	Nonhandicapped students attending integrated classes gave more positive ratings to EMR adolescents than did nonhandicapped students in segregated classes.	Females rated more positively than males.
*Walker, 1974		X	EMR	Made greater gains in social and/or emotional adjustment in special classes.	
*Gottlieb, Gampel, & Budoff, 1975	X		EMR	Better behavioral adjustment in mainstream.	
*Haring & Krug, 1975	X		EMR	Better behavioral adjustment in mainstream.	
*Budoff & Gottlieb, 1976	X		EMR	Better behavioral adjustment in mainstream.	
*Gerke, 1976		X	EMR	Made greater gains in social and/or emotional adjustment in special classes.	

TABLE 1 (continued)

Study	Supports Refutes (Mainstreaming)		Cate-gory	Cognitive	Social Affective		Other
				Academic	Handicapped/Self-esteem & behavior	Nonhandicapped/attitudes	
*Meyers, 1976	X		EMR	Greater gains in mainstream class.	Made greater gains in social and/or emotional adjustment in special classes.		
§Iano, Ayers, Heller, McGettigan, & Walker, 1977	X		EMR			Self-contained handicapped subjects were better accepted by nonhandicapped peers than mainstreamed, handicapped subjects.	
†Gottlieb, Semmel, & Veldman, 1978	X		EMR			Fulltime special class placement resulted in higher sociometric standing among nonhandicapped students than that of partially mainstreamed students.	
†Strang, Smith, & Rogers, 1978	X		EMR		Partially mainstreamed subjects had significantly higher self-concepts than self-contained subjects.		

– Study neither supported nor refuted mainstreaming
BD/ED Behavior Disordered/Emotionally Disturbed
LD Learning Disabled
EMR Educable Mentally Retarded
* Information from Carlberg & Kavale, 1980
† Information from Gottlieb, 1981
‡ Information from Gottlieb, Gampel, & Budoff, 1975
§ Information from Gresham, 1982

populations have fared about equally as well academically in the regular class as they did in special classes, but self-concept and social development improved with regular class placement (Anderson et al., 1980). Glass (1981) reported the results of the work of Carlberg's (1979) meta-analysis techniques to gain results from fifty efficacy experiments. These studies encompassed 27,000 students with the average IQ being 74 and average age being 11 years. The results indicated that when existing research is statistically integrated, placement in a special class is an inferior choice to placement in the regular class.

The efficacy issue becomes more clouded when the variable of age of the handicapped student is considered. Scholom, Schiff, Swerdlik, and Knight (1981) reported the results of a 3-year study of learning disabled students across self-contained and mainstreamed settings. Their results supported self-contained placement for younger learning disabled students. However, they also implied that as children approach adolescence identity issues and the influence of the peer group assume greater significance, and mainstreaming may be the best alternative. Clark (1978) cautioned against the wholesale mainstreaming of secondary level educable mentally retarded while maintaining that his position "in no way defends the inadequacies of the present special class model" (p. 5). Carlberg and Kavale (1980), evaluating the results of Carlberg's earlier study (1979), concluded:

> Regardless of whether achievement, personality/social, or other dependent variables were chosen for investigation, no differential placement effects emerged across studies. Similarly, variables such as IQ, age, percent of male subjects, duration of treatment, sample size, blindedness of measures, internal validity, and date of publication had little effect on the relative superiority of regular class placement to special class placement.
>
> Category of exceptionality, however, revealed differential placement effects. The obtained ES (Effect Size) suggested that the problems of LD or BD/ED (Learning Disabled or Behavior Disordered/Emotionally Disturbed) children were apparently more tractable in the special class than children whose primary problem was low IQ. Thus SLs (Slow Learners) and EMRs (Educable Mentally Retarded) experience negative consequences because of special class placement while positive effects from special class placement were found for LD and BD/ED children (p. 304).

IMPLICATIONS FOR THE PRACTITIONER

Few individuals will argue with the underlying moral reasons for mainstreaming. It would be difficult to find individuals who did not respect the attempts by the courts and governing bodies (state and national) to ensure equal educational opportunities for all America's children. The trouble begins when attempts are made to translate the idea into practice. Obviously, the effects of mainstreaming have been dramatic, sudden, and emotionally powered. Arguments among researchers, politicians, parents, and professionals persist, but the reality is that education in the least restrictive environment is law and implementation has been underway for more than half a decade. The task of implementation falls to the school district, through the administrators to the teachers. The impact has been both subtle and intense.

Service delivery models have shifted emphasis to more resource rooms and "pull-out" models (Glickling & Theobald, 1975). The content of the professional literature is filled with articles about resources rooms. Some (Freeman, Gavron, & Williams, 1981) contend that the three R's are taught in settings similar to those in use before PL 94-142 and that only art, physical education, and lunch are appropriate for mainstreaming. Graham and Harris (1980) claim that classes for the mild to moderately impaired have virtually disappeared. The consequence of this is that many students formerly served in these units have been "mainstreamed," have failed, and have been placed in classes once designated for the more severely handicapped. Vernon (1981) believes students have been "dumped" into regular classes and all too commonly left without support services. Add this to the noncategorical movement (Lilly, 1977) and special education is almost where it was at the beginning of the twentieth century.

Regular teachers are daily confronted with full or partial provision of educational programming for handicapped students. They must individualize instruction, establish cooperative learning environments, adjust braces, possess at least a rudimentary knowledge of signing, schedule time for IEP meetings, schedule time for special students to receive support services, and an infinite number of daily, but ultimately significant mainstreaming-related tasks. It is not surprising that many have felt unprepared to cope (Hirshoren & Burton, 1979; Middleton, Morsink, & Cohen, 1979) and teacher trainers have been busy attempting to fill the need.

Special educators are also being cast in the role of consultant (Salend, 1980) and diagnostician. They are asked to provide supportive services to children rather than direct services (Clark, 1978) and function as colleagues to regular educators. Administrators must facilitate this change in role and encourage integration and cooperation among faculty (Salend, 1980). Additional time must be spent coping with special transportation needs, adjusting schedules, and the size of classes. Discipline of special education students is a sensitive issue (Flygare, 1981) and administrators must proceed carefully.

The problems of practical implementation may be solved if the answers to two questions can be found:

1 How is the least restrictive environment determined? Which setting, combined with which teaching method and style, works best for which child with what needs? (Hannah & Parker, 1980; Heron & Skinner, 1981; Meyen & Lehr, 1980)

2 How is the transition from special to regular class optimally facilitated? (Dodd, 1980; Graham & Harris, 1980; Kesselman-Turkel, & Peterson, 1981)

THE STATE OF THE ART AND THE FUTURE

It is probable if not provable, that the individuals initiating the concept of main-streaming three-quarters of a century ago had little notion of the duration of the ensuing debate. Today, mainstreaming gives rise to a number of interrelated concerns. For example, the lack of a clear, concise definition of the concept is one of the many problems associated with conducting research on its effective-ness. The lack of unquestionable, conclusive evidence as to mainstreaming's efficacy, coupled with the practical impact on education, contributes to a sense of uncertainty about mainstreaming's future.

It may be surprising to some persons to discover that even though a common definition of mainstreaming has yet to evolve, and its effects remain undeter-mined, some have attempted to predict its future course. Ensher (1980) ex-pounded the contemporary success of mainstreaming and predicted that "mainstreaming as a slogan will disappear, while in practice its pedagogy will be routine within school and community" (p. 492).

Opposing opinions have been expressed by others (Reichart, 1981; Winschel, 1980; Ysseldyke & Algozzine, 1982). Winschel (1980) hypothesized that main-streaming is only a fad, likening it to hula hoops and progressive education. The impact of a troubled society on regular education combined with the growing disillusionment of those individuals working with handicapped students drown-ing in the mainstream is the reason offered by Winschel for the eventual failure of the ideal. Reichart (1981) and Ysseldyke and Algozzine (1982) support main-streaming as an ideal while indicating their belief that it will succumb to various unavoidable realities. Ysseldyke and Algozzine believe that the realities, "teacher attitudes and expectancies, as well as several dimensions of public policy, impede the full implementation of the innovative concepts of normaliza-tion, mainstreaming, and least restrictive environment embodied in the law" (p. 246). The concern for teacher attitudes and expectations is exemplified by the work of Corder (1981) and Hudson, Graham, and Warner (1979). Ysseldyke and Algozzine (1981) and Reichart (1981) agree, however, that perhaps of greater significance is the role that changing public policy will play in the future of special and regular education.

If one perceives PL 94-142 and mainstreaming as instruments of social re-form and reflections of societal attitudes, then mainstreaming is most likely doomed. The emergence of new social perspectives, economic considerations and the Reagan administration's social and budgetary policies signal a full-cy-cle return to the conservative politics of the past (Iannaccone, 1981; Reichart, 1981; Ysseldyke & Algozzine, 1982). Iannaccone (1981) predicted that special education would suffer, not so much from direct attacks as from federal-level "benign neglect." The probability of less federal intervention, whether in the form of decreased monies or monitoring, or both, raises the question of how many schools will, out of conscience or conviction, continue to invest in an ill-defined practice, whose cost and efficacy remain undetermined. Perhaps, as Reichart (1981) suggests, the concern will be more open:

> . . . "Those handicapped who can "make" it—fine, and those who have difficulties—too bad." The burden will again be upon the handicapped individual and his or her family. Services "required" of the school will be given, but these are not times of gentleness we are moving toward. They may well be times wherein the wheelchair in the regular classroom, those unfamiliar crutches, the uncomfortable need to change a prosthesis, the self-conscious need for toilet aid, for a place to rest, for someone to help with the colostomy bag may not seem viable as options in the midst of teacher cuts, salary freezes and the abolition of "sacred cow" programs. (p. 105)

It may be too much to hope that persons in position of power and responsibility in individual schools and some public school systems recognize that mainstreaming is not an all-or-nothing proposition. One classroom model, one cascade of services, one placement is not superior to any other. Optimistically, some individuals will have the wisdom to understand and to act upon the idea that a particular environment may be more supportive of a particular child than another environment in the effort to provide adequate educational services.

REFERENCES

Abeson, A., & Zettel, J. The end of the quiet revolution: The Education for All Handicapped Children Act of 1975. *Exceptional Children*, 1977, *44*, 114–128.

Aiello, B. Especially for special educators: A sense of our own history. *Exceptional Children*, 1976, *42*, 244–251.

Anderson, R. M., Martinez, D. H., & Rich, H. L. Perspectives for change. In J. W. Schifani, R. M. Anderson, & S. J. Odle (Eds.), *Implementing Learning in the Least Restrictive Environment—Handicapped Children in the Mainstream*. Baltimore: University Park Press, 1980.

Baldwin, W. D. The social position of the educable mentally retarded in the regular grades in the public schools. *Exceptional Children*, 1958, *25*, 106–108.

Barclay, J. R., & Kehle, T. J. The impact of handicapped students on other students in the classroom. *Journal of Research and Development in Education*, 1979, *12*, 80–92.

Bennett, A. *A Comparative Student of Subnormal Children in the Elementary Grades*. New York: Teachers College, Bureau of Publications, 1932.

Birch, J. W. *Mainstreaming: Educable Mentally Retarded Children in Regular Classes*. Reston, VA: Council for Exceptional Children, 1974.

Blatt, B. The physical, personality, and academic status of children who are mentally retarded attending special classes as compared with children who are mentally retarded attending regular classes. *American Journal of Mental Deficiency*, 1958, *62*, 810–818.

Bruninks, R., & Rynders, J. Alternatives to special class placement for educable mentally retarded children. In E. Meyen, G. Vergason, & R. Whelan (Eds.), *Alternatives for Teaching Exceptional Children*. Denver: Love Publishing Company, 1975.

Burton, T. A., & Hirshoren, A. The education of severe and profoundly retarded children: Are we sacrificing the child to the concept? *Exceptional Children* , 1979, *45*, 598–602. (a)

Burton, T. A., & Hirshoren, A. Some further thoughts and clarifications on the education of severely and profoundly retarded children. *Exceptional Children*, 1979, *45*, 618–625. (b)

Carlberg, C., & Kavale, K. The efficacy of special versus regular class placement for exceptional children: A meta-analysis. *Journal of Special Education*, 1980, *14*, 295–306.

Christopolos, F. Keeping exceptional children in regular classes. *Exceptional Children*, 1973, *39*, 569–572.

Christopolos, F., & Renz, P. A critical examination of special education programs. *Journal of Special Education*, 1969, *3*, 371–379.

Clark, G. Mainstreaming for the secondary educable mentally retarded: Is it defensible? *Focus on Exceptional Children*, 1978, *7*, 1–5.

Connor, F. P. The past is prologue: Teacher preparation in special education. *Exceptional Children*, 1976, *42*, 366–378.

Corder, B. Secondary teacher's perceptions toward the handicapped. *American Secondary Education*, 1981, *11*, 29–31.

Council for Exceptional Children. What is mainstreaming? *Exceptional Children*, 1975, *42*, 174.

Cruickshank, W. Least restrictive placement: Administrative wishful thinking. *Journal of Learning Disabilities*, 1977, *10*, 193–194.

Deno, E. Special education as developmental capital. *Exceptional Children*, 1970, *37*, 229–237.

Diamond, B. Myths of mainstreaming. *Journal of Learning Disabilities*, 1979, *12*, 246–250.

Dodd, J. Mainstreaming, *English Journal*, 1980, *69*, 51–55.

Dunn, L. Special education for mildly retarded: Is much of it justifiable? *Exceptional Children*, 1968, *35*, 5–22.

Dybwad, G. Avoiding misconceptions of mainstreaming, the least restrictive environment, and normalization. *Exceptional Children*, 1980, *47*, 85–88.

Ensher, G. L. Mainstreaming: The image of change. In J. W. Schifani, R. M. Anderson, & S. J. Odle (Eds.), *Implementing Learning in the Least Restrictive Environment—Handicapped Children in the Mainstream*. Baltimore: University Park Press, 1980.

Flygare, J. Disciplining special education students. *Phi Delta Kappan*, 1981, *62*, 670–671.

Freeman, R. N., Gavron, S. J., & Williams, E. U. Public Law 94-142: Promises to keep. *Educational Horizons*, 1981, *59*, 107–112.

Gearheart, B. R., & Weishahn, M. W. *The Handicapped Student in the Regular Classroom*. St. Louis, MO: C. V. Mosby Company, 1980.

Gickling, E. E., & Theobald, J. T. Mainstreaming: Affect or effect. *Journal of Special Education*, 1975, *9*, 317–328.

Glass, G. V. *Effectiveness of special education*. Paper presented at the Working Conference of Social Policy and Educational Leaders to Develop Strategies for Special Education in the 1980's, Wingspread, Racine, WI, September 1981.

Gottlieb, J. Mainstreaming: Fulfilling the promise? *American Journal of Mental Deficiency*, 1981, *86*, 115–126.

Gottlieb, J., Gampel, D. H., & Budoff, M. Classroom behavior of retarded children before and after integration into regular classes, *Journal of Special Education*, 1975, *9*, 307–315.

Graham, S., & Harris, K. R. The least restrictive alternative: An educational dilemma. *Educational Unlimited*, 1980, *2*, 12–14.

Gresham, F. M. Misguided mainstreaming: The case for social skills training with handicapped children. *Exceptional Children*, 1982, *48*, 422–433.

Guskin, S. L., & Spicker, H. H. Educational research in mental retardation. In N. R. Ellis (Ed.), *International Review of Research in Mental Retardation (Vol. 3)*. New York: Academic Press, 1968.

Hannah, E. P., & Parker, R. M. Mainstreaming vs. the special setting. *Academic Therapy*, 1980, *15*, 271–277.

Heron, T. E., & Skinner, M. E. Criteria for defining the regular classroom as the least restrictive environment for LD students. *Learning Disability Quarterly*, Spring 1981, *4*, 115–120.

Hirshoren, A., & Burton, T. Willingness of regular teachers to participate in mainstreaming handicapped children. *Journal of Research and Development in Education*, 1979, *12*, 93–100.

Hudson, F., Graham, S., & Warner, M. Mainstreaming: An examination of the attitudes and needs of regular classroom teachers. *Learning Disability Quarterly*, 1979, *2*, 58–62.

Iannaccone, L. The Reagan Presidency. *Journal of Learning Disabilities*, 1981, *14*, 55–59.

Johnson, G. O. A study of the social position of mentally handicapped children in the regular grades. *American Journal of Mental Deficiency*, 1950, *55*, 60–89.

Johnson, G. O. Special education for the mentally handicapped—a paradox. *Exceptional Children*, 1962, *29*, 62–69.

Jones, R. L., Gottlieb, J., Guskin, S., & Yoshida, R. K. Evaluating mainstreaming programs: Models, caveats, considerations, and guidelines. *Exceptional Children*, 1978, *44*, 588–601.

Koegh, B. K., & Levitt, M. L. Special education in the mainstream: A confrontation of limitations? *Focus on Exceptional Children*, 1976, *8*, 1–11.

Kesselman-Turkel, J., & Peterson, F. Taking the tough route of fairness. *American Education*, 1981, *17*, 6–13.

Kolstoe, O. P. Programs for the mildly retarded: A reply to critics. *Exceptional Children*, 1972, *39*, 51–56.

Lilly, M. S. Special education: A teapot in a tempest. *Exceptional Children*, 1970, *37*, 43–48.

Lilly, M. S. A merger of categories: Are we finally ready? *Journal of Learning Disabilities*, 1977, *19*, 56–62.

MacMillan, D. L. Special education for the mildly retarded: Servant or savant. *Focus on Exceptional Children*, 1971, *2*, 1–11.

MacMillan, D. L., Jones, R. L., & Aloia, G. F. The mentally retarded label: A theoretical analysis and review of research. *American Journal of Mental Deficiency*, 1974, *79*, 241–261.

McKinnon, A. J. Parents and pupil perceptions of special classes for emotionally disturbed children. *Exceptional Children*, 1970, *37*, 302–303.

Meyen, E. L., & Lehr, D. H. Least restrictive environments: Instructional implications. *Focus on Exceptional Children*, 1980, *12*, 1–8.

Middleton, E. J., Morsink, C., & Cohen, S. Program graduates' perception of need for training in mainstreaming. *Exceptional Children*, 1979, *45*, 256–261.

Peterson, N. L., & Haralick, J. G. Integration of handicapped and non-handicapped preschoolers: An analysis of play behavior and social interaction. *Education and Training of the Mentally Retarded*, 1977, *12*, 235–245.

Porter, R. B., & Milazzo, T. C. A comparison of mentally retarded adults who attended a special class with those who attended regular school classes. *Exceptional Children*, 1958, *24*, 410–412, 420.

Rapier, J., Adelson, R., Carey, R., & Croke, K. Changes in children's attitudes toward the physically handicapped. *Exceptional Children*, 1972, *39*, 219–224.

Reichart, S. Social perspectives of mainstreaming. *Educational Horizons*, 1981, *59*, 104–106.

Reynolds, M. C. A framework for considering some issues in special education. *Exceptional Children*, 1962, *28*, 367–370.

Reynolds, M. P. Mainstreaming: Historical perspectives. In P. A. O'Donnell & R. H. Bradfield (Eds.), *Mainstreaming: Controversy and Consensus*. San Rafael, CA: Academic Therapy Publications, 1976.

Roos, P. Trends and issues in special education for the mentally retarded. *Education and Training for the Mentally Retarded*, 1970, *5*, 51–61.

Salend, S. J. How to mainstream teachers. *Education Unlimited*, 1980, *2*, 31–33.

Scholom, A., Schiff, G., Swerdlik, M. E., & Knight, J. A three year study of learning disabled children in mainstream and self-contained classes. *Education*, 1981, *101*, 231–238.

Skodak, M. *A Follow-up and Comparison of Graduates from Two Types of High School Programs for the Mentally Handicapped* (Final report, U.S. Department of Health, Education, and Welfare, Project Number 6-8680). Dearborn, MI, 1970.

Smith, J. O., & Arkans, J. R. Now more than ever: A case for the special class. *Exceptional Children*, 1974, *40*, 497–502.

Sontag, E., Certo, N., & Button, J. E. On a distinction between the education of the severely and profoundly handicapped and a doctrine of limitations. *Exceptional Children*, 1979, *45*, 604–616.

Stephens, W. B., & Peck, J. R. *Success of Young Adult Male Retardates*. Washington, D.C.: Council for Exceptional Children, 1968.

Vacc, N. A study of emotionally disturbed children in regular and special classes. *Exceptional Children*, 1968, *35*, 197–204.

Vernon, M. Education's "three mile island": PL 94-142. *Peabody Journal of Education*, 1981, *59*, 24–29.

Warner, F., Thrapp, R., & Walsh, S. Attitudes of children toward their special class placement. *Exceptional Children*, 1973, *40*, 37–38.

Winschel, J. F. Mainstreaming: A still audible dissent. In J. W. Schifani, R. M. Anderson, & S. J. Odel (Eds.), *Implementing Learning in the Least Restrictive Environment—Handicapped Children in the Mainstream*. Baltimore: University Park Press, 1980.

Ysseldyke, J. E., & Algozzine, B. *Critical Issues in Special and Remedial Education*. Boston: Houghton Mifflin, 1982.

Competition as an Obstacle to Mainstreaming

Mara Sapon-Shevin

One often hears laments about the competitiveness of children, their need to be first, best, fastest, and prettiest. Children are aware of who is "the smartest boy in the class," "the slowest girl in our reading group," or "the last one picked at softball games." It is seldom acknowledged, however, that *we*—the adults, the teachers—have had a hand in making children the way they are. Although we may sometimes cringe at the fierce competitive behavior we observe, we seldom admit that we have some responsibility (credit or culpability) for such behavior.

I walk into a classroom of third graders doing independent seatwork, and I see that they have built themselves barricades of books so that their fellow students will not be able to see their papers. They curve their arms over the tops of their papers so that their neighbor's eyes will not see the answer. I wonder, where did they learn to do this?

I introduce a noncompetitive bingo game to a group of kindergarteners. We play the game through once, together, and when we reach the last number, they *all* win. Shouts of "Bingo!" "I won!" and smiles of delight fill the classroom and are soon followed by the plea, "Let's play again, huh?" I am pleased with the game I invented and pleased with the children. A second grader, older, wiser, wanders over to observe. At the end of the game he observes the same results—ten winners, all learning, all happy—and he looks at me with disbelief and says, "Hey, this is no fair. This is an 'everybody wins game': somebody's gotta lose."

Must the differences in reaction to the game be interpreted as a magical developmental milestone, or can we acknowledge that after 2 years of schooling, already the second grader has learned that "somebody's gotta lose"?

"So our children are competitive," many will argue, "so what? And what has all this got to do with mainstreaming?"

At the very heart of mainstreaming is the acknowledgement that all children are different, and that we must teach teachers and children to accept these differences and build upon them. Much has been written lately about teaching children about differences, and clearly we must move in the direction of helping children to understand each others' similarities and uniquenesses. Teachers trying to integrate exceptional children into their classes may implement special curriculum units designed to foster understanding and acceptance of differences and disabilities, but if we truly want children to behave differently, we must look beyond specific programs, no matter how well designed these may be to the overall social climate of the classroom. We must look not just at how

Sapon-Shevin, Mara. Who says somebody's gotta lose? Competition as an obstacle to mainstreaming. *Education Unlimited*, 1980, 2(4), 144–45. Reprinted by permission.

we treat the differences of special children, but at how schools treat differences in general; we must look not just at a specific curriculum, but at the day-to-day activities of the classroom and how these affect the ways in which children behave.

What are the conditions which promote competitiveness in children and how can they be altered? Among the many sources of competition in the classroom, two seem to be most directly accessible to the teacher's management. The first source of competitiveness springs from children's tendency to compare themselves to others around them and to then place (or have placed) value judgments on those differences. All children grow and change, do things today that they could not do yesterday, and it is natural and desirable for children to seek affirmation from their social environment concerning these changes.

Children compare themselves to others in order to answer the questions "Who am I?" and "How am I doing?" While the desire to define oneself and to document change is natural and desirable, there are two ways to engage in this process. One can engage in self-definition by looking at absolute standards ("I am 5 feet 2 inches,") or at comparative standards, by relating oneself to others ("I'm taller than Mike, but shorter then Beth"). Similarly, one can document change in oneself in the same two ways: *absolutely* ("I used to be able to run a 10 minute mile, but now I can run a mile in 8 minutes,") or *relatively* ("I used to be the slowest kid in the class, but now I run faster than three other kids").

There are clear parallels in the field of formal evaluation: norm-referenced and criterion-referenced tests. Considerable attention has been devoted recently to the limitations of norm-referenced testing, and the contrasting value of criterion-referenced tests in both describing what an individual can actually do and in enabling a student or a teacher to set clear goals for him/herself based on that description.

In the same way that different types of formal evaluations lead teachers or students to differing courses of action or instruction, the extent to which we provide children with norm-referenced evaluation, as opposed to descriptive evaluations of themselves and their behavior, will affect their own behavior and their own self-evaluations. Contrast "Suzy finished her spelling before any one else did" with "Terrific—you finished your spelling before gym." Finishing "before anyone else" is a distinction available to one child only, while finishing before gym is theoretically available to all.

Descriptive or criterion-referenced standards of evaluation encourage children to examine their own behavior in certain ways: What percentage of the problem did I get right? Was I able to stay under water for a whole minute? Standards of achievement which are constantly related to others leads to different kinds of behaviors: Not "Do I feel good about what I accomplished?" but "Did anyone else accomplish more?" If teachers help children to set reasonable standards for themselves, children can feel continuing success as they learn, grow, and achieve. When such absolute standards are missing, students will inevitably look to others for comparison, and this guarantees that the majority of them will experience continuing frustration, anger, or disappointment.

The kinds of evaluations children receive affect not only how they feel about themselves, but perhaps equally significantly, how they feel about their classmates. If evaluation is always comparative, then students who do better will be perceived as threats, that which keeps one from full success. ("No matter how hard I work or how much I learn, someone else has always done more or learned it before.") Students who do not do as well are either perceived as deserving of scorn or are looked upon with feelings of gratitude or relief, as it is their low standing which enables me to keep my position.

A related classroom condition also encourages students to engage in negative peer evaluation—scarcity. If a teacher is perceived as having a limited amount of love or praise, then those who receive it are likely to feel chosen, and those who do not, unappreciated. When success or praise are scarce, peer interaction is affected as well. When a teacher's praise is so scarce that her saying "Suzy did a really good job" implies that I am not likely to be praised this morning, then rather than being proud of Suzy, I am likely to see her as the *reason* that I did not get praised (hardly an auspicious way to encourage people to interact well with Suzy). When success is a limited commodity, as it must be in a competitive situation, then other students represent obstacles to be overcome, or at best, ignored in one's quest for success. Rather than encouraging positive peer interaction, competition fosters secretiveness and lack of communication.

What, then, can teachers do to decrease the frequency with which children compare themselves to another and increase children's positive feelings about themselves and others? In regard to providing descriptive standards of success, teachers can set individual goals for students and can also help students to set goals for themselves. This kind of individualization makes sense at both the academic and social levels. In addition to providing students with a more appropriate, personalized educational program, openly setting individual goals for students can allow other students to understand that (a) we are all different, (b) we have different things we are working on, and most significantly, (c) we can be proud of any individual who accomplishes his/her goals.

In visiting a mainstreamed classroom recently, one little girl proudly pointed to another girl and announced "Karen can tie her shoes now." Although the little girl who informed me of this had probably been able to tie her own shoes for many years, this did not in any way detract from her admiration of Karen's recent success. The teacher of this classroom has helped her students to see that different things are difficult for different people, and that an acomplishment is important, even if that other person's accomplishment seems "easy" to you. No child who has just succeeded likes to be told "Big deal—I've been able to do that for years."

Teachers must help students to see that differences are positive, and that different goals flow naturally from diverse needs. This must be contrasted to the feelings created by another teacher who, when asked "How come Billy gets to work on those workbooks and I don't" responded, "That's because Billy has a lot of problems you don't have." Such a response is likely to make children respond very differently to the student who has a differentiated program, making doing something different stigmatizing and undesirable.

When all children are routinely asked to do exactly the same work, then any deviations from this "norm" are likely to be attributed to handicaps or disabilities. This can become a problem at the opposite end of the spectrum as well, when gifted children are made to feel uncomfortable or rejected because their educational needs are different. When individualization is the order of the day, children tend to expect differential treatment and to accept the legitimacy of those differences.

Additionally, success must never be (or be seen as) a limited commodity in the classroom. In an effort to motivate students, teachers often place "star charts" on the wall, graphic demonstrations of who is succeeding and who is not. This tends to focus students' attention, not on what they are learning, or on feeling proud of their new skills, but on "who is winning." Research has shown that competition may be appropriate and motivating only under very limited conditions, one of those being when all involved have an equal chance of winning. In most classrooms, this is clearly not the case, and one must question how a star chart motivates those students with limited skills and no chance of winning. Classrooms should be organized so that all children really can succeed; in such classrooms, a teacher saying "Hey, Billy got a perfect paper" will then be a cause for other students' congratulations, as it will not imply that their chances for success or praise have in any way been decreased.

Minimizing competition in classrooms, however, is only a first step. The second step is much more difficult, but the rewards are also proportionately greater. Schools, little league and game manufacturers have done a thorough job of teaching children to compete, but rarely do children receive any systematic instruction in how to cooperate. Teachers must teach children how to give and receive help, and how to combine their talents and energies in working toward a common goal. Cooperation is not simply a mind-set; there are numerous specific skills which children need to be taught in order for them to cooperate with one another.

Let us take, for example, the skills involved in helping other students. Although teachers often use the term "help," what specifically do they teach children about appropriate and inappropriate ways of helping, and the value/desirability of such interaction? Take the following scenario: During a reading group, Jimmy is reading. He is a poor reader, and comes to a word he does not know. He tries to sound it out, stumbles, tries again, and becomes silent. The teacher says, "Who can help Jimmy?" and calls on Steve, who supplies the word effortlessly and is praised by the teacher. Has Steve *helped* Jimmy? In fact, Steve has read the word *instead* of Jimmy, received praise from the teacher, and possibly caused Jimmy some embarrassment.

Consider another lesson about helping. In Classroom A, the teacher observes Craig explaining a math problem to Mary that seems to have her confused. The teacher calls out, "Mary and Craig, move your desks apart! I don't tolerate cheating in this class." In Classroom B, the teacher observes one child struggling with a problem and asks for volunteers to assist the confused student. The interaction between the two children in the two classes is strikingly similar—what is different is that in Classroom A such behavior is labeled "cheating" and strenuously discouraged, and in Classroom B the behavior is termed "helping" and the teacher has spent considerable time with the students teaching them both how to help others ("Don't give answers, let them come up with the answer themselves,") and encouraging them to put these helping skills into practice. When students do help one another, we can often see ourselves as teachers reflected in their style. I observed one little boy correcting another's paper as follows: "Right, right right—ooops, this one needs to be looked at—right," as he marked big C's by the correct answers and left blank the errors. Clearly this 6 year old has learned his technique from his teacher.

Most children would profit from systematic instructon in how to give and receive help. Everyone has strengths and weaknesses, and therefore will both need help and be in the position to provide help to others throughout his/her life. An academically adept child may have poor physical coordination and need help learning to jump rope; a student who is blind will need help when things are written on the board, and smaller children will need help when a task requires strength or height.

The skills which people need in giving and receiving help can be analyzed into four categories:

- *Asking for help* in appropriate ways ("Can you please get my coat for me" rather than "Give me my coat")
- *Offering help* in appropriate ways ("Do you want me to help you?" rather than "You're too short—I'll get the ball" or simply doing something for another individual
- *Accepting help* in appropriate ways ("Thank you for getting my coat")
- *Refusing help* in appropriate ways ("No thanks—I can do it myself" rather than "Leave me alone, stupid, I'm not a baby—I can do it myself")

Although the strengths and weaknesses of children in mainstreamed classrooms may be more apparent than in supposedly "homogeneous" classrooms, all classrooms contain children who are different, and who would profit from learning appropriate ways of interacting with other children.

Teachers and schools surely did not invent competitiveness in children, but that does not mean that sensitive, conscientious teachers cannot change the ways in which children interact. The potential for teaching our students to be compassionate, caring human beings who potentiate rather than obstruct the success of others is great. Let us seize every opportunity, as parents and as teachers, to allow all our children to experience success and positive feelings of self-worth.

Mainstreaming Will Fail Unless There Is a Change in Professional Attitude and Institutional Structure

Charles Kunzweiler

There is much research being undertaken at the present time in an attempt to evaluate the 'mainstreaming' movement over the past ten years. Current reviews of research indicate that there is no significant differences in achievement between those handicapped children who are educated in special classes vs. those handicapped children who are educated in 'normal' classes. It is also indicated that temporal considerations (i.e., the amount of time spent in regular classes and special classes) is not a significant variable when evaluating academic achievement. (It appears to be independently controlled by administrative needs.) The current research does indicate that the most important variable in determining academic achievement for a 'mainstreamed' handicapped student is the quality of teaching between him/her and the teacher and the 'normal' student in his/her class.

Many papers have been written concerning the pros and cons of labeling and the possible effects, both negative and positive, that labeling may have on the individual. Many papers have been written concerning the whole area of testing and its alleged relationship to re-enforcing prejudice against minority groups and 'special' students vs. its supposed credibility in the 'real' world.

In short, the research today is full of findings that indicate that although there has been significant changes in special education legislation in the past ten years and consequent institutional *SHIFT* (i.e., there has really not been any significant *CHANGES* in institutional structure—the different use of time, space, and personnel) there has been very little, if any, change in professional attitude toward the handicapped, teacher training, and real institutional structural change.

The purpose of this paper is to re-enforce, before 'mainstreaming' meets its demise by being evaluated before its evolution is completed (i.e., it is a *PROCESS,* a very young one at that, not an instantaneous "cure-all" or "magic wand"), that educators must turn their attention to the next two "new frontiers" to be developed if 'mainstreaming' is to be successful. These two frontiers are teacher attitude and training, and institutional structural change.

TEACHER ATTITUDE AND TRAINING

Let us turn our attention to the kinds of attitudes that we as teachers bring into the classroom with us and the kinds of experiences we have in our teacher

Kunzweiler, C. Mainstreaming will fail unless there is a change in professional attitude and institutional structure. *Education,* Spring, 1982, *102*(3), 284–288. Reprinted by permission.

training. There will be no differentiation made here between "regular" teachers and "special" teachers since success for the handicapped student depends on her/his interaction with *both;* and the fact that with the exception of some individuals in both realms, teacher presentation of material and teacher technique does not vary greatly. "Special" educators have no "special bag of tricks."

Let us look first at attitude toward the handicapped. We know that development of attitudes toward the handicapped and contact with the handicapped is a tremendously complex issue. For the purpose of this paper, we will oversimplify and generalize by saying that the process is an individual phenomenon that takes into consideration such variables as, prior contact with the handicapped, attitude of parents toward the handicapped, attitude of peer group toward the handicapped, the visibility of the handicapped, etc. Individuals vary in their attitudes based on varying psychological needs. As a group, in general, cultural attitudes toward the handicapped are negative (although, again, it does not hold true for all individuals).

We come to our teacher training institutions as a rather large, generally middle class group, or at least a group that has adopted middle class values, with diverse prejudice and diverse levels of commonly shared learned prejudices. We go into an environment that stresses *ACADEMICS* and does virtually nothing to help us deal with our own growth as human beings. We have no formal structures or processes that help us deal with our spiritual and emotional growth as human beings and as educators. We have no (or limited) formal accepted institutional experiences that help us deal with our own ability to challenge pre-conceived beliefs and possibly develop some replacements that are more accurate because they are being processed by people who are more "whole" (i.e., have physical, intellectual, and spiritual being).

Because of this lack of formal structure and processes, if we come into college as a bigot, the chances are we will leave the college as a bigot who has earned the academic credentials to teach. Consequently, we could begin to build in our own teacher training programs structures and processes to deal with emotional and spiritual growth to aid perspective teachers to reach higher levels of consciousness and awareness so as to affect their contact with all children. Courses, sensitivity groups, clergy, etc., could be utilized to help perspective teachers, who in all probability are culturebound, to challenge pre-conceived attitudes and beliefs and different groups so that the label that gets "hung on" the student is used as a tool of communication and as a stimulus that evokes an appropriate educational response and an appropriate 'mindset' for treatment. These structures and processes must be built in for *all* teachers. If we do not "tear the walls down" between training for our "regular" teachers and training for our "special class" teachers on the University teacher training level and begin building those structures and processes for all teachers, it is doubtful that the quality of the interaction between teacher and 'mainstreamed' student will improve. (Another important variable in the acceptance of a handicapped student by 'normal' students is the attitude of the teacher towards the handicapped student.)

Let us now turn our attention to instruction. Current literature reflects the fact that there has been very little change in the methods of instruction in classrooms where 'handicapped' students have been 'mainstreamed.' This has adversely effected their level of achievement. Studies indicate that teachers spend approximately seventy-five percent (75%) of their time lecturing to the group. We know that there is little chance for academic success for main-streamed students unless the level of instruction is compatible with their needs (this is true for all children). Teacher training institutions re-enforce traditional teacher roles by stressing subject matter as opposed to technique. It is a moot argument that seeks superiority for the individualized curriculum—instruction approach over the traditional lecture approach. The simple fact of the matter is that without an individualized curriculum-instruction approach is it doubtful that the mainstreamed 'handicapped' student will benefit academically (unless, of course, the handicap has not affected the intellectual process). Teacher train-ing institutions could prepare all teachers to have the individualized curricu-lum-instructional approach in his/her repertoire of instructional techniques so that he/she can be flexible and have the ability to change techniques as the environment changes. That one is better than the other argument is no longer useful. We need to prepare teachers who have an understanding and command of all methods since, *under certain conditions,* all of them are valid.

Specialization has made the realm of the psychological off-limits to all but a relatively few special class teachers and even they get a very limited education in the area of psychological treatment of students in need. Their training is geared at methodologies that *CONTROL* behavior. Teacher training institu-tions could if 'mainstreaming' is to work, begin training all teachers in the treat-ment of psychological *PROCESS*. We could make them understand that non-compatibility with expected classroom behavior cannot be generalized into a label of "abnormal behavior", or "emotional disturbance", or "behavior prob-lem." The act of rebellion may be a temporal-special phenomenon that is nec-essary, and in fact healthy, for that particular student's total adjustment and sense of inner-balance in his own process. (Students who are frequently, and intensely either self-destructive or destructive to others for long periods of time must be looked at more closely when applying those labels.) They could be trained in the "anthropological perspective" so that they develop the ability to see the child as he is in inter-relation to his own unique inner growth process and his relationship to the culture and to his immediate surroundings. We could bring teachers out of the myopic view and understanding of behavior they have and help them to see the complexities that are involved. Teachers could be trained as therapists as well as academicians. They could learn new responses to *PROCESS* in their interactions with *all* students.

In sum, we could turn our attention to developing techniques to stimulate growth developing experiences for teachers—emotionally and spiritually as well as intellectually—in our College and Graduate School programs so that teachers' attitudes toward all differences in people will be enhanced and per-ceived on a more "whole" level. We could also deal with areas of instruction and the realm of the psychological. In short, we could change our teacher training method to produce flexible "Jacks of all trades—Masters of all." We could also produce new evaluation tools that are not testing old objectives in new environments and with new curriculum.

INSTITUTIONAL STRUCTURAL CHANGE

Earlier in the paper, I alluded to the difference between institutional *SHIFT* as opposed to *CHANGE*. Understanding the difference is very significant—in fact, *CRITICAL* when evaluating Mainstreaming.

As human beings within a culture, we have acquired "mindsets" or "constructs" concerning concepts such as time, space, and physical phenomenon (i.e., A year is 365 days, there are 52 weeks in one year, 7 days in one week, 24 hours in one day, 60 minutes in one hour; a square has four equal sides, a triangle has three equal sides; we sleep on a bed, someone who is in charge is "at the top", someone who is inferior is "on the bottom", etc.). As teachers, we have our own unique profession–based constructs in these areas (i.e., a school year is nine months, 180 days, a school day is six hours, a period is 45 minutes, a classroom has four walls and a blackboard, the teacher lectures from the front of the class, the student sits quietly and listens, etc.). These constructs or "mindsets" are constantly re-enforced by tradition and by the individual's need to maintain psychological homeostasis in his/her daily life. Consequently, we tend to see the world within the constraints these "mindsets" impose. For instance, a teacher might agree that he/she hasn't got the time to work individually with a 'mainstreamed' student because she has twenty-nine (29) other students and only forty-five (45) minutes per day to work with them. She just doesn't have time to do it. This teacher is viewing time within the contraints that the learned 'mindset' has imposed on her. It is possible to view time in a different way. Instead of five (5) forty-five (45) minute periods per day, we can say there are 225 minutes per week or 900 minutes per month (15 hours), etc. Time viewed this way might free the teacher psychologically to spend twenty (20) minutes per week developing an individualized program for the mainstreamed child.

Other areas that "mindsets" exist are the utilization of space and personnel. For most teachers, a classroom consists of one room with four walls with roughly thirty (30) chairs and his/her desk which is usually at the front of the room where he/she is located. That "construct" puts constraints on the creative potential to create environments that can successfully accommodate 'mainstreamed' students. For instance, a classroom can consist of one (1) large area that is broken up into sub-areas by moveable partitions. It can be broken up into: (1) subject areas, (2) quiet and noisy areas, and (3) instructional areas, etc. Teachers can be placed anywhere depending on: (1) subject being taught, (2) activity involved in, and (3) nature of instructions, etc. Mainstreamed children could all be serviced by one teacher within the area in a model such as mentioned above. One small classroom of thirty (30) students and one teacher with four (4) 'mainstreamed' students could be one large area with one hundred twenty (120) students and four (4) teachers and sixteen (16) mainstreamed students. They could be grouped together when necessary without ever leaving the "regular class' (perhaps with other students in the area who need similar help at that particular time). Resource teachers could come into the area to service the 'mainstreamed' students and any other students who need help. They could consult with other teachers right within the area. One teacher could assume responsibility for programming for all the 'mainstreamed' children, with the other teacher assuming some of his/her other teaching responsibilities. All kinds of learning arrangements and creative alternatives could be developed that are flexible enough to provide environments that could meet the needs of all students and teachers. Once again, the "open" class vs. the "traditional" class superiority argument is of no use to us anymore. We could develop alternative environments that are flexible enough to contain *both* approaches. *Under certain circumstances,* each is valid.

We could also take a hard look at our use of personnel. We have untapped resources within our schools that have not been touched. High school students who want to work in the helping professions can be trained (for social studies credit) in educational processes and used to teach younger mainstreamed children. Other creative alternatives can be developed.

What we have done in 'mainstreaming' amounts to an institutional structural "shift". We have "shifted" handicapped children from one environment to another without changing the "mindsets" that constrict us in our use of time, space, and personnel. What we have done is shift the handicapped child back to the very environment he was initially not successful in and expected him to somehow succeed without changing the very structures and processes that caused them to fall behind and to be segregated. We have set ourselves up to fail. We have to fail!

We have to grow through the traditional "mindsets," "constructs," and language in education and the consequent culturally conditioned teacher images and responses they illicit. We could give educators a "new set" of problems to work with that will encourage new sets of responses that are more appropriate to all kinds and ranges of students. We could foster real institutional structural change. We could attend to it in teacher training and by mandatory training for administrators.

In sum, if we do not deal with these 'new frontiers,' 'mainstreaming' will fail. It's failure will ultimately be the failure of education. If 'mainstreaming' does not have the chance to "play out" its evolution, it will not have the opportunity to do its real task—i.e., to move all teachers to a higher level of consciousness and awareness in the whole field of education, and as human beings.

ENABLING ACTIVITIES

To enable you to meet the objectives listed in the chapter study guide (p.1), the enabling activities listed below were designed to provide a variety of study directions and exploration activities ranging from the difficult and time-consuming to less complicated, straightforward tasks. It is important that you understand that you do not have to do every enabler listed: Choose only those that help you achieve a study guide objective or appeal to one of your interests in the chapter topic.

1 Summarize the arguments for mainstreaming presented in this chapter. For each argument, prepare a written rebuttal.
2 Interview a special education and a regular classroom teacher for their views on mainstreaming.
3 Identify two or three improvements that could be made in one of your community's buildings to help the handicapped. Interview the business manager of the school system to find out what it would cost to make the improvements and what procedures would have to be followed.
4 Locate and read Mainstreaming exceptional children: Some instructional design and implementation considerations, by Margaret C. Wang *(The Elementary School Journal,* 1981, *81*(4), 195–221). Prepare a 15-minute oral presentation comparing Wang's instructional design and implementation considerations and the four theoretical proposals for mainstreaming discussed by Chaffin (Will the real "mainstreaming" program please stand up! *Focus on Exceptional Children,* 1974, 6(5).
5 Using your best writing skills, develop a "position paper" stating your beliefs about the mainstreaming movement.
6 Locate and read Special education for the mentally handicapped, by G. Orville Johnson *(Exceptional Children,* 1962–1963, 29(2), 62–69) and Special education for the mildly retarded—Is much of it justified? by Lloyd Dunn *(Exceptional Children,* 1968, 35(1), 5–24).
7 You are a teacher in a system that does not mainstream exceptional students. Prepare an oral presentation justifying the mainstream concept that would be presented to the faculty members of your school.
8 Locate and read Mainstreaming handicapped students: Are your facilities suitable? by James Russo *(American Schools and Universities,* 1974, *47*(2), 25–32). Using this as a base, inspect one of your community buildings to see if the facilities are suitable for the handicapped. Devise a checklist that could be used to evaluate a school building's suitability for educating the handicapped.

SELF-TEST

True-False

1 The issue of mainstreaming gained popularity in the early 1900s.
2 When mainstreaming, particular attention should be given to the child's label.
3 Mainstreamed handicapped children perform better, both academically and socially, than their nonmainstreamed peers.
4 Self-esteem increases in handicapped children who are mainstreamed.
5 Most mainstreaming advocates agree that the handicapped must display adequate social and academic skills prior to being mainstreamed.
6 Nonhandicapped students interact more with mainstreamed handicapped than with self-contained handicapped students.
7 Severely handicapped populations have benefited the most from mainstreaming.

8 The state of the art on mainstreaming is "how should it be done" rather than "should it be done?"

9 Ruhl suggested that mainstreaming will continue to be successful because of past federal legislation and present societal interest.

10 The role of the special educator has not changed with mainstreaming.

11 Teacher attitudes toward the mainstreamed handicapped have no effect on public policy.

Multiple-Choice

12 Which of the following is not a responsibility regular teachers take on when mainstreaming is implemented?
   (a) diagnose and place students in appropriate educational settings
   (b) establish individualized educational programs
   (c) allot time for IEP meetings
   (d) know what types of support services are available

13 Normalization may be defined as:
   (a) the educational methods used by regular education teachers
   (b) the placement of learners with deviant behaviors in regular education classrooms
   (c) providing educational experiences to handicapped individuals that are similar to nonhandicapped peers
   (d) both a and c

14 The increased use of resource rooms caused:
   (a) more isolation for mildly handicapped individuals
   (b) a setback for the mainstream movement
   (c) highly specialized classes to be developed
   (d) nonhandicapped individuals with learning disabilities to be placed there

15 According to the concept of least restrictive environment:
   (a) every handicapped child must be placed in a normal classroom
   (b) each individual is placed in a setting that she/he chooses
   (c) an individual's placement depends on services within a particular setting which is closest to normal and still meets special needs
   (d) an individual can leave and enter a classroom without asking formal permission

16 Responsibility for the implementation of mainstreaming rests with the:
   (a) administration
   (b) teacher
   (c) mainstreaming advocates
   (d) school district

2

LEGISLATION AND LITIGATION

CHAPTER STUDY GUIDE

After reading the selections presented in this chapter and completing the enabling activities, the student should be able to:

1 Briefly describe the historical events that provided the foundation for present laws and litigation.
2 Differentiate between legislation and litigation and describe the impact of each on special education.
3 Summarize the constitutional foundation for most of the present special education legislation.
4 List four areas of special education directly affected by legislation and litigation.
5 Describe possible future legislation and litigation directions for special education.
6 Identify and discuss the significant provisions of Public Law 94-142 and Section 504 that are related to special education.

Legislation and Litigation

Rosalie Boone

The development of publicly supported special school programs began with the passage of compulsory education laws (Dunn, 1968). Rhode Island passed the first such law in 1840 and Massachusetts followed in 1851. Many early state constitutions had provisions for free public education. For example, in 1848 the Wisconsin Constitution contained the following article:

> The legislation shall provide by law for the establishment of district schools which shall be free to all children between the ages of four and twenty years. (Melcher, 1976)

Despite these early promises to provide a free public education to all children, the handicapped have waited well over a century for legislation guaranteeing fulfillment of the promise.

Traditionally, exceptional children received public education only to the extent states chose to provide such an education and "within whatever fiscal limits legislatures chose" (Ennis & Gitlin, 1973). Consequently, handicapped children were routinely denied the public school education assured normal children. In the last two decades, however, litigation and federal legislation have improved educational opportunities for America's handicapped children: courts abandoned their "hands off" policy regarding the affairs of schools; litigation stimulated legislation; and federal legislation culminated in laws reflecting "total commitment to provide services across the board for all handicapped persons" (LaVor, 1977, p. 96).

HISTORY OF FEDERAL LEGISLATION FOR THE HANDICAPPED

LaVor (1977) provides a comprehensive history of federal legislation for exceptional persons so only selected federal legislation will be reviewed here. The laws reviewed are significant either because they represent "firsts" in some area of legislation for the handicapped or because they affected a variety of handicapped individuals.

Federal legislation for the handicapped can be divided into four distinct periods. Federal laws passed between 1820 and 1870 are "early" federal laws (LaVor, 1977). The first piece of legislation related to the handicapped was passed in 1827. It did not deal with services for the handicapped, but provided a land grant to the Deaf and Dumb Asylum of Kentucky. Twenty years elapsed before Congress again passed legislation for the handicapped. This bill extended the time allotted for selling the lands granted to the Kentucky Asylum for the Deaf and Dumb.

In 1855 Congress enacted legislation establishing a federal facility for the insane in the District of Columbia. In 1857, Public Law 34-5 founded the Columbia Institution for the Instruction of the Deaf and Dumb and Blind (later to become known as Gallaudet College). A year later the first appropriation of federal funds for the handicapped was enacted. This law (Public Law 35-59) provided money for tuition, salaries, maintenance, and other expenses of the Columbia Institution for the Instruction of the Deaf and Dumb and Blind. Six years later, in 1864, President Lincoln signed a bill authorizing the Columbia Institution to confer degrees.

The passage of Public Law 45-186 in 1879 authorized, for the first time, federal funds to provide materials for a specific group of handicapped citizens. These funds permitted the establishment of the American Printing House for the Blind. During the 39 years following the enactment of Public Law 45-186 only one federal law for the handicapped was passed to provide special mailing privileges for the blind.

The second period of federal enactments for the handicapped was characterized by legislation stimulated by the impact of the world wars. Several authors (Melcher, 1976; Cruickshank (in Aiello), 1976; and LaVor, 1977) suggest that the First World War marked the end of a 40-year period in which no federal legislation for the handicapped was passed. Melcher (1976) notes that "Following World War II the United States was finally ready for a major thrust in serving the handicapped" (p. 128). Aiello (1976), in a bicentennial article chronicling the history of the field of special education, quotes William Cruickshank:

> Although it may seem peculiarly related to special education, the Second World War was a significant milestone for our field . . . As opposed to the First World War which was a killing war, the Second World War was a maiming war. Tens of thousands of young men and women who left their communities as normal persons returned as disabled citizens. But the fact that they spent their childhood as normal people resulted in an interesting change on the part of people in the community . . . Society became more aware of and more accepting of people with disabilities and this change in attitude was very significant." (p. 248)

According to LaVor (1977), the first significant federal act for handicapped persons in the twentieth century was the Soldier's Rehabilitation Act of 1918. This act provided services to disabled veterans of World War I. A bill (Public Law 66-236) providing comparable services for disabled civilians was enacted in 1920. The Soldier's and the Citizens Rehabilitation Acts provided federal money for training, to prepare disabled persons to fill the many vacancies created by war-induced manpower shortages. Although in 1943 the Citizens Rehabilitation program was expanded to provide services for the mentally ill and the mentally retarded, most legislation for the handicapped between the two world wars provided services for the blind. Twenty-five such pieces of legislation were enacted between 1919 and 1952.

Increased federal involvement in general education marked the beginning of the third period of legislation affecting the handicapped. Prior to the late 1950s the federal government was reluctant to become involved legislatively or financially in education. Although the Cooperative Research Act was passed in 1954, it was not until 1957 that Congress provided funds to implement the act. In 1957 approximately 66 percent of the $1 million appropriated for the act was directed to be spent on research relating to the education of the mentally retarded. This appropriation marked the first time Congress designated general funds specifically for services to the handicapped. In 1957 the Russians launched Sputnik and to ensure that American education kept pace with or surpassed Soviet education, the National Defense Education Act was enacted. This act indicated recognition that some extra services should be provided for exceptional and gifted students.

The federal government increased its involvement in general education and in special education in the 1960s. Federal support for training teachers of the deaf, the hard of hearing, the speech impaired, the emotionally disturbed, the crippled, and the visually handicapped became available with the passage of Public Law 87-276 in 1961 and its amendment in 1963. The passage of Public Law 89-750, the Elementary and Secondary Education Act, firmly established federal aid to education. Amendments to the Elementary and Secondary Education Act in 1965, 1966, and 1967 provided: *(a)* assistance to local education agencies to meet the needs of educationally deprived children, *(b)* grants to state agencies responsible for providing public education for handicapped children, and *(c)* funds to states to expand special education programs designed to meet the needs of handicapped children. Other federal legislation of the 1960s included the Handicapped Children's Early Education Assistance Act of 1968 and the Vocation Education Amendment of 1968, which provided that 10 percent of vocational education funds be spent for the handicapped. The Elementary and Secondary Education Act amendment of 1969 authorized technical assistance to programs for the gifted as well as funds for research and educational services affecting children with specific learning disabilities.

The 1970s ushered in the fourth period of federal involvement in the education of handicapped children. The Developmental Disabilities Services and Facilities Construction Amendments of 1970 assisted states in the design and provision of services and facilities to serve the mentally retarded and other developmentally disabled. The Developmentally Disabled Assistance and Bill of Rights Act of 1974 amended the Developmental Disabilities Act. Features of this amendment included the right to appropriate treatment, services, or rehabilitation; a list of minimum standards for the operation of residential facilities for the developmentally disabled; and the provision of individualized rehabilitation plans for clients served in Developmental Disabilities funded programs.

Both Section 504 of the Vocational Rehabilitation Amendments of 1974 and the Education Amendments of 1974 opened a new era of educational and rehabilitation rights and opportunities for handicapped individuals. Section 504 was the first federal civil rights law specifically to protect the rights of handicapped persons. This section was originally part of the Vocational Rehabilitation Act of 1973, which outlawed discrimination against the handicapped in employment practices. The passage of the Vocational Rehabilitation Amendments of 1974 expanded Section 504 to cover a larger spectrum of services for the handicapped. Thus, education services for the handicapped came to be protected by provisions similar to those of the Civil Rights Act of 1964 (Meyen, 1978). Public Law 93-380 amended the Elementary and Secondary Act of 1965. Section 801 of the amendment made a statement of national policy with regard to equal educational opportunity:

> Recognizing that the Nation's economic, political and social security require a well-educated citizenry, the Congress (1) reaffirms as a matter of high priority, the Nation's goal of equal educational opportunity and (2) declares it to be the policy of the United States of America that every citizen is entitled to an education to meet his or her full potential without financial barriers.

In 1975 President Ford signed an act that committed the federal government to substantial financial contribution toward the education of America's handicapped children. Public Law 94-142, the Education for All Handicapped Children Act, is the most comprehensive educational legislation ever enacted on behalf of handicapped children. It guarantees free, appropriate public education for every child with a handicapping condition, mandating: (1) provision of educational services in the environment least restrictive for the child, (2) nondiscriminatory evaluation, and (3) procedures for the protection of due process rights.

Finally, 148 years after the first federal legislation related to the handicapped and 135 years after passage of the first compulsory education law, education for handicapped children evolved from nebulous promise to legal reality. The transition from promise to reality was not accomplished by legislation alone. The 1970s' escalation of federal attention to the handicapped was, in large measure, stimulated by landmark court cases and litigation which established basic educational rights for the handicapped.

THE ROLE OF LITIGATION

Gilhool (1973) points out that when parents of handicapped children resort to litigation as a means of achieving educational services it is neither an act of hostility nor a declaration of war. According to him, resorting to litigation "is not different from resorting to the legislature by lobbying or from resorting to the executive by way of negotiations with statewide or local school officials" (1973, p. 599). The powers of the courts differ slightly from those of the legislature and the executive officer. Whereas "the art of accommodation characterizes decisions in the legislature and in the executive . . . in the courts it is not a question of accommodation, it is the art of the necessary" (Gilhool, 1973, p. 599).

The role of litigation in securing the rights of various groups and individuals has been described by several observers. Abeson (1973) indicated that litigation becomes appropriate when the constitutional or statutory rights of exceptional children are abridged and when administrative remedies for redress have proven either ineffective or inefficient in protecting those rights. Gilhool (1973) cites four uses of litigation. He notes that litigation may be used to:

1 Secure certain substantive rights
2 Create a new forum to which citizens may turn for the enforcement of their rights
3 Bring to the attention of the public facts that have not had previous visibility
4 Allow the aggrieved citizen to express himself or to redefine, change, or alter his own and others' notion of who and what he is.

Higgins and Barresi (1979) observe that litigation has been used historically to achieve equality in basic rights, to open doors that had been closed, and to break new ground in the public philosophic base. Weintraub and Abeson (1974) have also stressed the role litigation plays in reshaping public policy. Public policy is viewed as important by these authors because it:

1 Determines the degree to which minorities, in this case the handicapped, will be treated inequitably by the controlling majority.
2 Determines the degree to which those who are served will be vulnerable to abuse from those who provide the services.
3 Determines how society will perceive a class or group of individuals.
4 Influences how a class or group of individuals will feel about themselves (pp. 526–529).

The labor movement of the 1930s, the civil rights movement of the 50s and 60s, and the current women's movement relied heavily on the courts to achieve social change. In following this traditional use of the courts, handicapped citizens joined the ranks of blacks, the poor, women, and the elderly in asserting their rights.

Turnbull (1978) described the impact of court decisions on the education of handicapped children. According to him, court decisions have established the following five principles of special education law:

1 Zero reject—no handicapped child may be excluded from a free, appropriate public education.
2 Procedural due process—each handicapped child has the right to procedural safeguards and certain due process standards in identification, evaluation, and educational placement.
3 Appropriate education—each handicapped child must be provided with an education that meets his/her own unique needs.
4 Least restrictive placement—every handicapped child must, to the maximum extent appropriate, be educated with children who are not handicapped.
5 Nondiscriminatory evaluation—every handicapped child must be fairly assessed in a manner which will allow him/her to be appropriately placed and served in the public school.

An understanding of how these five principles became established through litigation can best be achieved by examining the precedent-setting court cases from which the principles were derived and by examining the constitutional foundations on which these cases were built.

CONSTITUTIONAL FOUNDATIONS

Education is not a fundamental right. A fundamental right (Flanagan, 1974) is one explicitly guaranteed by the Constitution. The Constitution does not explicitly guarantee an education to American citizens. The states guarantee this right. However, states also have the power to expel or exclude children from public education in the interest of providing "the greatest good for the greatest number" (Flanagan, 1974, p. 522). A vivid example of this exclusionary power was the 1919 ruling made in *Beattie v. State Board of Education*. This ruling excluded a mentally normal, academically achieving 13-year-old boy from regular public school classes because his physical handicap was said to have a depressing and nauseating effect on the teachers and other students.

An alternative definition (of fundamental right) defines it as a right "implicitly guaranteed by virtue of its close nexus with other rights which enjoy explicit constitutional protection" (Flanagan, 1974, p. 526). The Fourteenth Amendment provides that no state may deny to any person within its jurisdiction the equal protection of the laws. The Fifth and Fourteenth Amendments protect individuals against the loss of liberty without due process of law. Equal protection of the law and due process are fundamental rights explicitly guaranteed by the Constitution. During litigation in the 1960s and 1970s the nexus between education and these fundamental rights was established. Exclusion from education was viewed by the courts as a threat to individual rights. Once a state elected to educate any of its children, exclusion of the handicapped from a minimum level of education meant denial of equal protection. Total exclusion from public education was said to violate due process. Denial of education was also deemed a threat to the right to vote, since illiteracy was often a basis for precluding a citizen's participation in state elections.

Zero Reject and Appropriate Education: Significant Court Cases

Brown v. Board of Education, 1954, had great impact on litigation for the handicapped. The Warren court, in declaring school segregation illegal because it violated the equal protection clause of the Fourteenth Amendment, provided the legal base for subsequent right to education litigation. A second significant case was *Pennsylvania Association of Retarded Citizens v. Commonwealth of Pennsylvania*, 1971. PARC was a class action suit filed on behalf of all mentally retarded children aged 6 to 21. Pennsylvania statutes permitted children who were uneducable or untrainable to be excluded from public schools. As a result of this statute many mentally retarded children were denied an education.

The factual basis of the suit was that no child is uneducable or untrainable—that every retarded child can benefit from an education. The legal basis was the opinion rendered by the Supreme Court in *Brown v. Board of Education*:

> Education is required in the performance of our most basic public responsibilities. It is the very foundation of good citizenship. It is a principal instrument for awakening the child to cultural values, in preparing him for later training. If education is a principal instrument in helping the child adjust normally to his environment, it is doubtful that any child may reasonably be expected to succeed in life if he is denied the opportunity of an education. The opportunity of an education, where the state has undertaken to provide it to any, is a right which must be made available to all on equal terms.

The PARC case was settled out of court by a consent order which ruled that Pennsylvania had undertaken to provide a free public education to its nonhandicapped children and many of its exceptional children. Consequently, it could not deny any mentally retarded child equal protection or access to a free public education. The three-judge panel also held that no child in Pennsylvania could have his/her educational status changed without procedural due process and the PARC court declared the state obligated to place each mentally retarded child in a "free public program of education and training appropriate to his capacity" *(Pennsylvania Association of Retarded Citizens v. Commonwealth,* 334 F. Supp. 1257, 1971).

Mills v. Board of Education of the District of Columbia was an additional precedent-setting right to education case. The Mills Court expanded the right to a free, appropriate public education and to due process procedures to handicapped children other than the mentally retarded. The plaintiffs were seven handicapped children who brought suit for failure to provide all children with a publicly supported education. In 1972 an order and decree was issued providing:

1 A declaration of the constitutional right of all children, regardless of any exceptional condition or handicap, to a publicly supported education.

2 A declaration that the defendant's rules, policies, and practices which excluded children without a provision for adequate and immediate alternative educational services and the absence of prior hearing and review of placement procedures denied the plaintiffs and the class rights of due process and equal protection of the law.

In response to the defendant concern about the scarcity of funds available to afford the relief ordered by the court, the court stressed that the public interest in conserving funds could not justify the denial of education or the continuance of discriminatory practices (McCarthy & Thomas, 1977). The judge, in response to this concern, stated that "the inadequacies of the District of Columbia public school system, whether occasioned by insufficient funding or administrative inefficiency, certainly cannot be permitted to bear more heavily on the exceptional or handicapped child than on the normal child" *(Mills v. Board of Education of D.C.,* 348 F. Supp. 866, D.D.C. 1972).

The prevention of total exclusion, however, was not sufficient to solve the educational inequities to which handicapped children were subjected. Admittance to school did not assure a handicapped student would receive the education necessary to develop his/her capabilities to the highest possible level. The Court, in both Pennsylvania Association of Retarded Citizens and Mills, realized that functional exclusion (the denial of meaningful or appropriate educational opportunity) was tantamount to no education at all. Mills, therefore, required that a handicapped child's education be "suited to (his) needs" (348 F. Supp. 866, D.D.C., 1972). Likewise, Pennsylvania Association of Retarded Citizens ordered that education for the handicapped child be "appropriate to his learning capacities" (343 F. Supp. 279, 307 E.D. Pa., 1972).

Although the constitutional right of the handicapped to some level of appropriate education was established by Pennsylvania Association of Retarded Citizens and Mills, neither case was based on a constitutional right to treatment in establishing equal educational opportunity *(Stanford Law Review,* 1979). Two additional cases established a constitutional right to treatment.

Wyatt v. Stickney, 1971, was filed on behalf of mentally ill and mentally retarded individuals in two of Alabama's state institutions. Plaintiffs alleged that the institutions were understaffed and that programs of treatment and habilitation were inadequate. The judge in Wyatt agreed. The court set minimum constitutional and medical standards for these institutions, including the establishment of individual treatment plans, minimum educational standards, and the provision of the least restrictive setting necessary for habilitation. Wyatt was the first case in which the institutionalized mentally retarded were ruled to have a constitutional right to adequate treatment.

The applicability of the right to treatment was broadened and the concept of treatment enlarged in the case of *Lora v. New York City Board of Education,* 1978. Lora involved a class action suit brought by minority students who had been assigned to New York special schools because of emotional problems. In Lora, for the first time, the right to treatment was applied to handicapped persons who were neither institutionalized nor completely deprived of specialized services. The court in Lora ruled that New York's process for reassigning the plaintiffs to special schools constituted a deprivation of liberty sufficient to invoke due process protections. The state was ordered to improve its evaluation and placement process and the quality of treatment and education of handicapped students in its schools. The judiciary ruling in Lora was especially important because by requiring the state to make an even more substantial effort to educate handicapped students, it raised the "minimum" level of services required to satisfy the due process and equal protection clauses of the Constitution.

Least Restrictive Environment: Significant Court Cases

Denial of an appropriate education was recognized in litigative action as just one of the circumstances which might result in the "functional exclusion" of handicapped students. Unnecessary placement in self-contained or segregated special education programs was recognized by the courts as another circumstance in which handicapped children were denied the opportunity to receive an appropriate education. As a remedy for the functional exclusion resulting from segregated placement, courts expressed a preference for placement of handicapped children in regular programs. Pennsylvania Association of Retarded Citizens was "the first to apply the least restrictive alternative to the education of handicapped children" (Meyen, 1978, p. 89). The Pennsylvania Association of Retarded Citizens court stated:

> It is the Commonwealth's obligation to place each mentally retarded child in a free, public program of education and training appropriate to the child's capacity, within the context of the general educational policy that, among the alternative programs of education and training required by statute to be available, placements in a regular public school class is preferable to placement in any other type of program of education and training.

The court in Mills ruled that the principles stated in the Pennsylvania Association of Retarded Citizens case applied to all handicapped children in the District of Columbia. Pennsylvania Association of Retarded Citizens and Mills thereby established the principle of least restrictive placement.

LeBanks v. Spears, 1973, also supported the principle of least restrictive placement. The consent agreement reached in LeBanks specified that:

> All evaluations and educational plans, hearings and determinations of appropriate programs of education and training . . . shall be made in the context of a presumption that among alternative programs and plans, placement in a regular public school class with the appropriate support services is preferable to placement in special public school classes. (*LeBanks v. Spears*, Civil No. 71-2897 E.D. La., 1973)

Despite the importance of the Pennsylvania Association of Retarded Citizens, Mills, and LeBanks in establishing the principle of least restrictive placement, such placement was merely a judicial "preference" or guide rather than a strict rule. *Mattie T. v. Holladay*, 1975, was the first least restrictive placement case to be based on federal statutes (Turnbull & Turnbull, 1979). Relying on the Education for All Handicapped Children Act (Public Law 94-142), Section 504, and the Elementary and Secondary Education Act of 1965, plaintiffs in Mattie T. successfully challenged placement in self-contained classes on the grounds that such placement isolates handicapped from nonhandicapped students and fails to meet their educational needs.

Nondiscriminatory Evaluation and Placement: Significant Court Cases

Appropriate and least restrictive education is inextricably tied to the issue of fair evaluation and placement of children. Improper testing and misclassification have resulted in denial of the right to educational opportunity, unjustified stigmatization, and discriminatory treatment based on race or cultural background. The right of handicapped students to nondiscriminatory evaluation and procedural due process in assessment and placement was advanced by litigation. The constitutional foundation of this litigation is based on the Fifth and Fourteenth Amendments, which provide that states treat citizens equally and deprive no person of life, liberty, or property without due process of law.

Turnbull and Turnbull (1979) state that "because of the criticisms of testing—criticisms centering on the permanent and stigmatizing consequences of being labelled as 'mentally retarded' and on the racial differentiation that results from testing—courts in the early and mid 1970's began to make inroads on the testing practices and procedures of the schools" (p. 87). Ross, DeYoung, and Cohen (1971) cited five criticisms most frequently levied against traditional assessment and placement procedures:

1 Testing does not, for many children, accurately measure their learning ability.
2 The administration of tests is often performed incompetently.
3 Parents are not given an opportunity to participate in the placement decision.
4 Special education programming is inadequate.
5 The personal harm created by improper placement is irreparable (pp. 5–6).

Four court cases were significant in the establishment of standards, regulations, or mandates to protect handicapped children from inappropriate evaluation and placement. The ruling in *Hobson v. Hansen* (1967) declared that ability grouping or tracking based on pupil performance on standardized tests violated equal protection and due process clauses of the Constitution. The court in Hobson found that track assignments were dependent on student performance on standardized tests which were "completely inappropriate for use with a large segment of the student body" (*Hobson v. Hansen,* 269 F. Supp. 401, 1967, p. 481). The court relied on *Brown v. Board of Education* in holding that the tracking system and its methods "irrationally separated students on the basis of race and socioeconomic background and thereby violated their right to an equal educational opportunity" (Ross, DeYoung, and Cohen, 1971, p. 7). The tracking system in Washington, D.C. was therefore ordered abolished. Defendants appealed the ruling, but the District Court of Appeals in *Smuck v. Hobson* (1969) affirmed the lower court's decree abolishing the track system.

Diana v. State Board of Education (1970) was the first case of its kind to be filed in a federal court and is considered one of the most significant cases of special education litigation. Diana was filed on behalf of nine Mexican-American children from Spanish-speaking homes. The plaintiffs charged discriminatory placement as a result of having been improperly assigned to classes for the mentally retarded on the basis of culturally biased testing procedures and test content. The case was settled by a stipulated agreement that required:

1 Children must be tested in their primary language.
2 Mexican-American and Chinese children in classes for the educable mentally retarded must be retested and reevaluated.
3 Special efforts must be extended to aid misplaced children in their readjustment to the regular classroom.
4 The state must make immediate efforts to develop and standardize an appropriate IQ test (Weintraub & Abeson, 1976).

Covarrubias v. San Diego Unified School District (1971) was filed on behalf of twelve black and five Mexican-American children placed in classes for the educable mentally retarded. Plaintiffs relied on Diana and charged that culturally biased testing resulted in denial of their right to an equal education. While Covarrubias resembled Diana in the legal arguments presented, it differed on two points. First, Covarrubias sought money damages under the Civil Rights Act of 1871, claiming conspiracy by the school district to deprive plaintiffs of the equal protection of the laws. Second, Covarrubias maintained that "any revision of testing methods based on Diana must also recognize the cultural influences of the ghetto environment in determining a student's learning ability" (Ross, DeYoung, and Cohen, 1971).

Larry P. v. Riles (1972) was filed on behalf of six black children who charged inappropriate placement in classes for the retarded based on discriminatory testing procedures that:

1 Failed to recognize the children's unfamiliarity with the white middle-class culture.
2 Ignored their own culturally based learnings and experiences.

The court in Larry P. extended the principles of Diana to include black children who spoke English but did not belong to the white middle-class culture on which intelligence tests were normed (Gearheart, 1980). The court forbade the use of tests that did not properly account for the cultural background of students tested. School authorities were also enjoined from using intelligence tests to place minority students in classes for the educable mentally retarded if such placements result in racial imbalance in the composition of such classes. Finally, the court ruled that schools must justify their reliance on tests that have resulted in a racial imbalance.

Classification, evaluation, and special education placement are vital parts of the educational process. They allow planning, programming, and the appropriation of funds for handicapped students, facilitate appropriate services, assist in measuring the results of special education programs, and assist in the enactment of legislation to aid individuals with specific types of handicapping conditions (Turnbull & Turnbull, 1979, pp. 88–89). Unfortunately, positive aspects of testing and labeling have often been obscured by discriminatory and unwise use. The principles of nondiscriminatory testing, classification, and placement established by litigation provide protection for handicapped students and for those whose culture and/or language differ from that of the majority.

Procedural Due Process: Significant Court Cases

"Procedural due process—the right to protest and challenge school decisions —is a necessary prerequisite to putting. . . other claims into effect" (Turnbull, 1978, p. 526). The due process precedent was established by two cases not specific to the area of special education. In the first case, *Dixon v. Alabama State Board of Education,* the court delineated procedures which have been used as guidelines in subsequent special education cases involving the satisfaction of due process requirements. In the second case, *In re Gault,* 1967, the Supreme Court held that status as a juvenile does not negate the constitutional right to procedural due process (Kahan, 1974).

Pennsylvania Association of Retarded Citizens v. Commonwealth of Pennsylvania was the first case which dealt directly with the procedural due process rights of handicapped children in the public school arena. Plaintiffs in Pennsylvania Association of Retarded Citizens argued that deprivation of educational benefits, whether by special placement or continuing inappropriate placement, requires notice and the opportunity to be heard. A second argument presented was that labeling requires prior notice and the opportunity to be heard. In response to these arguments the court required that parents be given notice and the opportunity to be heard prior to any change in their child's educational placement. This case provided the first detailed set of requirements for placing or reassigning a child. However, these requirements applied only to the evaluation and placement of mentally retarded children (Turnbull & Turnbull, 1979).

Mills v. Board of Education extended the procedural rights of notice and opportunity to be heard to all children with handicaps. In most cases where classification was an issue, procedural due process became the primary mechanism by which to protect children from discriminatory classification. According to Turnbull and Turnbull (1978) and Abeson, Bolick & Haas (1975) procedural due process requirements related to evaluation and placement can be subsumed under three basic procedural safeguards:

1 The child's parent or guardian must be notified in writing
  A by a notice that describes the proposed school action, the reasons for it and available educational opportunities
  B in their primary language
  C before evaluation
  D before change in placement
2 A parent has the right to request an impartial hearing and if he/she does make such a request, the hearing must be conducted by a hearing officer indepen-

dent of the local school authorities, at a time and place convenient to the parent

A within a specified period after the parent's request

B in a meeting which is closed to the public unless the parents request otherwise

3 The hearing must be conducted according to due process procedures, which include the right of the parent to:

A review all records prior to the hearing

B obtain an independent evaluation prior to the hearing

C be represented by counsel

D call witnesses

E present evidence and testimony

F cross-examine witnesses

G receive a complete and accurate record of proceedings

H be assured that evidence he/she presents will come before the hearing officer and be considered by the officer

I be assured that no evidence not offered by him/her or the school will be considered

J appeal the decision

Litigation in various courts established the principles of zero reject, appropriate education, least restrictive placement, nondiscriminatory evaluation, and procedural due process. These principles have been mirrored by state and federal legislation. The true significance of litigation on behalf of handicapped children is perhaps best expressed by Turnbull and Turnbull (1979):

> Litigation . . . was the original source for establishing educational rights of handicapped children. Were it not for the landmark decisions (e.g., PARC, Mills, LeBanks, Larry P. and Diana), it is doubtful if subsequent litigation would have had such widespread success, if the "second generation" litigation (defining "appropriate" education) would have had any useful precedents, or if state and federal legislation would have been enacted . . .

FUTURE DIRECTIONS IN LAW AND LITIGATION

Many authors have attempted to predict the direction which special education law and litigation will take. McCarthy and Thomas (1977), for example, expressed concern that "the courts in accepting the very emotional arguments of special education proponents may be opening a Pandora's box for future legal battles involving students with other types of special needs" (p. 86). They posed six questions:

1 Should the federal government, under the guise of promoting the general welfare, be able to direct tax dollars to private schools for "special" but not for "normal" children?

2 Is there a denial of fundamental rights when stringent due process and accountability procedures are mandated for "special" children while the "normal" child's fate is left in the hands of school officials?

3 Will courts require that the needs of other classes of students such as the musically talented or academically gifted be addressed by public schools?

4 Will advocates of the "normal" child capitalize on precedents regarding special education to demand that public school programs appropriately meet the divergent needs of all students?

5 If so, will the total school program become diluted from well intentioned but misdirected attempts to provide equal educational opportunities?

6 Or will a double standard prevail regarding criteria to measure the quality of educational programs for "normal" versus "special" children?

John Melcher (1976) made ten speculations in law and litigation for the following decade. His speculations can be placed into one of three categories: actions of the courts, areas of new or increased litigation, and changes or modification of existing laws.

1 Actions of the courts:
   A To expedite service to children courts will use third-party negotiators skilled in both special education and the dynamics of adversary related proceedings.
   B The courts will avoid rendering irrevocable decisions. They will avoid premature resolution that might prove to answer only a legal technicality and not resolve the full problem inherent in a suit. Courts will maintain a higher case-surveillance level.
2 Areas of new or increased litigation:
   A Litigation against the schools will increase in the areas of program quality as opposed to program availability. Phrases such as "appropriate educational program" will be tested in the courts to determine the limits of parental veto of specific school programs.
   B Litigation between and among school groups will be expanded. Teachers of regular classes will determine the limits of their responsibility and involvement in meeting the educational needs of the severely handicapped. School boards will seek legislation and be involved in litigation to determine the role of residential facilities in providing for the needs of low-incidence handicapped populations.
   C Liability suits against school systems, teachers, support personnel, and administrators will increase markedly because of the issues of quality and accountability. These suits will produce legislation to protect "good Samaritans" against liability suits.
   D Post hoc damage suits will be brought by adults who feel that the special education they received or failed to receive as children has harmed their development.

3 Changes or modifications of existing laws:

   A Statutes will be sharply modified to emphasize the right of handicapped persons to be a direct party and involved in all procedures.

   B Laws will be modified to allow third parties to intervene on behalf of the child who needs service but whose parent, guardian, or surrogate has failed to seek or respond to suggested educational treatment programs.

   C Public laws will be enacted that will require school districts to offer alternative programs that give the child or his/her parents a choice of special educational methodologies and strategies.

   D Laws relating to compulsory attendance, exclusion, and expulsion will change. Review of all exclusions and expulsions by nonschool authorities prior to nonemergency expulsion will be demanded. Civil suits will ask for monetary awards for damages suffered by children affected by expulsion or exclusion.

Turnbull (1978) envisions broad challenges to self-contained special education. He suggests that the future issue is "whether courts and agencies will apply the least restrictive principle by taking into account the relative 'richness' or 'poverty' of educational services in separate programs and the likelihood that such programs will be more enhancing for the handicapped child . . . " (p. 526). According to Turnbull, laws aimed at eliminating bias in evaluation and placement procedures are particularly fertile grounds for future litigation. Therefore, with regard to future developments surrounding the principle of nondiscriminatory evaluation, Turnbull expects that:

   1 Tests themselves will come under attack in the courts.

   2 Battles will be fought over how tests are administered and interpreted.

   3 Adaptive behavior tests may be challenged.

   4 Attempts will be made to hold test producers, as well as test users, liable for allegedly validated tests later shown to be improperly validated or nonvalidated.

   5 Placement decisions based on "soft" data will be challenged.

Finally, Turnbull's survey of the issues related to the principle of procedural due process indicates to him that parent initiative will not remain the sole catalyst of special education school-parent confrontations. Turnbull believes that school-initiated due process hearings could become the order of the future.

THE FUTURE OF EDUCATION FOR THE HANDICAPPED

Progress of education for the handicapped has not been steady nor irreversible. We have, in the last 20 years, progressed via litigation and legislation, reaffirming the humanity and individuality of the handicapped and defending their basic right to life, liberty, and equality of opportunity. The extent to which this forward momentum can be maintained is unknown.

Current views regarding the future of educational advances for the handicapped vary from outright pessimism to tentative optimism. The late 50s and the 60s brought changes in our social perspectives which emphasized the human and civil rights of minorities including the handicapped. Many observers, however, now see a shift from the social activism of the 1960s and 1970s, and increasing economic malaise has prompted many citizens to demand a change in the social and economic priorities of our country. Iannaccone (1981) believes the mismatch between changing socioeconomic circumstances and governmental philosophy was instrumental in producing the Republican victory of 1980. He states that the "socioeconomic factors which gave saliency to education policies for over 20 years have now played themselves out" (p. 56). As the character of government in domestic affairs change, so do many policies affecting education. Education in the 1980s is not viewed as a significant area for national policy initiatives. Iannaccone suggests the federal government will assume a posture of benign neglect with regard to education: "The problems of education will not be central to the major political issues the Reagan administration and GOP leadership face. The stamp of irrelevance will be placed on them rather than of opposition by the Reagan administration" (p. 59).

Clark and Amiot (1981) in a tour of administrative, legislative, and association offices in Washington, D.C., interviewed congressional staff members and other officials, appointees, and members of the Reagan administration. As a result of these interviews they were able to gain an impression of the Reagan administration's attitude toward education. Interview responses indicated that the Reagan administration feels that:

- Education is not a core responsibility of the presidency and is therefore low on everyone's priority list.
- Education and schools are failing.
- This failure is largely attributable to federal programs and expenditures in education.
- Enforcement of regulations has converted government allies in education into adversaries.
- Federal involvement in education should be justified on the basis of economic self-interest rather than humanistic, welfare intentions.

Clark and Amiot describe the Reagan administration policy framework for education in terms of "the 5 D's":

1 Diminution—reduction of federal expenditures in education.

2 Deregulation—reduction of federal monitoring in the field of education achieved by revocation of rules and regulations and failure to enforce existing regulations.

3 Decentralization—encouragement and support of greater state and local control of education.

4 Disestablishment—probable eradication of a cabinet-level department of education.

5 Deemphasis—a narrowing of the focus of federal policy in education from general social concerns such as integration or equity to more specific educational and economic concerns (e.g. educational performance standards and specific job training) (p. 258).

Clark and Amiot contend that there is "no disagreement that the Administration intent is to modify the federal role in education substantially" (p. 261); however, they point out that there are numerous interpretations of the scope of change which will occur in educational policies. Some analysts envision an increasingly inactive federal role in education. Other forecasters (the majority of them, according to Clark and Amiot) view current changes as only the first steps toward total federal disengagement from education policy. A third group of analysts believe that lobbies and special groups will be able to develop and "maintain such an effective coalition that the impact of current Reagan policies will be dulled almost completely" (p. 262).

Clark and Amiot's projections for the future of education under Reagan include:

1 Obeisance to the core elements of past federal education policy (i.e.., special education, vocational education, educational equity, minority group education).

2 School improvement aimed at fostering the interests of the "New Right" (i.e., basic skills, achievement standards, private schools, free enterprise, moral and ethical values).

3 Extrication of the federal government from its "keystone role" in education policy.

4 Reversal of the pattern of education policy development that has persisted for 25 years but no revolutionary federal disengagement (p. 262).

What will befall the handicapped student in a national climate characterized by a less humanized social perspective and greater economic stress? How will the handicapped student fare educationally under an administration that does not view education as an overriding national interest? Iannaccone predicts that benign neglect will be seen in the administration of bilingual and special education programs. Reichart (1981) displays a more negative viewpoint when he predicts "a return to old practices and perspectives related to the handicapped" (p. 196). Reichart believes that homogeneous placements will again become a tenable solution to meeting the needs of the handicapped, that mainstreaming will continue as long as it does not cause too much trouble, that our social perspectives related to the common good and to collective behavior responsive to common institutional needs are very likely going to be tested against the fierce sounding boards of practical economics. With limited funds, greater competition for available monies, and the likelihood of fewer regulations, Reichart asks how many will eagerly invest the precious remaining dollars on the handicapped in the school setting?

Clark and Amiot admit that the Reagan administration's policy concerns in education have widespread public support, but they believe there are several considerations which may temper any changes in education policy being advocated by the administration:

1 Past commitments to minorities, the poor, the handicaped may be "too strong to sever or to reallocate solely to local discretion" (p.259).
2 The efforts of those antagonists who will attempt to thwart the administration's objectives have not yet been fully taken into account or implemented.
3 The very nature and characteristics of the field of education will act to depress the changes in educational policy by the administration.

Whatever predictions become reality, it seems likely that the 1980s may mark the beginning of another period in the history of treatment and education of handicapped individuals. Let us hope that history will record this period as enlightened and responsive to individual needs in spite of economic difficulties.

REFERENCES

Abeson, A., Bolick, N., & Hass, J. A primer on due process: Education's decisions for handicapped children, *Exceptional Children*, 1975, *41*, 68–74.

Abeson, A. (Ed.) *Legal Change for the Handicapped through Litigation*. Arlington, VA: The Council for Exceptional Children, 1973.

Aiello, B. Especially for special educators: A sense of our own history, *Exceptional Children*, 1976, *42*, 244–252.

Clark, D. L., & Amiot, M. A. The impact of the Reagan administration on federal education policy, *Phi Delta Kappan*, 1981, *63*, 258–262.

Dunn, L. M. Special education for the mildly retarded — is much of it justified? *Exceptional Children*, 1968, *35*, 5–22.

Ennis, B. J., Friedman, P. R., & Gitlin, B. *Legal Rights of the Mentally Handicapped*. New York: Practicing Law Institute, 1973.

Flanagan, R. Handicapped children, *Cornell Law Review*, 1974, *59*, 519–545.

Gearheart, B. R. *Special Education for the 80's*. St. Louis, MO: The C. V. Mosby Co., 1980.

Gilhool, T. K. Education: An inalienable right, *Exceptional Children*, 1973, *39*, 597–609.

Higgins, S., & Barresi, J. The changing focus of public policy, *Exceptional Children*, 1979, *45*, 270–276.

Iannaccone, L. The Reagan presidency, *Journal of Learning Disabilities*, 1981, *14*(2), 55–59.

Kahan, J. Due process for the retarded, *The George Washington Law Review*, 1033–1051.

LaVor, M. L. *Federal Legislation for Exceptional Persons: A History in Public Policy and the Education of Exceptional Children* (Ed. by Weintraub, Abeson, Ballard, & LaVor), The Council for Exceptional Children, 1977.

McCarthy, M. M., & Thomas, S. B. The right to an education: New trends emerging from special education litigation, NOLPE: *School Law Journal*, 1977, *7*(1), 77–87.

Melcher, J. W. Law, litigation, and the handicapped children, *Exceptional Children*, 1976, *43*, 126–130.

Meyen, E. *Exceptional Children and Youth: An Introduction*, Denver, CO: Love Publishing Co., 1978.

Reichart, Sanford. Social perspectives of mainstreaming, *Educational Horizons*, 59(3), 1981.

Ross, S. L. Jr., DeYoung, H. G., & Cohen, J. S. Confrontation: Special education placement and the law, *Exceptional Children*, 1971, *38*, 3–11.

Stanford Law Review. The right to treatment and educational rights of handicapped persons: Lora *v*. Board of Education, 1979, *31*, 807–815.

Turnbull, H. P., & Turnbull, A. P. *Free Appropriate Public Education Law and Implementation*, Denver, CO: Love Publishing Co., 1979.

Turnbull, H. R. III. The past and future impact of court decisions in special education, *Phi Delta Kappan*, 1978, 523–527.

Weintraub, F. J., & Abeson, A. New education policies for the handicapped: The quiet revolution, *Phi Delta Kappan*, 1976, *55*, 526–530.

Public Law 94-142 and Section 504:
What They Say about Rights and Protections

Joseph Ballard
Jeffrey Zettel

BASIC THRUST, OBJECTIVES, AND TARGET POPULATIONS

What is PL 94-142?

PL 94-142, the Education for All Handicapped Children Act, is legislation passed by the United States Congress and signed into law by President Gerald R. Ford on November 29, 1975. The "94" indicates that this law was passed by the 94th Congress. The "142" indicates that this law was the 142nd law passed by that session of the Congress to be signed into law by the President.

What are the purposes of PL 94-142?

PL 94-142 can be said to have four major purposes:

• Guarantee the availability of special education programming to handicapped children and youth who require it.

Ballard, Joseph, and Zettel, Jeffrey. Public Law 94-142 and section 504: What they say about rights and protections. *Exceptional Children*, 1977, *44*(3), 177–184. Reprinted by permission.

• Assure fairness and appropriateness in decision making with regard to providing special education to handicapped children and youth.

• Establish clear management and auditing requirements and procedures regarding special education at all levels of government.

• Financially assist the efforts of state and local government through the use of federal funds (refer to Section 3 of the Act).

What is Section 504?

Section 504 is a basic civil rights provision with respect to terminating discrimination against America's handicapped citizens. Section 504 was enacted through the legislative vehicle PL 93-112, the Vocational Rehabilitation Act Amendments of 1973. Though Section 504 is brief in actual language, its implications are far reaching. The statute reads:

> No otherwise qualified handicapped individual in the United States shall, solely by reason of his handicap, be excluded from the participation in, be denied the benefits of, or be subjected to discrimination under any program or activity receiving Federal financial assistance.

To whom do PL 94-142 and Section 504 apply?

PL 94-142 applies to all handicapped children who require special education and related services, ages 3 to 21 inclusive. Section 504 applies to all handicapped Americans regardless of age. Section 504 therefore applies to all handicapped children ages 3 to 21 with respect to their public education both from the standpoint of the guarantee of an appropriate special education and from the standpoint of sheer regular program accessibility. Close coordination has thus been maintained between the provisions of PL 94-142 and those of the Section 504 regulations (refer to Section 611 of PL 94-142 and background statement of the Section 504 regulation).

What is the relationship of PL 94-142 to the older federal Education of the Handicapped Act (EHA)?

PL 94-142 is a complete revision of only Part B of the Education of the Handicapped Act. Part B was formerly that portion of EHA addressing the basic state grant program. The other components of the Act (Parts A-E) remain substantially unchanged and continue in operation. Parenthetically, all programs under the aegis of the EHA, including the PL 94-142 revision of Part B, are administered through the Bureau of Education for the Handicapped under the US Office of Education.

Was there a forerunner to PL 94-142?

Many of the major provisions of PL 94-142, such as the guarantee of due process procedures and the assurance of education in the least restrictive environment, were required in an earlier federal law—PL 93-380, the Education Amendments of 1974 (enacted August 21, 1974) PL 94-142 was enacted approximately one year and three months later, on November 29, 1975.

How are handicapped children defined for purposes of this Act?

Handicapped children are defined by the Act as children who are:

> mentally retarded, hard of hearing, deaf, orthopedically impaired, other health impaired, speech impaired, visually handicapped, seriously emotionally disturbed, or children with specific learning disabilities who by reason thereof require special education and related services.

This definition establishes a two pronged criteria for determining child eligibility under the Act. The first is whether the child actually has one or more of the disabilities listed in the above definition. The second is whether the child requires special education and related services. Not all children who have a disability require special education; many are able and should attend school without any program modification (refer to Section 4 of the Act).

If a child has one or more of the disabilities listed in the preceding definition and also requires special education and related services, how does PL 94-142 define special education?

Special education is defined in PL 94-142 as:

> specially designed instruction, at no cost to parents or guardians, to meet the unique needs of a handicapped child, including classroom instruction, instruction in physical education, home instruction, and instruction in hospitals and institutions.

The key phrase in the above definition of special education is "specially designed instruction . . . to meet the unique needs of a handicapped child." Reemphasized, special education, according to statutory definition, is defined as being "special" and involving only instruction that is designed and directed to meet the unique needs of a handicapped child. For many children therefore, special education will not be the totality of their education. Furthermore, this definition clearly implies that special education proceeds from the basic goals and expected outcomes of general education. Thus, intervention with a child does not occur because he or she is mentally retarded but because he or she has a unique educational need that requires specially designed instruction (refer to Section 4(a) (16) of the Act).

How are related services defined in PL 94-142?

Equally important to understand is the concept of related services that are defined in the Act as:

> transportation, and such developmental, corrective, and other supportive services (including speech pathology and audiology, psychological services, physical and oc-

cupational therapy, recreation, and medical and counseling services, except that such medical services shall be for diagnostic and evaluation purposes only) as may be required to assist a handicapped child to benefit from special education, and includes the early identification and assessment of handicapping conditions in children.

The key phrase here is "as required to assist the handicapped child to benefit from special education." This leads to a clear progression: a child is handicapped because he or she requires special education and related services; special education is the specially designed instruction to meet the child's unique needs; and related services are those additional services necessary in order for the child to benefit from special educational instruction (refer to Section 4(a) (17) of the Act).

RIGHTS AND PROTECTIONS

A Free Appropriate Education

What is the fundamental requirement of PL 94-142, from which all other requirements of this Act stem?

PL 94-142 requires that every state and its localities, if they are to continue to receive funds under this Act, must make available a free appropriate public education for all handicapped children aged 3 to 18 by the beginning of the school year (September 1) in 1978 and further orders the availability of such education to all children aged 3 to 21 by September 1, 1980 (refer to Section 3(c) of the Act).

What about preschool and young adults under PL 94-142?

For children in the 3 to 5 and 18 to 21 age ranges, however, this mandate does not apply if such a requirement is inconsistent with state law or practice or any court decree. Refer to regulations for further expatiation of this provision (refer to Section 612 (2) (B) of the Act).

What does Section 504 say regarding the right to an education?

Section 504 makes essentially the same requirement. However, the 504 regulation says "shall provide." PL 94-142 says "a free appropriate public education *will be available*."

The 504 regulation does not refer to specific age groups per se. Instead, it refers to "public elementary and secondary education," and, therefore, the traditional school age population. With respect to that school age population, the 504 regulation accedes to the September 1, 1978, date of PL 94-142 as the final and absolute deadline for the provision of a free appropriate public education. However, the Section 504 regulation also precedes that requirement with the phrase "*at the earliest practicable time* but in no event later than September 1, 1978." (Refer to #84.33(d) of the 504 regulation.)

What is required with respect to preschool and young adult programs under Section 504?

The 504 regulation appears simply to say that preschool and adult education programs will not discriminate on the basis of handicap, and further that such program accessibility is to take effect immediately. On the other hand, PL 94-142, as previously noted, explicitly states that there shall be available a free appropriate public education for children ages 3 through 5 and youth ages 18 through 21 unless such requirement is inconsistent with state law or practice or the order of any court. Again, PL 94-142 does not require such availability until September 1, 1978 (refer to #84.38 of the 504 regulation).

Since Section 504 and PL 94-142 are making, in essence, the same fundamental requirement of a free, appropriate public education, are federal monies authorized under Section 504 as they are under PL 94-142?

No. Section 504 is a civil rights statute, like Title VI of the Civil Rights Act of 1965 (race) and Title IX of the Education Amendments of 1972 (sex).

Must there be compliance with the fundamental requirement of PL 94-142 (as reiterated in Section 504 regulations) if PL 94-142 is not "fully funded"?

It is most important to note that compliance with this baseline guarantee of the availability of a free, appropriate public education is in no way dependent upon whether this Act receives appropriations at the top authorized ceilings, or in other words, is "fully funded." If a state accepts money under this Act, regardless of the amount of actual appropriations, it must comply with the aforementioned stipulation.

What does "free" education, as required in both PL 94-142 and Section 504, mean?

"Free" means the provision of education and related services at no cost to the handicapped person or to his or her parents or guardian, except for those largely incidental fees that are imposed on nonhandicapped persons or their parents or guardian (refer to #84.33(c) (1) of the 504 regulation).

What if a public placement is made in a public or private residential program?

If both the school and parents jointly agree that the most appropriate educational placement for the child is in a public or private residential facility, then such a program placement, including nonmedical care as well as room and board, shall be provided at no cost to the person or his or her parents or guardian (refer to #84.33(c) (3) of the 504 regulation).

Does "free" mean that no private funds can be used?

No. Private funds are not prohibited. To reiterate: there must be no cost to the handicapped person or to his or her parents or guardian.

What does "appropriate" education mean?

"Appropriate" is not defined as such, but rather receives its definition for each child through the mechanism of the written individualized education program (IEP) as required by PL 94-142. Therefore, what is agreed to by all parties becomes in fact the "appropriate" educational program for the particular child.

Individualized Education Programs

What are the basic concepts of the IEP?

The term *individualized education program* itself conveys important concepts that need to be specified. First, *individualized* means that the IEP must be addressed to the educational needs of a single child rather than a class or group of children. Second, *education* means that the IEP is limited to those elements of the child's education that are more specifically special education and related services as defined by the Act. Third, *program* means that the IEP is a statement of what will actually be provided to the child, as distinct from a plan that provides guidelines from which a program must subsequently be developed.

What are the basic components of an IEP?

The Act contains a specific definition describing the components of an IEP as:

> a written statement for each handicapped child developed in any meeting by a representative of the local education agency or an intermediate educational unit who shall be qualified to provide, or supervise the provision of, specially designed instruction to meet the unique needs of handicapped children, the teacher, the parents or guardian of such child, and whenever appropriate, such child, which statement shall include (A) a statement of the present levels of educational performance of such child, (B) a statement of annual goals, including short-term instructional objectives, (C) a statement of the specific educational anticipated duration of such services, and appropriate objective criteria and evaluation procedures and schedules for determining, on at least an annual basis, whether instructional objectives are being achieved.

(Refer to Section 4(a) (19) of the Act.)

May others be involved in the development of an IEP?

Good practice suggests that others frequently be involved. However, the law only requires four persons be involved (i.e., the parents or guardians, the teacher or teachers of the child, a representative of the local educational agency or intermediate unit who is qualified to provide or supervise the provision of special education, and whenever appropriate, the child). If a related service person will be providing services, then it seems to make sense that they be as involved as the teacher. Also, good practice indicates that parents often want to bring an additional person familiar with the child to the meeting.

Who must be provided an IEP?

Each state and local educational agency shall insure that an IEP is provided for each handicapped child who is receiving or will receive special education, regardless of what institution or agency provides or will provide special education to the child: (a) The state educational agency shall insure that each local educational agency establishes and implements an IEP for each handicapped child; (b) The state educational agency shall require each public agency which provides special education or related services to a handicapped child to establish policies and procedures for developing, implementing, reviewing, maintaining, and evaluating an IEP for that child.

What must local and intermediate education agencies do regarding IEP's?

• Each local educational agency shall develop or revise, whichever is appropriate, an IEP for every handicapped child at the beginning of the school year and review and if appropriate revise its provisions periodically but not less than annually.

• Each local educational agency is responsible for initiating and conducting meetings for developing, reviewing, and revising a child's IEP.

• For a handicapped child who is receiving special education, a meeting must be held early enough so that the IEP is developed (or revised, as appropriate) by the beginning of the next school year.

• For a handicapped child who is receiving special education, a meeting must be held within 30 days of a determination that the child is handicapped, or that the child will receive special education.

(Refer to Section 614(a) (5) of the Act.)

Do the IEP requirements apply to children in private schools and facilities?

Yes. The state educational agency shall insure that an IEP is developed, maintained, and evaluated for each child placed in a private school by the state educational agency or a local educational agency. The agency that places or refers a child shall insure that provision is made for a representative from the private school (which may be the child's teacher) to participate in each meeting. If the private school representative cannot attend a meeting, the agency shall use other methods to insure participation by the private school, including individual or conference telephone calls (refer to Section 613(a) (4) (B) of the Act).

Is the IEP an instructional plan?

No. The IEP is a management tool that is designed to assure that, when a child requires special education, the special education designed for that child is appropriate to his or her special learning needs and that the special education designed is actually delivered and monitored. An instructional plan reflects good educational practice by outlining the specifics necessary to effectively intervene in instruction. Documenting instructional plans is *not* mandated as part of the IEP requirements.

What procedures should education agencies follow to involve parents in the development of their child's IEP?

• Each local educational agency shall take steps to insure that one or both of the parents of the handicapped child are present at each meeting or are afforded the opportunity to participate, including scheduling the meeting at a mutually agreed on time and place.

• If neither parent can attend, the local educational agency shall use other methods to insure parent participation, including individual or conference telephone calls.

• A meeting may be conducted without a parent in attendance if the local educational agency is unable to convince the parents that they should attend. In this case the local educational agency must have a record of its attempts to arrange a mutually agreed on time and place such as: (a) Detailed records of telephone calls made or attempted and the results of those calls, (b) copies of correspondence sent to the parents and any responses received, and (c) detailed records of visits made to the parent's home or place of employment and the results of those visits.

• The local educational agency shall take whatever action is necessary to insure that the parent understands the proceedings at a meeting, including arranging for an interpreter for parents who are deaf or whose native language is other than English.

When must handicapped children be guaranteed the IEP?

• For handicapped children counted under the fiscal funding formula of PL 94-142, not later than the beginning of school year 1977-1978.

• For all handicapped children in each state, regardless of the delivering agency, not later than the beginning of school year 1978-1979.

What does Section 504 say with respect to the IEP?

As just discussed, PL 94-142 requires the development and maintenance of individualized written education programs for all children. The 504 regulation cites the IEP as "one means" of meeting the standard of a free appropriate public education (refer to #84.33(b) (2) of the 504 regulation).

Least Restrictive Educational Environment

PL 94-142 requires that handicapped children receive a free appropriate public education in the least restrictive educational environment. What does this mean?

It is critical to note what this provision *is not*:

• It is not a provision for mainstreaming. In fact, the word is never used.
• It does not mandate that all handicapped children will be educated in the regular classroom.
• It does not abolish any particular educational environment, for instance, educational programming in a residential setting.

It is equally critical to note what this provision *does* mandate:

• Education with nonhandicapped children will be the governing objective "to the maximum extent appropriate."
• The IEP will be the management tool toward achievement of the maximum least restrictive environment and therefore shall be applied within the framework of meeting the "unique needs" of each child.
• The IEP document(s) must clearly "show cause" if and when one moves from least restrictive to more restrictive. The statute states that the following component must be included in the written statement accompanying the IEP "and the extent to which such child will be able to participate in regular educational programs."

(Refer to Section 612(5) (B) of the Act.)

Correspondingly, what does the Section 504 regulation say with respect to least restrictive educational environment?

The language of the 504 regulation is, in most important respects, nearly identical to the least restrictive statute in PL 94-142. There remains one notable distinction, however. The 504 regulation would seem to consider the "nearest placement to home" as an additional determinant of instructional placement in the least restrictive environment (refer to #84.34(a) of the 504 regulation).

Procedural Safeguard

Under PL 94-142, what happens if there is a failure to agree with respect to what constitutes an appropriate education for a particular child?

States must guarantee procedural safeguard mechanisms for children and their parents or guardians. Those provisions of previously existing law (PL 93-380, the Education Amendments of 1974) toward the guarantee of due process rights are further refined in PL 94-142, and their scope is substantially enlarged.

Basically, the state education agency must guarantee the maintenance of full due process procedures for all handicapped children within the state and their parents or guardian with respect to all matters of identification, evaluation, and educational placement whether it be the initiation or change of such placement, or the refusal to initiate or change. Interested individuals are strongly urged to read Section 615 of the Act ("Procedural Safeguards") in its entirety.

It should be observed that the PL 94-142 refinements take effect in the first year under the new formula, that is, fiscal 1978 (school year 1977-1978). In the meantime, those basic features of due process as authorized in the prior Act (PL 93-380) must be maintained by the states.

It should be further noted that, when the parents or guardian of a child are not known, are unavailable, or when the child is a legal ward of the state, the state education agency, local education agency, or intermediate education agency (as appropriate) must assign an individual to act as a *surrogate* for the child in all due process proceedings. Moreover, such assigned individual may not be an employee of the state educational agency, local educational agency, or intermediate educational unit involved in the education or care of the particular child (refer to Section 615 of the Act).

Does the Section 504 regulation also require the maintenance of a procedural safeguards mechanism?

Yes. However, though most of the major principles of due process embodied in PL 94-142 are clearly presented in the 504 regulation, *all* of the stipulations of PL 94-142 are treated only as "one means" of due process compliance under Section 504 (refer to #84.36 of the 504 regulation).

What does PL 94-142 say with respect to assessment of children?

PL 94-142 carries a provision that seeks to guarantee against assessment with respect to the question of a handicapping condition when such assessment procedures are racially or culturally discriminatory. The statute does not provide a comprehensive procedure of remedy with respect to potential discrimination but does make two clear and important stipulations in the direction of remedy:

- "Such materials and procedures shall be provided in the child's native language or mode of communication."
- "No single procedure shall be the sole criterion for determining an appropriate educational program for a child."

The provision, in effect, orders that assessment procedures be multi-factored, multi-sourced, and carried out by qualified personnel. The regulations governing this provision should therefore be carefully reviewed (refer to Section 612 (5) (C) of the Act).

What does the Section 504 regulation say with respect to the assessment of children?

The objectives of Section 504 and PL 94-142 are identical of this matter, and the regulatory language for both statutes are also identical (refer to #84.35 of the 504 regulation).

What does PL 94-142 say with respect to the confidentiality of data and information?

PL 94-142 contains a provision that addresses the question of abuses and potential abuses in school system record keeping with respect to handicapped children and their parents. PL 94-142, as did the prior PL 93-380, simply orders a remedy and does not go beyond. The governing statutes for this provision are contained in the larger "Family Educational Rights and Privacy Act" (often referred to as the "Buckley Amendments" after the author, US Senator James Buckley of New York). That measure sets forth both the access rights and privacy rights with respect to personal school records for all of the nation's children and youth, and their parents.

Thus, readers should study the Act itself (contained in PL 93-380), the accompanying regulations for the "Buckley Amendments," and the modest addendums to those provisions contained in the regulations for PL 94-142 (refer to Section 617(c) and Section 612 (2) (D) of the Act).

What then, in summary, are the rights and protections of PL 94-142 (which, for the most part, are also affirmed in Section 504) that must be guaranteed?

PL 94-142 makes a number of critical stipulations that must be adhered to by both the state and its local and intermediate educational agencies:

• Assurance of the availability of a free, appropriate public education for all handicapped children, such guarantee of availability no later than certain specified dates.

• Assurance of the maintenance of an individualized education program for all handicapped children.

• A guarantee of complete due procedural safeguards.

• The assurance of regular parent or guardian consultation.

• Assurance of special education being provided to all handicapped children in the "least restrictive" environment.

• Assurance of nondiscriminatory testing and evaluation.

• A guarantee of policies and procedures to protect the confidentiality of data and information.

• Assurance of an effective policy guaranteeing the right of all handicapped children to a free, appropriate public education *at no cost* to parents or guardian.

• Assurance of a surrogate to act for any child when parents or guardians are either unknown or unavailable or when such child is a legal ward of the state.

It is most important to observe that an official, written document containing all of these assurances is now required (in the form of an application) of every school district receiving its federal entitlement under PL 94-142. Correspondingly, such a public document also exists at the state level in the form of the annual state plan, which must be submitted to the US Commissioner.

Problems in Legislation as a Vehicle for Educational Change

Laurence Iannaccone

The years following World War II provided a benign economic environment for Americans that accented the plight of the poor, particularly the black minority. Concern over social and economic inequalities and the Cold War led the United States to embark on a dramatic change in federal-state intergovernmental relations in education. President Lyndon B. Johnson's Great Society programs were a federal overlay of existing government initiatives. Early resistance to federal legislation was largely overcome by the promise of grants-in-aid. This ideological promise of federal intervention to change education had been largely played out by the latter half of the 1970s, however. Economic conditions became grim. Federal legislation and agency regulation then turned increasingly to punitive actions rather than to rewards to achieve compliance.

A cursory examination of the past 20 years of governmental reforms quickly confirms that the intention of legislation has been to alter the organizational, governance, personnel, and program planning functions of education as well as school finance. Nevertheless, unfavorable indicators of student achievement and related outcomes resulting from recent policy changes—lower scores on standardized achievement tests, higher rates of school violence and vandalism, and lower levels of public satisfaction with schooling effectiveness, for example—offer little comfort to those who expect legislative action to have direct or immediate effects on school performance. Today there is only a fragmentary and inadequate understanding of how the passage of any legislation is linked to changes in the actual operation of schools, let alone student learning. Even without other supporting data, of which there are many sorts, it is plain that the poor performance of the schools, especially in their governance and control systems, comes from their being overcentralized and vastly overbureaucratized (Wise, 1979).

Iannaccone, Laurence. Problems in legislation as a vehicle for educational change. *Exceptional Education Quarterly*, 1981, 2(2), 69–79. Reprinted by permission.

The lessons of the postwar experience with educational reform policies suggest an approach that takes account of "the school as an institution with a life, a climate, and ongoing transactions of its own" (Passow, 1976). This approach suggests that policy is most appropriately influenced by mutually interdependent levels of government and by the multiple groups of organized participants who respond to legislation. Specifically, local differences in the roles and work orientations of school personnel and patrons and local variations in the customs, rules, and procedures used by decision makers should be accommodated. Otherwise the mismatch between legislative policy and local purposes will continue to frustrate both, exacerbating conflicts between levels of educational governance and heightening conflicts among the various lay and professional groups at each level. Continued escalation of existing policy conflicts is threatening to end legislated educational reform policies and to cause the abandonment of legislative responsibility for educational leadership. The fault for the present state of affairs lies as much or more in ill-conceived legislation as it does in the resistance of local teachers and citizens to legislated policy. Good legislative intent is not enough to make good policy, nor are good lobbying tactics. What is needed is equal attention to school systems, to the targets of legislation, to the basic character of schools, and to natural responses to the impact of legislative interventions (Mitchell & Iannaccone, 1980).

SCHOOL SYSTEM TARGETS FOR LEGISLATIVE POLICY

Schools are complex organizations serving to stimulate and coordinate the activities of many different people to achieve goals for children's learning and development. Improving education, therefore, means changing three control systems: *structural units*, such as school districts, teacher organizations, and special program offices, with specific powers and responsibilities; *procedures* used in making the administrative and political decisions that control day-to-day activities and program operations; and *role and work orientations* (normative beliefs and commitments) of individual participants in responding to opportunities and demands for action. Each of these control systems affects different aspects of the school, and each is constrained by unique social forces and historical circumstances beyond the reach of legislated efforts to alter or enhance its performance. Thus effective legislation must be based on a careful assessment of how proposed policies will affect each of the school system's control systems and their interaction.

Structural Units

Public policy makers are consistently faced with two basic problems in structuring the distribution of powers within the schools. First, they have to wrestle with the problem of how to assign appropriate powers and responsibilities to each of several different levels of school organization (federal, state, district, and individual school). Second, they must decide which powers at each level should be assigned to professional educators and which should be reserved to lay citizens or political leaders. The competitive demands of each group are rooted in legitimate values and concerns. Professionals need discretionary latitude to deal with variations among pupils' needs, and the public has a need to protect pupil welfare from the private vested interests of professionals. Consequently, PL 94-142 explicitly requires the interaction of parents and teachers in determination of individualized education programs.

Procedures

Decision-making procedures control organizational performance by determining how available resources will be used and by assigning tasks and responsibilities to specific individuals. Legislative policy affects school decision-making procedures by specifying *who* can participate in various decision-making structures and *what* decisions they can legitimately make. PL 94-142, for example, in both its individualized education plan (IEP) requirements and its procedural safeguards, specifies who can participate in making which decisions.

Legislation specifying school decision-making procedures must deal with two problems. First, although increasing the number of people involved in making a decision makes the outcome more representative, it also complicates and slows down the decision process. Thus all decision-making processes must strike a balance between the need for efficiency in producing timely and appropriate decisions and the need to represent all legitimate interests at the time they are made. The second problem is found in the relationship between program planning and performance accountability decisions. Effective educational programs have to be tailored to the unique conditions in particular schools and communities. Programs may be adjusted to local conditions either by decentralizing planning or by giving local agencies latitude in implementing program plans. If both planning and implementation decisions are dominated by centralized state and federal agencies, then the schools are unable to accommodate critical variations in local conditions and needs. Conflict between governance levels is the result. Educational programs then become rigid and ineffective. If both planning and accountability are turned over to local agencies, however, the legislative intent may be subverted. Separating the responsibility for planning and accountability results in discontinuity and slippage between planned programs and their implementation. Thus legislation must strive to balance the need for cooperation between governmental levels with the need to ensure that universal program standards are generated and enforced.

Role and Work Orientations

Prior training and job experience produce orientations toward an individual's work that determine the perceived importance of tasks and influence the approach of that individual toward each task. These role and work orientations are extremely important in determining whether individuals will be responsive to particular legislative policies and what factors will reinforce or inhibit their willingness or capacity to implement the intended programs.

Examples of the ways in which legislative policy contributes to the formation of work orientations in the school include the creation of staff training and development programs; the adoption of credentialing requirements; and the identification of specific norms and behavioral expectations for educators, students, citizens, or school board members. A balance must be struck between providing teachers with the discretionary latitude to decide how best to teach each child and the need for standard practices and accepted techniques. These are matters of work orientation rather than structural or decision-making problems because they are reflected much more intensely in the ways individual teachers approach their work than in any structural arrangements or formal decisions taken outside the classroom. Legislation may attempt to specify too precisely the details of teaching and curriculum, as did the curriculum innovations following the first launching of Sputnik in 1957 and the federal search for "teacher proof" materials. Tampering with ill-understood work norms of people is a counterproductive activity.

LIMITATIONS IN LEGISLATION

No matter how intensely legislators may wish to improve the teaching by teachers and the learning by students, they have only limited powers of doing so. To be effective, legislative policy must be formulated into legal statutes. These statutes can control only specific and rather narrow aspects of the educational system. In formulating policy the legislature has at its disposal three qualitatively different types of controls that are embodied, separately or in combination, in every statute. Every statute must allocate resources to various school programs or organizational units. It must also formulate legal rules that constrain individual behavior and distribute formal authority and power within the school system, and it may also have to articulate important ideological beliefs, goals, or legislative intentions aimed at guiding the thinking and behavior of educators or lay citizens.

Each of these types of policy has its own unique and limited impact on the schools, and each must meet certain conditions to be effective. Thus the legislative influence on the schools is circumscribed both by the repertoire of available policy tools and by the complexity of the schools.

Resource Allocation

Given the political and economic realities, discussion of several problems inherent in fiscal legislation has been omitted here. However, it should be noted that even if the current fiscal problems are adequately answered by legislation, that legislation will not be effective unless there is consistency among its provisions for resource allocation, its legal rules, and the ideological beliefs it articulates. (See the article by Gerber in this issue for a discussion of resource allocation.)

Rule Making

There are two kinds of rules, which are an expression of policy. One kind defines the governance system in society and serves to distribute or redistribute power. A law that changes the rules about access to decision making is a strategy for redistributing power. For instance, PL 94-142, Section 613 (a)(12), requires states to provide an advisory panel with the power to (a) advise the state education agency, (b) comment publicly on proposed regulations and procedures for distributing funds, and (c) assist in reporting data and evaluation. These powers may be a significant base of influence for the constituencies represented on that panel, or they may be allowed to fall into disuse through purely ceremonial activities.

Three conclusions about rule-making legislation that creates new structures in governance can be drawn. First, all structural changes in access to decisions carry the inherent potential for some redistribution of power. Second, whether that potential is turned into significant influence or allowed to lapse into ceremonial disuse depends on the decisions and actions of the participants given access by the new structure and of the constituents they represent. Such a law can produce the conditions necessary for influence, but it is not sufficient by itself. Third, the exploitation of the opportunities and conditions produced by legislation to redistribute power almost always provoke political conflict.

Consequently there are two important considerations that special education strategists should take into account in proposing additional legislation aimed at redistributing power. One consideration is the existence of constituencies that have the capacity and willingness to exploit the opportunity. If these constituencies do not exist, then there are likely to be petty political conflicts and minor skirmishes around existing power distributions that will reinforce the status quo. Another consideration is that redistribution of power takes time. Successfully altering any organization is a confusing and anxiety-producing process that requires extended effort and patience. Even when everyone is ready and willing to change, it is often a matter of years before a major reorganization effort is adequately understood by all those who are affected by it and it is usefully incorporated into the established pattern of activities. If legislation tries to reorganize the power structure too often, confusion and uncertainty result, and there is a rapid growth in resistance or cynicism. There seems to be little point in responding to current policy because it can shortly be expected to change anyway. The proverb, "The more things change the more they stay the same," is especially true about legislated redistributions of power.

A second kind of rule specifies how individuals must behave in particular situations. Examples may be found in PL 94-142, Section 617, on administration; Section 618, on evaluation; Section 613, on state plans; and elsewhere throughout the statute.

To be effective, rules must be enforceable. Enforceable rules must meet at least four conditions. First, they must apply to behavior, not to intentions, desires, or attitudes. Second, they must provide for specific rewards or penalties. Legal rules that can be violated with impunity or that offer no incentive for the reluctant citizen cannot be expected to actually control behavior. Third, they must form a consistent set. If rules make contradictory demands, it is impossible to comply with all of them. Finally, enforceable rules must be understandable and sensible to those who are expected to comply. Rules that are confusing or call for behavior that seems silly encourage people to subvert or simply ignore them, making enforcement impossible. It is also impossible to enforce rules effectively when there are too many of them.

The positive effects of even well-formulated rules are not without some serious costs. Even the best rules tend to create apathy and alienation among those who are expected to follow them. Rules, by their nature, specify a minimum level of acceptable performance rather than a desired or optimal level; because of this they make it possible for people to do as little as is necessary to fulfill requirements. This tends to encourage apathetic rather than enthusiastic participation in any program and tends to produce compliance with the letter rather than the spirit of the law. Rules contribute to alienation by emphasizing standardization and routinization of all actions. Such standardization blunts the capacity of schools to respond to the unique personal meanings and rich human dimensions of all teaching and learning processes. Too often policy makers and interest group leaders try to cope with apathy and alienation by expanding the number of rules and increasing their specificity. The result is a vicious circle in which the final result shows up on the sort of administrative opportunism documented by the Rand Corporation studies of federal programs or the development of the wooden, mindless overcompliance found in recent Early Childhood Education evaluation studies (Berman & McLaughlin, 1978; Baker et al., 1977).

Ideological Beliefs

The third and least well understood mechanism by which legislation can have an effect on schools is legislative development and sharing of ideas. Education legislation frequently articulates ideas about how schools should be governed, how the processes of teaching and learning should be valued, and what the appropriate attitudes of school people toward their work are. Ideologies form the basis for policy development and implementation by describing and interpreting the tension between what is and what ought to be in society. Thus PL 94-142 states a congressional perception of the current situation in special education and what Congress believes the situation ought to be. (See, for example, section 3, entitled "Statement of Findings and Purpose.") Legislative language reflects legislators' reading of the hearts and minds of others; when the reading is accurate, as it is more often than many people realize, it builds or strengthens an ideological consensus, without which legislation is at best a poor vehicle of change, and at worst counterproductive.

The elements of legislation are interactive, and this is particularly significant for the problems that legislators must confront in dealing with educational change. The essential discretionary latitude at the nexus of pupil-teacher inter-action dictates that neither resource allocation nor rules can be effective unless there are shared ideological commitments among the persons required to abide by the law.

POLITICAL RESIDUE OF PREVIOUS LEGISLATION AND ITS IMPLICATIONS

In the 1980s, new educational legislation (federal and state), intended to change education, must conform to or cope with the political backlash resulting from previous governmental interventions. This backlash is of at least three kinds: (a) that resulting from the perceived failure of intervention programs to im-prove scholastic achievement, (b) that reflecting public reaction to being over-governed, and (c) that produced by the perception that schools are being used inappropriately to solve social problems that are outside their proper mission. Although the core interest groups represented by each of these kinds of politi-cal backlash may be different, the mutual interests of these groups have pro-duced political coalitions of overwhelming influence. Their mutual goal is to stop the expansion of efforts to legislate learning.

Backlash of Scholastic Failure

Previous legislative attempts to change educational achievement, spanning a period of over 20 years, have been remarkably unsuccessful in improving the production functions of education. Whatever the causes, the data indicate a correlation between the growth of federal and state intervention programs and a general decline in achievement scores. The correlation may be spurious; causal links may not exist. In the realm of political philosophy and action, however, an unproved hypothesis that is believed becomes truth. The student achievement results of programs imposed on the schools by federal and state interventions, including legislation, generate little political support from the general public for further legislation to change education—except measures that might reduce federal and state intervention. Additional legislative inter-ventions to improve the quality of education are suspect from the start; they carry the stigma of previous failures in similar efforts.

Hence, for the sustained support of special education, it becomes particular-ly crucial to avoid overly optimistic learning outcomes in advocating whatever additional legislation may be needed. Special education does not have to prove itself to the public for support through marked improvement in academic achievement scores, although gains in the scores are not to be ignored. PL 94-142 includes terms such as "effectiveness of efforts" of special education and "unique needs" of exceptional children, but the emphasis throughout the statute is on unique needs. Even the evaluation section of the statute emphasizes process rather than outcome. More specific and to the point, Section 618(d)(2) on reports to the commissioner addresses "effectiveness of procedures" in reference to placement in the "least restrictive environment," a procedural rather than an outcome criterion. Ironically, extravagant promises of learning outcomes, in the hope of making legislation easier to pass, are more likely to come from enthusiastic advocates of special education than from legislative needs or the general public's demand. The promises of today's advocate who is a true believer can easily become the specter of tomorrow's evaluation.

Backlash of Overgovernment

The past 20 years have produced an accelerating centralization of all four levels of educational government: federal, state, local district, and individual school. This centralizing process has decreased discretionary latitude at the individual school level because of compliance with state and federal mandates. State-level powers have been curtailed, largely in response to federal government grant programs. Both federal and state education agencies have suffered reduction in their discretionary latitude in response to civil rights legislation and related judicial decisions. Moreover, this fundamental alteration of educational government was never demanded by most of the American citizenry, nor were even the separate pieces of this new governmental system demanded by the public. Instead the pieces of what, viewed as whole, may now be seen as a new centralized system of intergovernmental relations were separately tolerated as the necessary price that had to be paid for the additional funds required to mount each new program as it emerged and cope with the demand for equity without sacrificing the benefits it was believed the public schools had already provided. Even prior to the reforms legislated in the late 1950s, U.S. public schools were already burdened by significantly more bureaucratic control procedures than were needed for coordination of teaching/learning as such. Even then the bureaucratic procedural overburden reflected local and state governmental needs for assurances of accountability; such assurances were given at the expense of the discretionary latitude required by professional teachers to do their best work. The imbalance or overload of control has been severely worsened by the accretion of over 20 years of legislation, agency guidelines, administrative regulations, grant application procedures, form-filling demands, evaluation requirements, and other procedural prescriptions. Such regulations and guidelines often have no effect on the classroom and its teaching/learning processes. When they do have an effect, it is largely to decrease the discretionary latitude of the teacher, which is intrinsic to optimizing the outcomes of schooling.

In response to federal and state legislation, the last decade has seen an even more rapid issuance of agency rules of every sort. A punitive rather than a rewarding style of management has come to be seen as the trademark of governmental action. The anticipated benefits had earlier made increased overbu-reaucratization seem tolerable, but the punitive style made it less and less pal-atable. Misperception or not, on the eve of the 1980 presidential election U.S. domestic policy, including educational policy, was seen as a punitive expansion of centralized government, as an intrusion into the private and domestic affairs of local citizens. In education, as in domestic policies generally, one legacy of success in centralization and bureaucratization is a strong political backlash against being overgoverned. The general public stance toward government also greatly strengthens the probability of political backlash by organized teachers against additional legislation, which might further burden the schools' bureau-cratic controls. Taken together, the responses to new legislative proposals are likely to block legislation and lead to compromises that satisfy the demands of special interests for educational change at the symbolic level but provide signif-icant escape hatches at the operational level. That condition, in turn, can be expected to produce increased litigation, heighten frustration, and feed the fires of further political backlash against the education system as a whole.

The temptation to call for additional legislation must be resisted. When such legislation is deemed essential, it should be combined with significant reduc-tions in the bureaucratic demands already placed on school personnel. When-ever possible, concerted, serious efforts should be made for joint sponsorship of legislation by special education constituencies and other education groups, especially teacher organizations. Extensive collaboration may mean delays, but the delays are worth tolerating to obtain better legislation and increase its chances of proper implementation. Implicit also in dealing with the backlash against overgovernance is the necessity of giving present special education pro-grams time to become fully implemented in the schools. Again, this requires the commitment of time and effort by special education constituencies to working through and gaining an adequate understanding of school staffs, at the individ-ual school level especially. These tasks require dull, foot-slogging, day-to-day work, but it is work that special education groups have demonstrated an ability to do well in the past. In the political climate of today, to shirk such work for the goal of inhabiting the corridors of legislative power temporarily and passing a few new bills is an unintelligent decision.

Backlash and the Schools' Mission

Federal intervention efforts have produced yet a third sort of political back-lash, involving definition of the schools' proper mission. Since the mid-1950s, and especially since the late 1960s, federal policy has attempted to place the school in the vanguard of social change. Education law, at least systematically and incrementally, has represented an attempt to rearrange priorities, tilting them toward a redefinition of the school as the prime instrument of social change to produce socioeconomic equality. As legislation became more spe-cific and regulatory, it dealt with more precisely defined categories of prob-lems, as in such programs as affirmative action, bilingual education, PL 94-142, and busing. The legislation itself strengthened the public perception of government intervention as special interest law that is inimical to the welfare of the larger society. The election rhetoric of those who won the 1980 national elections rejects the definition of the school as the prime instrument of socioeconomic change and conceptualizes the school's mission in narrower educational terms.

Fortunately for special education, PL 94-142 and subsequent state legislation, while resting in part on the concept of equity, has not yet come to be seen by the general public as part of the "social engineering" that misdirects the schools' mission. Given the political climate of the day and the probable redirection of federal education policy under the Reagan administration. (Iannaccone, 1981), legislative strategy for special education should optimize its educational virtues rather than its socioeconomic promises. Both learning and social change are implicit outcomes of special education programs, but the slogans that are more likely to garner broad public support in the years ahead are those symbolizing improved educational services rather than social change.

REFERENCES

Baker, E., et al. *Evaluation of the Early Childhood Education program.* (California Department of Education interim report on the special study of selected Early Childhood Education Schools with increasing and decreasing reading scores). Sacramento, Calif.: State Department of Education, 1977.

Berman, P., & McLaughlin, M. W. *Federal programs supporting educational change* (Vol. 3): *Implementing and sustaining innovations.* (Prepared for the U.S. Office of Education: R-1589/8-). Santa Monica, Calif.: Rand Corporation, 1978.

Iannaccone, L. The Reagan presidency, *Journal of Learning Disabilities*, 1981, *14*(2), 55–59.

Mitchell, D. E., & Iannaccone, L. *The impact of California's legislative policy on public school performance.* (California Policy Seminar Monograph No. 5). Berkeley: Institute of Governmental Studies, University of California, 1980.

Passow, A. H. *Secondary education reform: Retrospect and prospect.* New York: Columbia University Press, 1976.

Wise, A. E. *Legislated learning: The bureaucratization of the American classroom.* Berkeley: University of California Press, 1979.

ENABLING ACTIVITIES

To aid you to meet the objectives listed in the chapter study guide (page 39), the enabling activities listed below were designed to provide a variety of study directions and exploration activities ranging from the difficult and time-consuming to less complicated, straightforward tasks. It is important that you understand that you do not have to do every enabler listed—choose only those that help you achieve a study guide objective or appeal to one of your specific interests in the chapter topic.

1 Read all the material published in the "Law Review" section of *Exceptional Children* since 1970. Prepare a written summary for use by teachers and administrators.
2 Review the procedures that are required for due process in identification, evaluation, and educational placement of handicapped children. Devise what you consider to be a model procedure for identifying and placing students in special education classes.
3 Review the Iannaccone article and prepare a rebuttal to his conclusions.
4 Organize and participate in a debate on the question "Should the public schools provide an education for every child regardless of exceptionality?"
5 Review the reading selections in this chapter to identify legal issues in special education placement, and then examine the legislative requirements for providing educational services to the children of your state.
6 Locate and read "Ethnic and social status characteristics of children in EMR and LD classes" by D. J. Franks (*Exceptional Children*, 1971, *37*, 536–537). Complete a similar survey for the schools in your community. Compare your findings with the results of the Franks study.
7 Prepare a panel discussion about the requirements a state must meet in order to receive federal funds for the education of the handicapped as stated in the Education Amendment of 1974.
8 Interview the chief administrator for public school education in your community to determine the assessment and placement procedures currently in use.
9 Prepare a 20-minute oral presentation on the topic "Special education services and the rights of the student" for an audience of parents.

SELF-TEST

True-False

1 The federal government has always been extensively involved with education.
2 Traditionally, all state legislatures provided the same services for exceptional children.
3 The first significant federal act for handicapped individuals was the Soldier's Rehabilitation Act of 1918, which provided services to disabled soldiers.
4 Section 504 of the Vocational Rehabilitation Amendments prohibits discrimination against the handicapped in employment practices.
5 An education is a fundamental right guaranteed by the Constitution.
6 According to Iannaccone, the federal government will continue to support special education through legislation.
7 Physically impaired children were the first to gain specific placement and evaluation criteria through procedural due process.

Multiple-Choice

8 Federal legislation allotted money for tuition, salaries and other expenses to the Columbia Institution for the Instruction of the Deaf and Dumb and Blind during the period of:
  (a) early federal laws
  (b) World Wars
  (c) general education interest
  (d) 1970s and 1980s

9 In 1957 the National Defense Education Act was enacted:
   (a) which recognized that extra services should be provided to exceptional and gifted students
   (b) because the Russians launched Sputnik
   (c) to ensure that American education kept pace with or surpassed the Soviet's
   (d) all of the above

10 Which of the following is not a provision to the Elementary and Secondary Education Act?
   (a) Funds must be provided to states to expand special education services.
   (b) Assistance must be given to local education agencies to help the educationally deprived.
   (c) Educational settings must be equipped with ramps and elevators to accommodate physically handicapped students.
   (d) Grants must be allocated to state agencies responsible for public education for handicapped children.

11 Public Law 94-142, the Education for All Handicapped Children Act, guarantees:
   (a) a free, appropriate public education for every handicapped child
   (b) nondiscriminatory evaluation
   (c) educational services in the least restrictive environment
   (d) all of the above

12 Which of the following is not a use of litigation according to Gilhool?
   (a) secure substantive rights
   (b) maintain the rights in the Constitution
   (c) allow the aggrieved citizen to express himself
   (d) alert the public to facts that have not been visible before

13 "Each handicapped child must be provided with an education that meets his own unique needs" comes under the principle of:
   (a) zero reject
   (b) procedural due process
   (c) appropriate education
   (d) nondiscriminatory evaluation

14 Clark and Amiot's assessment of the Reagan administration indicated:
   (a) the quality of education and schools are improving
   (b) federal involvement in education should be justified on the basis of economic self-interest
   (c) military build-up takes priority over education
   (d) education policies should be handled through the Department of Education

15 Why is traditional assessment criticized?
   (a) Tests are often administered incorrectly.
   (b) Some tests do not validly measure a child's ability.
   (c) Tests are not given in the child's primary language.
   (d) all of the above.

3

DISCIPLINE

After reading the selections presented in this chapter and completing the enabling activities, the student should be able to:

1 Formulate a definition of discipline.
2 List three categories into which discipline approaches can be placed.
3 Describe the relationship between student self-direction and school discipline.
4 Formulate a definition of punishment.
5 Differentiate between corporal and other forms of punishment.
6 Describe any differences between disciplining special education students and regular education students.
7 List three general competencies teachers need for successful classroom discipline.
8 List five ways school staff contributes to discipline problems.
9 List five alternative programs to school suspension.
10 Discuss the moral and ethical considerations inherent in a system of classroom discipline.

Discipline

Lee Clark

There are many aspects of the job that teachers find nettlesome: low salary, overcrowded classrooms, poor community support, low status, and insensitive administrators. There is one, however, that teachers struggle with daily. It has been the subject of inservice and college courses, journal articles, textbooks, and teacher conferences. Discipline—or the lack of it—separates good teachers from bad, contributes to "burnout," and consistently remains controversial.

In Gallup polls taken annually since 1968, discipline is reported as one of the major problems facing public schools. Parents cited it as the number one problem in 1977, and in 1981 discipline once again headed the list of major problems facing schools (Gallup, 1981). Teachers, parents, and even students are asking, "How can we prevent or eliminate discipline problems and create a better teaching and learning environment in the classroom?"

Historically, discipline of children was physical punishment. Numerous authors (Williams, 1979) have traced physical punishment to antiquity, when "infanticide" as well as subjecting children to cruel religious rituals was widely practiced. Two factors (among others) may have contributed to the consistent use of physical punishment in childrearing practices.

1 The Christian notion that children are inherently evil. In colonial America, Calvinist and Puritan traditions demanded stern treatment for children, since pleasure was considered evil and man corrupt and in need of reform. "He that spareth his rod hateth his son, but he that loveth him, chasteneth him" (Proverbs 13:24) was and still is one of the most widely quoted maxims regarding the disciplining of children.

2 The notion that children are property—an economic resource—and the father is the master. This authoritarian concept permeated all of society including education. The American school system was founded on such principles and has been supported by authoritarian models (Cremin, 1964). In describing school discipline, Manning (1959) notes that a century of strict disciplinary practices, which included corporal punishment, were wholeheartedly supported by parents and public. As a consequence, American schools placed little emphasis on self-discipline.

DeMause (1974) suggests a slow but general improvement in child care leading to less harsh forms of physical punishment. Various explanations have been provided for this trend, including improved economic and demographic factors, the growing psychic maturity of society, the promulgation of Judeo-Christian ideas, and the American belief in freedom, democracy, due process, and individual rights. With the gradual improvement in childrearing practices over the past two centuries, education has evolved toward channeling impulses into acceptable means of expression.

Several aspects in American society contributed to the gradual limitation of harsh physical punishment. Physical punishment decreased as the number of women teachers increased. Another factor was the belief that American schoolteachers were not as competent as teachers in England. Thus, parents were less willing to relinquish their authority to schools. Hyman (1979) and Manning (1959) suggested that as Americans moved west, both life and school were less violent, and the improvised punishments were less stringent.

As the mid-twentieth century approached, childrearing was characterized by increased permissiveness in education and attitudes toward discipline. This permissiveness was contributed to by "progressive" educators who consciously avoided the term "discipline" (Kandel, 1943) and associated it with the evils of pedagogical formalism (Tanner, 1979). Thus, discipline was not mentioned in educational methods. If a student was "interested," he would develop self-discipline. This philosophy produced a myriad of experimental education methods culminating in the free school movement in the late 1960s and early 1970s.

This "gradual" move toward permissiveness was not universally accepted. Many people today support the view that children should be totally obedient and conforming (Gil, 1970). In education this is reflected in the emphasis on deportment as an important part of the learning process. Trends, social mores, and values appear cyclic in nature. Having experienced a permissive cycle, it appears, as we move into the 1980s, that a return to the "basics" and "old fashioned discipline" is beginning.

DEFINING DISCIPLINE

The *Britannica World Language Dictionary* (1980) defines discipline as "systematic training or subjection to authority; especially the training of mental, moral or physical powers by instruction and exercise." In this context discipline is achieved through training, and importance is associated with the trainer or teacher. LaGrand (1969) supports the "teaching" concept by defining discipline as the habit of teaching restraint, orientation, and organization, essentials necessary if learning is to prevail. Madsen and Madsen (1974) define discipline as a process whereby certain relationships are established. It is a way of behaving conducive to productive ends. They further state discipline must first be taught, then it can be learned. It this context, discipline is achieved when the teacher presents and the student receives, both sharing responsibility. Discipline is taught!

Etymologists inform us that the word discipline shares its derivation with "disciple," connoting a process of learning. Since learning is a student-related responsibility, Bushell (1973) defines discipline as a set of procedures designed to eliminate behaviors that compete with effective learning. If the student is responsible for learning, then he or she assumes the task of eliminating behaviors not conducive to learning. The teacher's role is facilitation rather than arbitration.

Definitions are sometimes developed as a reaction to a specific crisis rather than as a careful examination of all the factors that have an impact. The interpretation of the role of the teacher, student, and organization coupled with the emphasis placed on each will significantly affect any definition of discipline under these conditions. Those who place a high degree of importance on the role of the organization would support the notion that the needs of the group come first and are best accomplished through external control. Various definitions (Haralson, 1979; Wingo, 1963) say just that; Ausubel (1961) defines discipline as the imposition of external standards and controls on individual conduct, and Curwin and Mendler (1980) define a discipline problem as a situation in which the needs of a group are in conflict with those of a group member. According to Chesler, Crowfoot, and Bryant (1979), discipline policies in the schools are primarily oriented toward maintaining order.

With the various definitions available, it is little wonder that discipline, like the weather, is a term often used but rarely understood. To the parent, it may imply corporal punishment for recalcitrant offspring, to the athlete it conjures a routine of vigorous training, and to the teacher it may evoke the image of a quiet and orderly classroom.

In reality the classroom is often less than quiet and orderly. It is the vehicle in which two prime goals should be accomplished. First, the immediate satisfaction of the learning tasks set for society's young; and second, long-term goals (which depend on self-discipline) of successful personal development. Self-disciplined students are one of the major goals of classroom discipline—citizens educated not only to the point of graduation, but also trained for subsequent achievement. Discipline, then, is the organization of the learning environment to efficiently and orderly permit satisfaction of immediate learning tasks and the inculcation of self-discipline.

APPROACHES TO DISCIPLINE

While most attention has focused on appropriate ways of dealing with discipline problems after they occur, strategies have been developed to eliminate problems before they occur. Glickman and Wolfgang (1980) describe eight "discipline models." They position them on a continuum from child-centered to teacher-directed. These models cluster into three categories: relationship/listening, confronting/contracting, and rules/punishment.

Relationship/Listening

Strategies in this category assume students to be rational and that a minimum of "power" is needed for response to students. This category includes Teacher Effectiveness Training (Gordon, 1974); Transactional Analysis (Berne, 1964; Harris, 1969); and Values Clarification (Rath, Hormin, & Simon, 1966).

Teacher Effectiveness Training (TET)   Teacher Effectiveness Training is based on the assumptions that a positive teacher-learner relationship is essential, the student is rational and wants to behave appropriately, and through a warm personal relationship learning will more readily occur. In order to establish this quality relationship, teachers need to be sensitive, warm, and noncritical. Gordon (1974) provides a number of specific actions needed to achieve this. He further provides specific methods the teacher can use to attain an effective student/teacher relationship. Discussion of "active" and "critical listening," appropriate ways to acknowledge responses, "door openers," and "I" messages are emphasized as tools for assisting the student to gain an understanding of his or her emotional state and behavior. Gordon also provides the teacher with techniques for resolving a conflict in a democratic manner.

Strengths of this strategy include an emphasis on a "no-lose" situation when resolving problems. TET assists the teacher in establishing ownership for the problem. The student is expected to resolve problems supported by teacher facilitation. This approach emphasizes a democratic system for setting rules and purports to develop responsibility in the student.

There are limitations with this strategy—especially for the special education teacher. The assumption that children are rational and able to make appropriate decisions may be faulty for some exceptionalities. Further, it may be difficult to keep a warm, nonthreatening, no-lose relationship when dealing with a violent student who is physically and emotionally out of control.

The emphasis on verbalization may also be a limitation if a student has limited language. TET requires dialogue to be effective. The amount of time necessary to listen and aid a student resolving a problem is often not practical. Empirical evidence supporting or critical of this strategy is limited, due to the subjectivity of interpreting many of the variables involved. Hyman (1979) investigated TET in terms of effectiveness for the inservice training of teachers. He found that the data base was weak, with many of the investigators attempting to measure global results such as improvement in achievement scores. He did suggest, however, that this approach helped teachers humanize their approaches to children as measured by a variety of attitude scales.

When considering this model as an alternative to traditional discipline methods, the following factors should be considered:

1 The teacher should perceive his/her role as one of facilitation.
2 The student must have an active role in the learning process.
3 The structure of the classroom must facilitate dialogue.
4 Harsh punishment techniques cannot be considered.
5 The severity of the behavior and the rational ability of the student population must permit continued dialogue.

Transactional Analysis (TA)   Transactional Analysis is a strategy to provide a framework to ascertain if verbal interactions are conducive to dealing with misbehaving students (Glickman & Wolfgang, 1980). Developed by Eric Berne and Thona Harris, TA is psychodynamically oriented.

When two or more people encounter each other, sooner or later one of them will speak or acknowledge the other. This is the "transactional stimulus." The other will respond to the stimulus and this is the "transactional response" (Harris, 1969). These transactions emanate from various aspects of the personality and affect the individual's decision making process. For example, problem solving is greatly impaired if the student or teacher is responding from a part of the personality that is not conducive to rational thinking. Transactional Analysis provides the teacher and student with a means to decode responses and identify which personality aspect is responding. Once identified, a common framework can be established from which to resolve problems.

The strengths of Transactional Analysis include provision for determining the relationship between a person's emotional state and what they are communicating. This may eliminate many communication barriers so the real problem can be addressed. TA also enables a teacher to evaluate critically verbal and nonverbal student interactions.

The primary limitations of TA for classroom discipline is the generality of the approach. It describes what is occurring between a student and teacher yet provides no specific remedies for changing behavior. As with TET, some special education populations may be inappropriate for TA because language and rational thinking are requisite.

Empirical evidence supporting Transactional Analysis as an effective strategy for resolving discipline problems is limited. One effort by Hestorly (1974), however, suggests benefits from the program that included increased teacher praise and better self-image for students.

The following should be minded when considering Transactional Analysis as a possible discipline strategy.

1 The teacher must be a facilitator.
2 The student must have an active role in the learning process.
3 The structure of the classroom must facilitate dialogue.
4 Teachers must be willing to develop specific interventions independently once the dialogue type has been identified.
5 Punitive strategies will probably be counterproductive.
6 The student must possess some ability to think and communicate rationally through the "adult" state.

Values Clarification Values Clarification (Rath, Hormin, & Simon, 1966) is based on the assumption that behavior problems result from the lack of personal codes or values of conduct. A second assumption is that if values are clarified, students will become more consistent and rational in their actions. A non-judgmental, supportive environment is needed to accomplish this. To internalize values the student must freely choose those values.

A major strength of this model is the integration of the value system process into the everyday curriculum. By permitting the student to raise questions, explore alternatives, and make choices without fear of being corrected, even the low-achieving student can develop a sense of worth and satisfaction.

As in many strategies, the strength of Values Clarification can also be a limitation. Teachers must be alert not to infuse their own values into a situation. At times this may be difficult. For example, dealing with students who feel one may steal (as long as they don't get caught) could create a situation in which a teacher cannot accept stealing as a legitimate value. As with Transactional Analysis, Values Clarification has no direct method for dealing with inappropriate behaviors. Its value is in long-term effects and must be used over an extended period before results are evident.

The following should be evaluated when considering Values Clarification as a possible discipline strategy.

1 The teacher must be open-minded, nonjudgmental, and a facilitator.

2 The student has the primary role in the learning process.

3 Classroom structure must allow exploration of ideas, mistakes without judgment, and facilitation of dialogue.

4 Punitive consequences could not be considered, as they would impede the student's free will.

5 The student must possess the ability to think rationally and be willing to explore alternatives.

6 The community attitudes must be conducive to this strategy.

Glickman and Wolfgang's (1980) second group of strategies include what they call the confronting/contracting models. Like the first group, the confronting/contracting models assume a need for a nonpunishing relationship between teacher and student, but they confront the student and make him/her choose a plan that will initiate change—a contract of sorts. Strategies representative of this group include Dreikurs's Social Discipline Model (1972) and Glasser's Reality Therapy (1969).

Social Discipline Model   The social discipline model was developed by Rudolph Dreikurs (1957) and is based on the individual psychology of Alfred Adler. Basic to this approach is the concept of individuality of each child and the individuality of each child's goals. Children are primarily motivated by the need to belong and be accepted. With regard to misbehavior Dreikurs identified four related goals: (*a*) using disability as an excuse, (*b*) attention getting, (*c*) revenge, and (*d*) struggling for power. He developed a four-step system to identify which goal is dominant.

1 Observation and data collection concerning the student and interactions with peers and family.

2 Develop a hypothesis as to which goal is motivating the student.

3 Verifying the goal by reflecting on how the behavior makes the teacher feel.

4 Verify the hypothesis by confronting the student with the hypothesis.

Dreikurs further developed the system so students will more readily understand the logical consequences of their behavior. Punishment was deemphasized with the substitution of natural and logical consequences. Central to this approach is a belief in the child's rational capabilities and that the teacher can redirect a child's misplaced goals through logical consequences.

The strengths of the Social Discipline Model include mutual respect. The student is permitted to solve his/her own problems facilitated by the class and the teacher with natural and logical consequences increasing socialization. Both the student's and teacher's roles are defined and unlike the nonintervention strategies, the teacher takes an active role.

The major limitation of Social Discipline is the assumption that the teacher can determine the student's social goal. Where language, intelligence, and teacher/student relationships are limited, determining the social goal of a student may be very difficult—especially if the student chooses not to cooperate. The student has the responsibility for goal setting and the motivation to do so. Another limitation of the Social Discipline theory is the difficulty in determining appropriate logical consequences given the spontaneity of classroom interactions.

Factors to be considered with the Social Discipline Model include:

1 While the teacher need not be as much a facilitator as in earlier models, he must be a "guide."
2 The student must be a partner in the learning process.
3 Classroom structure must permit group interaction and individualized attention coupled with a nonthreatening classroom atmosphere.
4 Punishment and punitive consequences cannot be considered.
5 A certain degree of rational thinking is required of the student.

In reviewing the research evaluating the effectiveness of the Social Discipline Strategy, Hyman (1979) found ten "reasonable studies." Few of these, however, were even quasi-experimental. Despite the lack of empirical support, a great number of testimonials have been offered supporting the approach (Hyman, 1979).

Reality Therapy   Reality Therapy's basic premise (Glasser, 1969) is the notion that all students have the capacity to be rational and responsible for their actions. The student may, however, need direction and motivation. The teacher assumes the role of a "confronter," asking students to examine the problem and insisting on a commitment to make a plan to correct the problem. Once a plan is developed, the teacher assumes the role of enforcer. The plan provides a clearly defined course which includes not only the problem behavior(s) but a commitment from both the student and teacher for remediation.

A major strength of Reality Therapy is the clear delineation of both the student's and teacher's role in the problem solving process. Responsibility for the success of the plan falls on the student, but if the plan fails the teacher assumes control until a new plan can be developed.

Criticism of Reality Therapy centers around some of Glasser's assumptions. He states that it is the teacher's responsibility to produce a relevant classroom environment for successful student experiences. School district procedures, community standards, and fiscal considerations all influence what goes on in a classroom and may be ouside the control of the teacher. Thus, determining relevancy is not always the prerogative of the teacher or the student.

Glickman and Wolfgang's (1980) third set of strategies are the rules/punishment models. These strategies call for the establishment of rules for acceptable behavior, which are backed up with rewards and punishment. Student participation in the establishment of rules is not required. The teacher using these strategies is very much in control. Examples of rules/rewards and punishment include suspension and punishment models.

Suspension   Despite the importance placed on school participation by compulsory attendance laws, "schools may punish misbehavior by depriving students of access to education" (Kaeser, 1979). While some argue that suspension has little if any educational benefits and that it does little to change a particular behavior, some educators find it a useful tool to provide an immediate and inexpensive response to rule breaking. It is also a serious enough action to capture the attention of the student's parents.

There are, however, enough negative consequences to make one question the benefits. First, the student is temporarily denied guaranteed access to public education. Suspension may also label a student as a troublemaker, which can lead to more failure and suspensions. The Children's Defense Fund (1974, 1975) investigated national data on suspended students and concluded that suspended students frequently have learning disabilities or inadequate academic skills, and even brief suspensions may harm their progress. The data also indicated that suspensions are not uniformly applied to all groups. They found that nonwhite and male students are suspended disproportionately to females and whites. "Few school districts specified their disciplinary practices in writing and dramatic increases in suspensions occurred after desegregation" (Nielson, 1979).

Suspensions become an even more undesirable alternative when discussing special education students. According to Lichtenstein (1980), recent legislation and court decisions have circumscribed the school authority to impose such punishment equally on all students. "Handicapped students cannot be deprived of an educational program for more than two days, have their programs changed without strict adherence to prescribed procedures, not be refused the public school's services unless an appropriate private placement is provided at the school district's expense" (Lichtenstein, 1980). This is primarily due to Public Law 94-142. According to Lichtenstein, Congress's intent was to increase handicapped children's educational opportunities, but one of the act's unexpected side effects has been to supplant the disciplinary procedures of local school districts in the areas of suspension and expulsion. This has been reinforced through various court decisions (*Stuart v. Nappi*, 1979; *Mills v.*

Board of Education of the District of Columbia, 1972). The net effect is to separate the handicapped child from the school and deny him/her access to school programs, people, and resources. The only time a handicapped student may be deprived even temporarily of a program is when he/she presents a danger to the health, safety, or welfare of the balance of the student body. Regardless of the position educators take with regard to suspensions, it is virtually always considered a last alternative.

Numerous viable alternatives to suspension have been reported. One such alternative is in-school suspension. By removing disruptive students from classrooms, others are assured an environment conducive to learning, and the attempts of students to seek home suspension as a holiday from school are undermined (Nielson, 1979). Other benefits of in-school suspension include the continuation of the educational process. Academic assignments can continue to be completed. If in-school suspension programs have well-trained staff members, many times the root of the problem can be discovered. Documented advantages of programs such as these are numerous (Clark, 1978; Mizell, 1977; McClung, 1975; Mendez, 1977). There are other alternatives to in-school suspension programs that have had varying degrees of success and some of these are presented in Table 1.

Punishment   Traditionally, discipline problems have been resolved through punishment. Punishment is an approach which implies control through fear. It involves the use of negative consequences to discourage unacceptable behavior. The theory behind this method of changing behavior is explained by Thorndike's Law of Effect:

> Of several responses made to the same situation, those which are accompanied or closely followed by satisfaction to the animal will, other things being equal, be more firmly connected with the situation, so that when it recurs, they will be more likely to recur; those which are accompanied or closely followed by discomfort to the animal will, other things being equal, have their connection with the situation weakened so that when it recurs, they will be less likely to occur. The greater the satisfaction or discomfort, the greater the strengthening or weakening of the bond (Thorndike, 1911).

Sigmund Freud gave another explanation for using punishment as a deterrent through his pleasure-pain principle. The pleasure principle states that the organism attempts to function in such a way as to achieve pleasure and avoid the opposite (Brenner, 1955).

Punishment, as it is described here, often takes the form of corporal punishment. Miller (1980) states that when the teacher, having exhausted other approaches, feels only physical punishment will prove corrective, then that choice should not be denied. This position is supported by a Supreme Court decision—*Ingraham v. Wright* (1977)—in which the court ruled that corporal punishment in the public schools was not a violation of the Eighth Amendment's prohibition against cruel and unusual punishment. In response to the criticism that corporal punishment produces negative feelings toward school

TABLE 1
ALTERNATIVE PROGRAMS TO SUSPENSION

Program	Description
1 Human Relations Staff	A central committee advises schools and parents on discipline problems. (Foster, 1977)
2 Cooling-off Rooms	Angry or disruptive students leave class and seek counseling in the cooling-off room. Results were a 27 percent reduction in suspensions. (National School Public Relations, 1976)
3 Behavior Clinic	Three hours of weekly group counseling for misbehaving students provides training in school skills. (NSPR, 1976)
4 TALK	Individual and group counseling is arranged weekly with a teacher for "high risk" students, (NSPR, 1976)
5 Guided Group Interactions	teachers identify school leaders and assign them randomly to heterogeneous groups including all students in the school. Peer counseling occurs for 12 weeks, with graduation from the group for improved conduct being rewarded with a certificate. (NSPR, 1976)
6 Teacher Advocate	One teacher counsels regularly with the same group of students for several years and helps resolve their conflicts with other teachers. Results were less truancy, vandalism, and misconduct. (NSPR, 1976)
7 Alternative Schools	Evening or day schools are created for students who cannot function in traditional public schools. Common elements are individualized instruction, contingency contracting, and low student-teacher ratios. (Christen & McKinnon, 1977; NSPR, 1976)
8 Police Referral Center	Police and School personnel create a counseling center for suspended students. (NSPR, 1976)
9 Student Advocate	Teachers and counselors choose a council of 36 student leaders including influential delinquents. When fights occur, the offenders each select an advocate from this council and the students resolve the problem. Results were some negative leaders becoming positive influences, and problems were resolved effectively. (NSBA, 1977)
10 Schedule Changes	Discipline problems were charted according to frequency and time of day. Periods were then rotated so the same course did not always occupy the most disruptive time of day. (NSBA, 1977)
11 SOS—Save One Student	School personnel, including custodial and secretarial workers, choose one disruptive student to counsel and support throughout the year. (NSBA, 1977)
12 Buddy System	Two students create a team to assist each other in avoiding trouble. (NSBA, 1977)
13 Parent–Study Committees	A community group identifies the most frequent student offenses and devises alternatives in lieu of suspensions. (Kemper, 1975)

(continued)

TABLE 1 (CONTINUED)

Program	Description
14 Teacher Release Time	Teachers who are least effective with students are given one free day to follow some of their most disruptive students to perceive school from the child's point of view. (NSPR, 1976)
15 Principal's Round Table	The principal periodically selects 15 students who represent various populations in the school. The group presents ideas regarding discipline prevention and punishment. (Bozym, 1977)
16 Detention Halls	Students are retained after school for their misbehavior. Academic assignments must be completed during the detention. (Williams, 1977)
17 Smoking Clinic	Students who would otherwise be suspended for smoking must attend an evening clinic for a week. The clinic informs as to the hazards of smoking and methods for quitting. A parent must accompany the student. Results indicated that suspensions had dropped (over a 3-year period) from 45 percent of all suspensions for smoking to 20 students a year. (Jorgensen, 1977)
18 Referral Forms	Before the principal disciplines a student, the referring teacher must complete a parent and student conference, after school detention, consultation with the counselor, and changes in student seating and schedules. (NSPR, 1976)
19 Parent Phone Calls	Before any suspension decision, school personnel must phone parents and discuss alternatives. Conferences among parents, students, and staff often result. (NSBA, 1976)
20 Work Programs	Students must eliminate their misconduct demerits by working weekends or after school on campus custodial projects. Results indicated that suspensions decreased. (Betteker, 1975; NSPR, 1976)
21 Truancy Prevention Programs	Nationally the largest proportion of suspensions result from nonattendance, cutting classes, or truancy. Several projects successfully decreased truancy through contingency management systems. (NSPR, 1976)

Adapted from "Let's Suspend Suspensions: Consequences and Alternatives" by Linda Nielson.

and teachers, Miller suggests that given the background of some students, the failure of the teacher to use corporal punishment in an aggravated situation may reinforce the student's negative concept of the teacher, the school, and society. He concludes, "Those who would absolutely deny teachers the right to exercise their judgment as to the efficacy of corporal punishment are not only divorced from the realities of the classroom, but are also expressing very directly their doubt that teaching is a true profession" (p. 22).

On the other hand, Brodinski, et al. (1981) suggested that research challenges Miller's position. Corporal punishment has not been shown to be a deterrent to disruptive behavior. The idea that some students only respond to
corporal punishment means that they have not been exposed to other means.
With regard to using corporal punishment as a protection for teachers, the
authors state "tabulation of the incidence of physical punishment shows its
greatest frequency occurs in primary grades" (p. 2). What are teachers in
the primary grades being protected from that requires physical punishment?
Feshback and Feshback (1973) found a positive correlation between physical
punishment and deviant behavior. Kenneth Clark (1980), a member of the
Board of Regents for the State of New York, goes even further in his objection
to the use of corporal punishment when he states, "there is reason to believe
that the adults who resort to this method of discipline are manifesting symptoms of personal instability. These adults are communicating to children that
violence is a legitimate way of seeking to resolve tensions" (p. 22).

SUMMARY

Empirical research reported about discipline models is limited at best. According to Glickman and Wolfgang (1980), there are no teacher-student interaction models that do not have their critics. There is not now, and probably never
will be, research reported that provides indisputable documentation that one
model is predominantly superior to others. This is true for a variety of reasons,
the most important of which is the failure of studies to compare strategies (Hyman, 1979).

Another reason for the inconclusiveness of discipline research is that most
studies evaluate success based on teacher self-reports. When teachers receive
training for a specific approach and they believe in it, they will generally report
success. The actual behavior change remains to be verified independently.

Intervention strategies aimed at altering a student's behavior or establishing
a classroom behavioral program based on one model has a rather narrow conceptual foundation. Programs designed in this manner often appear successful
in that they are frequently associated with limited, short-term changes in behaviors. However, if the teacher's goal is to assist students in becoming self-
disciplined, functional, healthy members of society, teachers cannot be satis-
fied with program results that are incomplete and short-lived. Teachers will
certainly do their students a disservice if they accept this limited definition of
success. Rather than pick a specific strategy, one should examine as many as
possible, choosing the aspects of each that are most compatible with the teaching style, classroom structure, and other organizational factors unique to the
dynamics of each individual classroom.

Since research cannot take all possible variables into consideration, the ultimate responsibility for validation lies with the classroom teacher. This responsibility takes an added significance for the special education teacher. The impact of Public Law 94-142, court cases concerning discipline interventions, the

increasing number of students being identified as exceptional, and the severity of certain exceptionalities all demand that the special education teacher address the discipline issue thoroughly. Only through innovative, open-minded, and resourceful experimentation can the special education teacher hope to develop strategies that can successfully establish and maintain discipline.

REFERENCES

Ausubel, D. P. A new look at classroom discipline, *Phi Delta Kappan*, 1961, *43*, 1.
Berne, E. *Games People Play: The Psychology of Human Relations*. New York: Grove Press, 1964.
Betteker, D. Suspensions: Get rid of them. *Thrust for Educational Leadership*, 1975, *5*, 26–27.
Bozym, M. Discipline as a multi-colored act. *Creative Discipline*, 1977, *1*, 2.
Brenner, C. *An Elementary Textbook of Psychoanalysis*. New York: Doubleday, 1955, p. 73.
Britannica World Language Dictionary. Chicago: Encyclopedia Britannica, 1980.
Brodinski, B., et al. *Practical Applications of Research*, newsletter of Phi Delta Kappan: Center on Evaluation Development and Research. Vol. 4, no. 1, Bloomington, IN, September, 1981.
Bushell, D. *Classroom Behavior*. Englewood Cliffs, N.J.: Prentice-Hall, 1973.
Chesler, M., Crowfoot, J., & Bryant, B. Organizational context of school discipline—analytical models and policy options. *Education and Urban Society*, 1979, *11*, 465–510.
Children's Defense Fund. *Children out of School in America*. Cambridge, MA.: Washington Research Project, Inc., 1974.
Children's Defense Fund. *School Suspensions: Are They Helping Children?* Cambridge, MA.: Washington Research Project, Inc., 1975.
Christen, W. L., & McKinnon, B. E. Opportunity Hall: Place for dropouts–truants–kickouts. *Personnel and Guidance Journal*, 1977, *55*, 605–607.
Clark, K. Should corporal punishment be abolished in the elementary school—yes. *Instructor*, March 1980, 2.
Clark, L. *The impact of an in-school suspension center—Winston-Salem–Forsyth County Schools*. Winston-Salem, NC, June 1978.
Cremin, L. A. *The Transformation of the School*. New York: Random House, 1964.
Curwin, R. L., & Mendler, A. N. *The Discipline Book: A Complete Guide to School and Classroom Discipline*. Reston, VA: Reston Publishing Co., 1980.
deMause, L. The evolution of childhood. *History of Childhood Quarterly*, Spring 1974, *1*, 504–575.
Dreikurs, R. *Psychology in the Classroom: A Manual for Teachers*. New York: Harper and Row, 1957.
Dreikurs, R., & Cassell, P. *Discipline without Tears: What to Do with Children Who Misbehave*. New York: Hawthorn Books, 1972.
Feshback, S., & Feshback, N. Alternatives to corporal punishment. *Journal of Clinical Child Psychology*, Vol. 2, Fall 1973.
Foster, G. *Discipline Practices in Hillsboro Schools*. Coral Gables, FL, April 1977.
Gallup, G. H. Thirteenth annual Gallup poll of the public's attitudes toward the public schools. *Phi Delta Kappan*, 1981, *63*, 33–47.

Gil, D. G. *Violence against Children*. Cambridge, MA.: Harvard University Press, 1970.

Glasser, W. *Reality Therapy: A New Approach to Psychiatry*. New York: Harper and Row, 1969.

Glickman, C. D., & Wolfgang, C. H. *Solving Discipline Problems: Strategies for Classroom Teachers*. Boston: Allyn & Bacon, 1980.

Gordon, T. *T.E.T.: Teacher Effectiveness Training*, New York: David McKay Co., 1974.

Haralson, E. Advocacy groups and school discipline. *Education and Urban Society*, August 1979, *11*, 527–546.

Harris, T. A. *I'm OK—You're OK: A Practical Guide to Transactional Analysis*. New York: Harper and Row, 1969.

Hestorly, S. O. *How to Use Transactional Analysis in Public Schools*. Little Rock Arkansas Public Schools, 1974.

Hyman, I. A. Discipline in American education: An overview and analysis. *Journal of Education*. Spring 1979, *61*, 51–70.

Ingraham v. Wright, 430, U.S. 651, 1977.

Jorgensen, J. An alternative to suspension for smoking. *Creative Discipline*, 1977, *1*(4), 5.

Kaeser, S. Suspensions in school discipline. *Education and Urban Society*, August 1979, *11*, 465–484.

Kandel, I. L. *The Cult of Uncertainty*. New York: Macmillan Publishing Co., 1943.

Kemper, R. *Coping with Discipline Problems*. Your Schools, Columbia, SC, May 1975, 11–12.

LaGrand, L. E. *Discipline in the Secondary School*. West Nyack, New York: Parker Publishing Co., 1969.

Lichtenstein, E. Suspensions, expulsion and the special education student. *Phi Delta Kappan*, March 1980, 459–461.

Madsen, C. H., & Madsen, C. K. *Teaching/Discipline: A Positive Approach for Educational Development*. Boston: Allyn & Bacon, 1974.

Manning, J. Discipline in the good old days. *Phi Delta Kappan*, December 1959, 94–99.

McClung, M. Alternatives to disciplinary exclusion from school. *Inequality in Education*, 1975, *20*, 58–73.

Mendez, R. School suspension—Discipline without failure. *NASSP Bulletin*, 1977, *61*, 11–14.

Miller, C. Should corporal punishment be abolished in the elementary school—no. *Instructor*, March 1980, 22.

Mills v. Board of Education of District of Columbia, 348 F. Supp. 866 (1972).

Mizell, H. *Designing a Positive In-school Suspension Program*. Columbia, SC, September 1977.

National School Board Association Report (Nielson L. Auth.) Garden City, Kansas, March 1977.

National School Public Relations—Suspensions and expulsions (Nielson L. Auth.) Arlington, VA, 1976.

Nielson, L. Let's suspend suspensions: Consequences and alternatives. *Personnel and Guidance Journal*, May 1979, 442–445.

Rath, L., Hormin, M., & Simon, S. *Values and Teaching*. Columbus, OH: Charles E. Merrill Publishing Co., 1966.

Stuart v. Nappi, 443 F. Supp. 1235 (1978).

Tanner, L. N. A model of school discipline. *Teachers College Record*, May 1979, *80*, 734–742.

Thorndike, E. L. *Animal Intelligence*. New York: Macmillan Publishing Co., 1911, p. 244.

Williams, G. Social sanctions for violence against children: Historical perspectives. In I. Hyman & J. Wise (Eds.), *Corporal Punishment in American Education*. Philadelphia: Temple University Press, 1979.

Williams, W. Report. *Mind in La: Webster Parrish School Board*, September 1977.

Wingo, G. *Elementary school student teaching, 3d ed*. Boston: Scott, Foresman, 1963.

Classroom Discipline: The Unclaimed Legacy

Regina S. Jones
Laurel N. Tanner

> The treasure which you think not worth taking trouble and pains to find, this one alone is the real treasure you are longing for all your life. — Treasure of the Sierra Madre

Numerous public opinion polls rank discipline as the biggest problem facing the public schools.[1] But for university professors, those who study and write about problems of education, discipline is not a problem of great importance. If it were, the professional literature would reflect that concern. As Edward Wynne points out, "Discipline is not ignored as a topic, but it is apparently not a matter of high concern."[2] Substantial scientific research on classroom discipline is rare.

Clearly, professionals from the university have turned their backs on the public. During the late 1960s and early 1970s, while the public was naming discipline as the worst school problem, many university professors (who were never allies of the lower schools) joined the romantic critics of the schools (e.g., Herbert Kohl and Charles Silberman) in calling for the liberation of children from the tyranny of school.[3] Surely many Americans must have perceived this as undermining discipline in the schools. One must wonder about the political impact; the perception that the education profession was exacerbating the discipline problem (or, at the very least, was unresponsive to it) may well be contributing to a continuing unwillingness to underwrite the costs of education.

Although professorial unresponsiveness to the public is not politic, it is defensible on the ground of academic freedom. In a free society, university professors have the right, indeed the obligation, to select their own problems for research (although sociopolitical forces and government policy deeply affect

Jones, Regina S., and Tanner, Laurel N. Classroom discipline: The unclaimed legacy. *Phi Delta Kappan*, 1981, *62*, 494–497. Reprinted by permission.

choices). But more than academic freedom is at issue here. The field of education is intimately related to public authority. Professors of education are not removed from public accountability and should be responsive to public anxiety about the schools.

Even if the public were not worried about discipline, however, discipline should still be a matter of grave concern for professors of education. Knowledge of the theory and methodology of classroom discipline is of paramount importance to those preparing to enter the teaching profession. In fact, for more than half a century surveys have identified discipline as the primary concern of prospective and beginning teachers.[4] Yet the term "discipline" (or "class control," for that matter) rarely appears in the index of educational methods texts. Professionals from the university seem to have turned their backs on practitioners in the schools as well as on the public.

True professionalism requires scientific investigation of the practical problems of a profession in order to improve practice and provide a solid base for it. As John Dewey pointed out more than half a century ago in *The Sources of a Science of Education,* one of the first principles in the development of a science of education is that the problems that researchers attempt to solve must derive from the educational situation.[5] Writing on virtually the same problem in 1978, N. L. Gage concluded that research workers should "look straight at the problems of teaching."[6] Surveys and polls reflect the consistency with which discipline has been identified as the top problem in public education; it must be systematically studied to effect improvement. But researchers have seemed, on the whole, uninterested in such study.

Occasionally, teacher educators have been chided for ignoring the problem of discipline in the schools. In 1961 David Ausubel alleged that colleges of education were maintaining "a conspiracy of silence about the existence of disciplinary problems in the schools."[7] There is, of course, no evidence to support the idea of a continuing coverup, Watergate style; commentators on the issue have tended to present the problem in deceptively simple terms. However, such claims prevent us from seeing clearly the background of the problem, which we must understand in order to know ourselves and our own historical/political commitments.

THE LEGACY

University professors acquire an interest in the research problems that occupy them through their own education and through exposure to the literature in their specialties. As Thomas Kuhn points out in his discussion of the scientific enterprise, such problems normally are "closely modeled on previous achievements."[8] Building an educational science is a "plodding enterprise," Gage tells us.[9] In any science be it education or economics, the purpose of research is the steady extension of knowledge. Participation in a science requires that the student learn the bases of the field—its heritage of research and conceptualization.

The real question is, of course, whether there is a heritage of conceptual ideas on discipline that affects (or should affect) our own thinking and methods and upon which contemporary researchers can build. Thus if Dewey ignored discipline in his conception of educational method (Dewey is still, without question, the leading figure in the theory and practice of American education), we could conclude that contemporary educators are in the grip of a tradition that excludes discipline. The influence on modern education of the progressive education movement during the first half of the 20th century has been well documented. According to Lawrence Cremin, Dewey was "the chief articulator of the movement's aspirations."[10] Of immediate importance however, is that the movement left a legacy of ideas about the methods and meaning of education to which we are heirs.[11] That legacy has manifested itself in the school curriculum. Inquiry learning and the idea of meeting individual differences are only two of the ideas handed down to us as part of our inheritance from the era of progressive education.[12] Are there significant conceptions about discipline in the legacy?

The progressives did not ignore discipline. In fact, they handed down a strong legacy in which discipline is viewed as inseparable from pedagogical aim and method.[13] For the progressives, the democratic commitment of schooling is to help the young become self-directing. According to Dewey, discipline requires training or experiencing if it is to become self-directing.[14] In short, discipline is an educational problem. This is the leading conceptual idea in the legacy. The progressives believed that discipline—that is, development toward self-direction and social responsibility—is part of everyone's education. Developing a curriculum based on this notion was actually the central problem faced by progressive educators. Today, self-direction and social responsibility are central, but neglected, goals of education in U.S. society. In a very real sense they are an unclaimed legacy.

There are other concepts in the legacy. In a recent study, a group of progressivists—scholars and activists who experienced educational reform during the progressive education era—identified self-direction, interest, and motivation as the leading concepts relative to classroom discipline held by progressive educators.[15] The panel of progressivists included Hollis L. Caswell, president emeritus, Teachers College, Columbia University; Arthur W. Foshay, professor emeritus, Teachers College, Columbia; Paul R. Hanna, professor emeritus, Stanford University, who was associate director of the Lincoln School, Teachers College, Columbia; Maurice L. Hartung, professor emeritus, University of Chicago, who was associate director of evaluation for the Eight-Year Study of the Committee on Relation of Schools and Colleges of the Progressive Education Association; J. Paul Leonard, president emeritus, San Francisco State University; Alice Miel, professor emeritus, Teachers College, Columbia; A. Harry Passow, professor, Teachers College, Columbia; Harold G. Shane, University Professor, Indiana University; B. Othanel Smith, professor emeritus, University of Illinois, who was editor of *Progressive Education;* and Ralph W. Tyler, now on the staff of Science Research Associates, who was director of evaluation for the Eight-Year Study.

The idea of *interest* lay at the heart of the progressive conception of educational method. Thus, as Foshay points out, the progressivists believed that "order proceeds from interest, and that it was therefore up to the teacher to maintain interest," for "much trouble proceeds from boredom." Closely allied with interest is *motivation;* according to Foshay, the progressive idea was that "children are eager to learn, and will if given a reason to." Foshay notes that this legacy continues "almost unaltered" in middle-class schools, but "in working-class schools, discipline has always been more harsh, and it continues to be so."[16]

Foshay's perception of the progressive viewpoint reflects in general the experience of others on the panel. As Tyler reports, interest was linked conceptually by progressives to learning and self-discipline. In the project method, for example, there is "learning involved as the student carries on an activity which he chooses and plans. He disciplines himself to carry through the project." The project method is a part of the legacy but no longer flourishes in the curriculum, with the exception of such fields as agricultural education and home economics. Unfortunately, as Tyler recalls, "many teachers found it difficult to manage classes seeking self-discipline."[17] One reason was, undoubtedly, the child-centered emphasis of William Kilpatrick's version of the project method. Kilpatrick, as Cremin writes, "in seeking to make Dewey's ideas manageable for mass consumption by the teaching profession, ended by transforming them into versions quite different from the originals."[18] Yet in the hands of competent teachers the project method was (and is) an effective teaching technique, as shown by the outcomes of the Eight-Year Study.[19]

The progressives believed that pupil interest in the program of the school was the key to good discipline. In the words of Caswell, who was himself a pioneer in the field of curriculum, "The fundamental basis of good discipline in a school situation is a curriculum in which appropriate recognition is given to the interests, needs, and status of the pupils to be taught."[20] This too is in the legacy, yet its implementation varies enormously from classroom to classroom, from school to school.

The progressives were always optimistic. They believed in education as a means of realizing innate individual potential. They believed in human intelligence as the key to human behavior. As Tyler noted, a concept of discipline held by progressive educators was that "intelligent understanding of what was to be learned would stimulate self-discipline."[21] Their objectives for youth were developmental; their approaches to discipline, positive. Thus it is hardly surprising that they believed that physical coercion was undesirable. Smith puts it this way: "The belief was that physical coercion would in many cases terminate the disruptive behavior, but the basic disposition of the individual would not thereby be altered in desirable directions. In other words, the aim was to bring about inner changes consonant with good conduct."[22] Concern for helping the student develop constructive self-control and a sense of responsibility is in the legacy. As Leonard observes, teachers tend to teach as they themselves were taught. "Therefore the greatest residual of these ideas is in schools where the teachers are students of teachers who were trained in the key progressive concepts."[23]

Today, while virtually everyone agrees that schools have the responsibility to teach self-direction, there is deep disagreement as to what this means in actual classroom practice. This disagreement can be traced to a basic philosophical argument among progressive educators and a subsequent schism in the progressive education movement. In Dewey's opinion, for instance, choosing one's actions intelligently in a given set of circumstances does not come automatically; it is learned through practice. A disciplined person, Dewey argues, is one who is trained to consider his or her actions and undertake them deliberately.[24] Discipline is, for Dewey, a universal developmental problem.

This idea was badly misconstrued by Dewey's disciples, including Kilpatrick, who held the notion that the child is, from the start, able to decide what is best. But as Foshay tells us, "Progressive teachers and other field people knew that children require a framework or they act at random."[25] Theorists in the 1920s abandoned Kilpatrick's misconstruction of Dewey as unworkable. In the free school movement of the late 1960s and early 1970s, educational reformers once again advanced the idea of the child's inherent possession of self-discipline, and with predictably disappointing results. The romantic view of the self-direction is operationally impossible because it is theoretically unsound. Nevertheless, it was Kilpatrick's theoretical position—that children are automatically ready for self-discipline and need only to be left to themselves to follow their own interests—that became identified with progressive education. Hartung recalls, "It was quite commonly believed that many progressive educators were quite permissive and that they tolerated behavior that was disruptive."[26]

But we are also heirs to the Deweyan legacy of discipline as developmental. As Caswell points out, it was rather generally accepted by progressive educators that, "in seeking to develop self-disciplined living on the part of pupils, teachers must start with pupils where they are, adjusting methods of control so that gradually self-control is achieved." But he identified the problem when he added: "This concept is the one upon which there would have been the greatest disagreement."[27]

Even when educators agreed that teachers should follow a developmental approach to self-direction, theory tended to remain just that. Progressive educators had immense difficulty in translating theoretical ideas into detailed strategies for teachers. Obviously this was nowhere more apparent than in teacher education. In 1933 Willard W. Beatty, who was president of the Progressive Education Association and superintendent of schools in Bronxville, New York, charged, "In the majority of instances, those institutions which are offering even the slightest training for the newer type of school are devoting most of their time to talking about it."[28] On the whole, teachers were simply not prepared to implement a developmental approach to self-discipline. Thus, as Hanna recalls, the "potential good" in the Deweyan approach "was undone by the excessive dependence of untrained teachers on pupil self-discipline."[29] Today teacher education is still deficient in this area. The result, Hanna notes, is that "few teachers have the necessary skills to set teaching/learning tasks that stimulate pupils to self-discipline."[30]

But the situation today is not the same as it was in the progressive era, when practitioners were eager to implement progressive ideas. The negative experiences of unprepared teachers with progressive methods have led to disillusionment with the underlying progressive ideas. A fundamental problem facing educators today is that self-direction has become negatively associated with discipline, and the preparation of children for responsible citizenship has been neglected.

Although self-direction and social responsibility are both in the legacy, they have been treated as antagonists in the past, and this has also created problems for modern educators. As early as 1902 Dewey wrote of the importance of viewing the child and society as interactive rather than as conflicting elements in educational theory. "It is easier to see the conditions in their separateness, to insist upon one at the expense of the other, to make antagonists of them," he observed, warning that when that happens, instead of seeing the educational problem as a whole, "We get the case of the child versus the curriculum; of the individual nature versus social culture."[31]

Dewey's analysis was more than academic; child-centered pedagogical protest against the traditional school was already creating a child-versus-society schism in educational thought. A quarter of a century later Harold Rugg and Ann Shumaker wrote about the conflict between society and self as orientations for educational reform. "If neither one alone, how shall the two be reconciled?" they asked.[32] Each orientation had its heyday in the progressive education movement—child-centered pedagogical reform in the 1920s and society-centered reform in the 1930s—but both were in the mainstream of progressive thought. Each sect (for that is what they were[33]) thought that its particular emphasis should be the organizing center for progressive education. The society-centered sect was concerned with social problem solving via the development of social responsibility. As Miel points out, "shared management with students" (called group or cooperative planning in the 1940s and 1950s) represented an effort to develop social responsibility.[34] Also, as noted by Passow, the idea that "children and youth should participate in establishing the rules and guidelines which will guide their behavior rather than have them imposed from above by some adult authority" was held in principle (if not practice) by many teachers.[35] The child-centered sect, as noted earlier, was concerned with individual self-realization, through encouraging enough freedom for pupils to pursue their interests.

The conflict between the child and society as centers for progressive educational theory boded ill for discipline in the schools; it caused the elements for a unified theory, self and society, to be placed in opposition rather than interwoven. Dewey saw them whole, but his disciples tended to cast the school in either a child-centered or a society-centered mold. In either case an important dimension for educational reform was missing. Reform without the other half of the talisman was (and is) foredoomed to failure. This split in the progressive education movement of a half century ago is the source of our periodic peda-gogical leaps from one center to the other—from do-your-own-thing to con-formity and close monitoring of behavior. Educators would do well to use the holistic model provided by Dewey and try to help each child develop toward self-direction and social responsibility.

IMPLICATIONS

The most pressing and persistent problem with which educators must concern themselves today is self-direction as an unclaimed legacy. There can be only one position on this problem: Any educational program in the public schools that does not promote the development of self-direction in pupils is gravely flawed. Unfortunately, there has been a tendency of late to view discipline as a managerial problem. This is not to say that classroom and school management are unimportant for discipline but that they are not enough. The progressives knew this, but most of the proposals for dealing with discipline today miss this point. Vandalism, for example, is dealt with as a problem of school design. Obviously, schools without windows can reduce the strain on education bud-gets incurred by property loss, but such approaches do not address the aim of discipline, which is to make people self-controlling and self-responsible. This is an educational matter; to talk about discipline is to talk about education in its most significant sense.

Ironically, most proposals for dealing with disciplinary problems in the schools miss the central point of the nature of discipline: namely, that it is part of everyone's education. A leading example is the Safe School Study of the National Institute of Education, which was a response to congressional con-cern about school crime and how it can be prevented. The report lists two "means of prevention": security devices and "a strong, dedicated principal . . . who instituted a firm, fair, and consistent system of discipline."[36] Although schools exist for educational reasons, one would not know it from this report, for it ignores the educational possibilities for dealing with the problem. It con-cerns itself only with symptoms.

In a later report Francis Ianni, who was an author of the Safe School Study, badly undermines the school's fundamental role of preparing children for re-sponsible citizenship. "Certainly the traditional reliance on the school as the primary medium for resolving social problems is no longer tenable," he de-clares. "We may never be able to 'teach' solutions to the problem of school crime as part of the school's curriculum."[37] He then suggests organizational changes in the school as the solution to school crime. Ianni's pessimistic con-clusion about the curriculum as a means of countering school crime is not based on research in which the curriculum was a variable; it must be dismissed as mere rhetoric. Had Ianni taken the trouble to investigate, he would have found that, although responsible citizenship has been a traditional goal of schooling in the U.S., it tends to be given short shrift in the curriculum. By defaulting in this area, schools have also missed an opportunity to enhance discipline. Like many social scientists, Ianni tends to look at the limitations of schools rather than at their possibilities. (What a striking contrast with the progressives!) More important, his narrow prescription is a dangerous base on which to form public policy, for it seeks to do away with the responsibility of the school to students as future citizens. This responsibility is twofold: to help students learn to govern their own behavior and to prepare them to cope with the social problems of our time. It is also a dangerous base for public policy because it reflects outright hostility to the idea of progress (the changeability of human beings). We need a policy that looks to the possibilities of education for developing thoughtful and responsible behavior in individuals, and such possibilities are limitless. *Discipline should be viewed as an educational problem, not just an administrative or managerial problem.*

Clearly, we have a powerful heritage of conceptualization on discipline, and professionals from the university would do well to build upon it. The proper education of teachers must include a developmental approach to discipline in which discipline is linked to the purposes of education.[38] As Smith observes, all too few colleges of education have incorporated disciplinary concepts and practices in their professional programs.[39] And those that have done so tend to teach methods of discipline without the theories on which the methods are based. This is no longer (nor was it ever) enough. If we are to make our rightful claim to the legacy, teachers will have to choose their strategies in light of the legacy. In 1845 Horace Mann, leader of the public school movement, wrote: "If there are no two things wider asunder than freedom and slavery, then must . . . the course of training which fits children for these two opposite conditions of life be as diverse as the points to which they lead."[40] Nearly a century and a half later, it is still 'true that training children for freedom requires other kinds of plans and structures than training them for slavery. It is time to claim our legacy.

REFERENCES

1 George H. Gallup. "The 12th Annual Gallup Poll of the Public's Attitudes Toward the Public Schools," *Phi Delta Kappan,* September 1980, p. 34.

2 Edward A. Wynne, "Behind the Discipline Problem: Youth Suicide as a Measure of Alienation," *Phi Delta Kappan,* January 1978, p. 307.

3 Herbert R. Kohl, *The Open Classroom* (New York: Random House, 1969): and Charles E. Silberman, *Crisis in the Classroom* (New York: Random House, 1970).

4 Frances F. Fuller, "Concerns of Teachers: A Developmental Conceptualization," *American Educational Research Journal,* March 1969, pp. 207–26; and Thomas J. Coates and Carl E. Thorensen, "Teacher Anxiety: A Review with Recommendations," *Review of Educational Research,* Spring 1976, p. 164.

5 John Dewey, *The Sources of a Science of Education* (New York: Liveright, 1929).

6 N. L. Gage, *The Scientific Basis of the Art of Teaching* (New York: Teachers College Press, 1978), p. 93.

7 David P. Ausubel, "A New Look at Classroom Discipline," *Phi Delta Kappan*, October 1961, p. 30.

8 Thomas S. Kuhn, *The Structure of Scientific Revolutions* (Chicago: University of Chicago Press, 1970), p. 47.

9 Gage, op. cit., p. 41.

10 Lawrence A. Cremin, "The Free School Movement—A Perspective," *Today's Education*, September/October 1974, p. 71.

11 Lawrence A. Cremin, *The Transformation of the School* (New York: Alfred A. Knopf, 1961).

12 Daniel Tanner and Laurel N. Tanner, *Curriculum Development: Theory into Practice* (New York: Macmillan, 1980), pp. 398–440.

13 Regina S. Jones, "An Inquiry into the Classroom Discipline Legacy from the Progressive Education Movement" (Doctoral dissertation, Temple University, 1980).

14 John Dewey, *The School and Society* (1899; reprint ed., Chicago: University of Chicago Press, 1915), pp. 23, 24; 30, 31.

15 Jones, op. cit.

16 Ibid., p. 182, Appendix.

17 Ibid., pp. 168, 169.

18 Cremin, *The Transformation of the School*, op. cit., p. 221.

19 A study instituted in 1933 in which Ralph Tyler and his associates systematically assessed the outcomes of progressive methods. It was found that the graduates of 30 progressive high schools did as well as or better in college than the graduates of traditional high schools. See Wildord M. Aikin, *The Story of the Eight-Year Study* (New York: Harper and Row, 1942); see also Tanner and Tanner, op. cit., pp. 364–72.

20 Jones, op. cit., pp. 175, 176.

21 Ibid., Appendix.

22 Ibid., p. 169.

23 Ibid., p. 183.

24 John Dewey, *Democracy and Education* (New York: Macmillan, 1916), p. 151.

25 Jones, op. cit., p. 188.

26 Ibid., p. 175.

27. Ibid., p. 173.

28 Willard W. Beatty, "Training the Teacher for the New School," *Progressive Education*, May 1933, p. 247.

29 Jones, op. cit., p. 173.

30 Ibid., Appendix.

31 John Dewey, *The Child and the Curriculum* (Chicago: University of Chicago Press, 1902), pp. 4, 5.

32 Harold Rugg and Ann Shumaker, *The Child-Centered School* (New York: World Book Co., 1928), p. vii.

33 See John Dewey, *The Child and the Curriculum*, op. cit., p. 4.

34 Jones, op. cit., p. 190.

35 Ibid., Appendix.

36 National Institute of Education, *Violent Schools—Safe Schools*, The Safe School Study Report to Congress, Vol. 1 (Washington, D.C.: U.S. Department of Health, Education and Welfare, January 1978), p. vi.

37 Francis A. J. Ianni, "The Social Organization of the High School," in National Institute of Education, *School Crime and Disruption: Prevention Models* (Washington, D.C.: U.S. Department of Health, Education, and Welfare, June 1978), p. 22.

38 By way of example, Lauren N. Tanner, in *Classroom Discipline for Effective Teaching and Learning* (New York: Holt, Rinehart and Winston, 1978), proposes developmental stages of discipline (see, in particular, pp. 19–40).

39 Jones, op. cit.

40 Horace Mann, "Ninth Annual Report to the Massachusetts Board of Education, 1845," in Lawrence A. Cremin, ed., *The Republic and the School: Horace Mann on the Education of Free Men* (New York: Teachers College Press, 1957), p. 59.

Taking Charge of Student Behavior

Lee Canter

There is an answer to the discipline problems at your school. The Assertive Discipline Program, a competency-based approach to discipline has been field tested by over twenty thousand teachers and principals nationwide. These educators report that the program has reduced behavior problems by 80 percent in their classrooms or schools.

Assertive discipline is designed to give an educator the skills and confidence necessary to "take charge" in the classroom. It advocates a systematic approach to discipline that enables teachers to set firm, consistent limits for students, at the same time keeping in mind each student's need for warmth and positive support.

Why is this kind of competency-based training necessary? To be frank, you and your teachers simply were not trained to deal with the behavior problems today's students present. Nationwide between 15 and 30 percent of all students exhibit emotional or behavioral problems at one time or another during the school year. Over 90 percent of these students are in regular, not special education, classrooms, yet less than 5 percent of all classroom teachers (and even fewer principals) have been trained to work with them. Research shows that, without specialized training, the educator's effectiveness in dealing with disruptive students is severely limited.

Assertive discipline is the result of seven years of research and evaluation into effective classroom discipline skills. The basic question in our research was, how can teachers get students to behave appropriately in the classroom? To find the answer, we studied master teachers who, given all the problems faced by today's teachers, can still get their students to behave. We found that these master teachers respond to their students in an "assertive" manner, by which we mean that they clearly and firmly express their wants and needs and are prepared to back up their words with appropriate actions. In other words, they say what they mean and mean what they say.

Canter, Lee. Taking charge of student behavior. *National Elementary Principal*, 1979, *58*, 33–41. Reprinted by permission.

Assertive teachers take the following stand in their classrooms: "I will tolerate no student stopping me from teaching. I will tolerate no student preventing another student from learning. I will tolerate no student engaging in any behavior that is not in his or her own best interest and in the best interests of others. And most important, whenever a student chooses to behave appropriately, I will immediately recognize and reinforce that behavior." Finally, assertive teachers are the bosses in their classrooms. They have the skills and confidence necessary to take charge.

In our research, we also focused on what types of teachers do not respond effectively to student behavior. We labeled such teachers either nonassertive or hostile.

Nonassertive teachers do not clearly or firmly communicate their wants and needs to the students, or if they do, they are not prepared to back their words up with actions. They are passive or wishy-washy with their students, and lack the skills and confidence necessary to deal effectively with disruptive behavior.

Hostile teachers, on the other hand, get the students to do what they want, but in so doing they violate the best interests of the students. These teachers often verbally or physically abuse their students.

The following example shows how each of these three types of teachers would deal with a student's disruptive behavior. Suppose the teacher wants the children to do their work without talking or disrupting each other. During the work period, one boy puts his work aside and begins to talk loudly to the children around him. What should the teacher do?

In such a situation, the nonassertive teacher would typically walk up to the boy and ask him to get to work. When he doesn't, the teacher shrugs and says, "I just don't know what to do with you." The hostile teacher would typically storm up to the boy and yell, "You have the biggest mouth I've ever seen. Shut it or you'll be sorry!" But the assertive teacher would typically walk up to the boy, look him in the eye, and tell him firmly, "Stop talking and get to work now. If you don't, you will have to finish your work during free time."

Now, here is an example to illustrate how the three types of teachers respond when a student behaves appropriately. Suppose one girl in the class tends to become disruptive during the transition periods between the activities. She gets very excited, fails to follow directions, and often runs around the room yelling. Finally, the teacher sets firm limits, and one afternoon the girl cleans up her activity appropriately and comes directly to the reading corner when she is asked to.

The nonassertive teacher would typically not recognize or support the girl's appropriate behavior, either verbally or nonverbally. The hostile teacher would typically say to the girl, "It's about time I didn't have to chase you around the room to get you to clean up and sit down!" But the assertive teacher would typically say to the girl, "I like the nice job you did cleaning up and following directions. You did so well that you can sit on my lap and pick a story for me to read to the class."

GETTING YOUR TEACHERS TO BE MORE ASSERTIVE

In order for your teachers to become more assertive and thus more effective in dealing with behavior problems, they need both confidence and skills.

Most teachers do not have the confidence necessary to lay down the law in their classrooms because they have little confidence in their ability to deal with problem students. Many teachers (and many educators in general) believe that certain types of students "cannot" behave appropriately at school. Among the most common misconceptions are these: If the child has emotional problems, the teacher says, "He is just too disturbed for me to handle in my class." If the child has neglectful parents, the teacher says, "Coming from those parents, how can you expect her to behave normally?" If the child is from a low socio-economic background, it's "What can you expect from a child raised in that kind of neighborhood?" If the child belongs to a racial minority group, it's "You know how some black kids are; there is no way to get them to behave." And if the child is educationally handicapped, it's "She's EH—you can't expect her to behave."

These misconceptions are ridiculous. All students can behave appropriately at school. It does not matter whether children are neglected, neurotic, or deprived; they still can behave. The only children who cannot behave are those with organic problems, such as brain damage. Problem students can behave— they simply do not want to behave. When problem students are with teachers who expect them to behave, however, and who assertively communicate their expectations to the students through both words and actions, the students will choose to behave appropriately. The first step in dealing with students assertively, then, is for teachers to develop higher expectations of their own ability to deal with all students. When expectations are raised, confidence levels will be raised as well.

Along with increasing their confidence, your teachers must increase their skills in dealing with students who have behavior problems. The following are the competency skills guidelines your teachers should follow in order to deal assertively with student behavior.

- *The teacher must know at all times what he or she wants the students to do.* Typical behavior teachers want from students includes: following directions; staying in their seats; raising their hands when they want to speak; getting to class on time; keeping hands, feet, and objects to themselves and bringing pencils, books, and paper to class. The teacher must communicate these wants to students both verbally and visually.

- *The teacher must know how to systematically set limits when the students do not behave properly.* Consistency is the key to limit setting. A teacher must provide a negative consequence every time a student chooses to behave inappropriately. The consequence must be included in a systematic discipline plan. (See the box in page 110 for guidelines for an effective plan.)

- *The teacher must know how to systematically reinforce the appropriate behavior of students.* Effective positive reinforcement of appropriate behavior is the key to dealing assertively with discipline problems. For verbal reinforcement at the elementary school level, first give directions to the students, then praise two students who comply with them. If one or more students have not followed the directions, list their names on the board, in accordance with your discipline plan. Be sure to praise every student every day. The most effective way of backing up verbal reinforcement is with action, such as sending positive notes home. Send two notes per class per day.

Classwide reinforcement enables all students to earn a positive consequence for appropriate behavior. One form of classwide reinforcement—the "marbles in a jar" incentive system—can be used with difficult classes. Whenever one or more students behave appropriately, they earn a marble for the entire class. Each marble equals one point. When the class has earned a predetermined number of points, the student gets a reward, such as free time. The younger the students, the more frequent the rewards must be. The same goes for problem students, who should have a chance to earn, say, three to five marbles a day, as compared with one a day for regular students. At the end of each day or period, count up the marbles earned and keep a running total. When the class has earned one reward, set a new goal. (Remember that the reward must be something the students really want.)

• *The teacher must know how to elicit the cooperation of the principals and the parents in discipline efforts with the problem student.* A teacher's discipline plan, to be effective, must be shared with the principal and the parents, and it must systematically spell out when and how they are to cooperate with the teacher in implementing the plan.

WHAT ASSERTIVE DISCIPLINE CAN DO FOR YOUR SCHOOL

What can you, the principal, expect if you use assertive discipline at your school? Here's a typical example of what happens. In September 1977, the faculty of Rice Elementary School, along with all their coworkers in the Santa Maria Elementary Schools, Santa Maria, California, were trained in assertive discipline.

In the days following the training, the teachers set up systematic discipline plans in each classroom, according to the basic guidelines in the box on page 110. Each teacher's plan was approved by the principal, and copies were sent home to the parents.

The students were told that they were expected to adhere to a few basic rules of behavior and that disruptive behavior would no longer be tolerated. Each teacher consistently followed the discipline plan every time any student broke any rule for any reason. If the initial plan did not work with serious behavior problems, more severe plans were developed.

All of the teachers balanced negative consequences with positive consequences when students behaved appropriately. They praised each student each day. They sent positive notes home to the parents. They set up classwide reward programs by which the student's appropriate behavior could earn extra free time or some other reward. If the students chose to behave, they chose to have the teacher's positive attention; if they chose to disrupt, however, they chose immediate punishment from the teacher.

A separate discipline plan was established to cover student behavior in the school year. First, rules of behavior were set down: follow directions, stay in assigned areas, use equipment properly, no fighting, no dangerous objects. If a student breaks a rule, he or she is given a pink slip, and a copy of the pink slip is sent to the teacher and to the principal or vice-principal. The first pink slip means the student is benched for the remainder of the period. The second pink slip means the student is benched and the parents are called. With the third pink slip, the student forfeits yard play for five days, in addition to being benched and having his or her parents notified. With the fourth pink slip, a parent conference is set up. For any severe disruption, the student is sent immediately to the principal.

If the students behave in the school yard, on the other hand, they are rewarded. For example, students who go five weeks without receiving a pink slip get to attend a special reward assembly to see an interesting film or participate in other enjoyable activities.

Reactions to the assertive discipline programs at Rice Elementary School have been positive. Third-grade teacher Barbara Zarling said, "It works very well. I haven't raised my voice so far this year. With this system, you don't have to; it's so cut and dried. The children really learn to take responsibility for their own actions."

Parents have also supported the new discipline program. One mother said, "Assertive discipline is a good thing. They should have done it a long time ago." And another mother added, "I think it's great. It's about time. It's also a good thing for parents because we have been slipping in the things we should be doing."

The students at Rice Elementary School gave the program mixed reviews, however. One sixth-grader stated, "It's not too good because there's a lot of things I want to say that I don't because I will get a check mark next to my name." Two fellow classmates responded, "That's the point, there's been too much talking. It's a whole lot better now—you can study more." Another student added, "I don't like getting my name on the board and staying after school." Finally, one fifth-grader concluded, "I'm glad we have the program because I get to think harder."

Gordon Herrmann, Rice's principal, agrees. "Assertive discipline makes consistent what was haphazard before," he said. "Now the students know what the consequences of their actions will be, and that's what makes discipline work. When a name goes up on the board and a check is added to it, there's no question what will happen: the student will be staying fifteen minutes after school. It was hard to keep discipline consistent from class to class before this system came along. We usually let the student off whenever there was a question. But now we can say, 'This is it—this is the way it is, and the way it's going to be.' The children definitely benefit from that firm stand."

"What's more," said Herrmann, "the teachers have taken more responsibility for discipline at the school. This year I have had only about one-tenth of the kids sent to the office that I used to have. Teachers are now laying down the law, and the students are keeping themselves in line."

Programs similar to the one at Rice Elementary School have been set up in hundreds of other schools in California and throughout the nation, with similar success. For the faculties of these schools—and perhaps for yours as well—taking charge of student behavior has been the answer to the discipline problem.

GUIDELINES FOR AN EFFECTIVE DISCIPLINE PLAN

1. Set down some basic general rules of behavior, such as: follow directions; raise hand before speaking; stay in seat; keep hands, feet, and objects to yourself; no cursing or teasing.

2. Allow a maximum of five negative consequences for disruptive behavior. Here is a hypothetical plan. The first time a student breaks one of the rules, his or her name is put on the board as a warning. The second time, a check mark is put next to the name and the student must stay after school for fifteen minutes. The third time, a second check is made, which means thirty minutes after school. The fourth time means three check marks and thirty minutes after school, plus a phone call to the student's parent. The fifth means four check marks and the student is sent to the principal or vice-principal.

3. At the end of the day, all names and check marks should be erased. Never erase a name or check mark as a reward for good behavior, however.

4. In cases of severe disruption, the student is sent immediately to the principal.

5. The principal is always the last consequence of the plan; he or she must approve the teacher's plan before it is put into operation and must be notified if any changes are made in it. In addition, the principal and the teacher should decide in advance what will be done with students who are sent to the principal's office.

6. A copy of the discipline plan should be sent to all parents.

7. The plan applies to all students in the classroom. If after three days or so the plan does not appear to be working with one or more of the students, make the plan stricter.

8. For students who present more severe behavior problems, the teacher should consider other consequences, such as one of the following:

Send the student to an in-school suspension room. The student is suspended from class and sent to an isolation room where he or she does academic work in silence, monitored by another teacher or an administrator. The student does not participate in recess or lunch; he or she eats alone and is escorted to the rest room. Disruptive behavior in the suspension room earns the student extra hours of isolation.

Record disruptive behavior. Place a cassette tape recorder next to the student and turn it on if he or she disrupts the class. The tape is then saved to be played at a conference with the parents and the principal.

Send the student to another classroom instead of to the principal's office. The disruptive student should be sent to a well-run classroom, at a different grade level, where he or she will spend half an hour sitting quietly in the back of the class doing academic work. The student takes no part in class activity. If the student is disruptive again, he or she is sent for an additional thirty minutes to another classroom. (Note: teachers should plan in advance with other teachers if they intend to use this technique.)

How the Adults in Your Schools Cause Student Discipline Problems—and What to Do About It

Daniel Linden Duke

If you wonder why your students spend so much time in your principal's office, or trying to explain their behavior to your dean of discipline, take a close look at the behavior of your teachers and school administrators.

During a study I conducted in San Francisco area high school—a suburban school with a large white majority student body and allegedly with few discipline problems—I stumbled on areas of student tension and conflict that, upon closer examination, could be traced to the behavior of adults. While I originally went to Bay High School (not its real name) to look at patterns of student discipline problems, I discovered quickly that the behavior of teachers and administrators was perhaps a more fertile field of inquiry. For example, out of 30 discipline-related issues raised during the school's faculty meetings, 19 touched on the inappropriate behavior of teachers and administrators. In other words, the school's adults were complaining about their own actions.

As the research continued, six separate categories of adult behavior that lead to student discipline problems were identified, and quickly became clear that in the school, adult behavior and student behavior were closely linked.

The six categories: (1) Inconsistent rule enforcement; (2) Noncompliance with discipline policies; (3) Insensitivity; (4) Lack of data; (5) Lack of classroom management skills; (6) Inadequate administration of disciplinary polices. Let's examine each.

Inconsistent Rule Enforcement   Nearly 20 percent of the items discussed during faculty meetings concerned two types of teacher inconsistency. "Per-

Duke, Daniel Linden. How the adults in your schools cause student discipline problems—and what to do about it. *The American School Board Journal,* 1978, *46,* 29–30. Reprinted by permission.

sonal inconsistency" describes a teacher who usually neglects certain rules and then begins suddenly to enforce them. "Between-teacher inconsistency," on the other hand, describes the situation in which one teacher may enforce a rule while another teacher may choose to ignore the same school policy. Both types of inconsistency, unfortunately, create student disrespect for school policies and headaches for both teachers and school administrators.

Students are particularly sensitive to personal inconsistency—as are adults. Think of how you feel when stopped by the police for speeding while other cars traveling at the same speed drive merrily by. It's this simple: People—including students—tend to expect the same treatment as everyone else, at least where rule enforcement is concerned.

The reasons for teacher inconsistency vary. Many teachers at Bay High School admit they discipline students inconsistently because they regard "police work" as beneath their status; others believe that a reputation for being "tough" on discipline undermines teaching effectiveness, and a few are afraid to enforce rules because they fear student reprisals. Several teachers justify their inconsistent behavior on the ground that there simply are too many school rules to enforce effectively. But when asked how many school rules there were at Bay High, 70 percent admitted they did not know, while responses from the rest ranged from five to 100. The point: Many teachers—unaware of school rules—believe that what goes on inside their own classrooms is their only concern. Until all teachers decide to share responsibility for the total school atmosphere, some teachers will continue to feel isolated and vulnerable, and students will remain confused and resentful of inconsistent and arbitrary rule enforcement.

Noncompliance   It's one thing to enforce rules inconsistently, and it's quite another to fail deliberately to comply with school discipline policies. Unfortunately, at Bay High School, noncompliance by teachers was far from uncommon. At one point, several teachers complained that their colleagues failed to show up for their duties as school monitor, thus leaving corridors, school grounds and parking lots unattended. Since few teachers relish these duties, the result was predictable: Many teachers tended not to talk or complain about out-of-class student behavior problems because the result might be an increase in monitoring assignments for themselves and other teachers. In other words, teachers think it's better to keep quiet than to spend every lunch period nabbing student smokers.

Ironically, one of the teachers most frequently cited for failing to appear for monitor duty was a vocal champion of strict discipline policies. Unfortunately, he also thought that discipline was an "administrative" matter. The school principal admitted that the school had "four or five hard hats" like this teacher, and that their attitudes created more discipline problems than they corrected.

Other common types of noncompliance by teachers: neglecting to check re-admission slips as a safeguard against illegal absences; basing student grades on classroom conduct; and not filling out or following procedures specified on student referral forms. These referral forms—first suggested by faculty representatives—are intended to encourage teachers to work out problems with students before sending students to the dean's office. While it's hard to pinpoint why teachers do not comply with certain rules, it's clear that students don't know what to expect when teachers ignore even "trivial" school rules.

Insensitivity   "All of the Bay High faculty is divided into three parts," according to the school's principal. The "hard hats"—all of whom teach elective courses and complain about everything—ascribe to the "teach the best, forget the rest" philosophy. Any student who doesn't submit to their personal codes of conduct is simply told to find another class. Teachers of required courses argue that they are not free to banish poorly motivated or uncooperative students in this manner. This generates a certain degree of tension among the faculty, and creates an extralegal set of "unofficial" rules.

A second group, comprising about half of the faculty, doesn't complain much, but sends students to the principal's office at the first hint of problem behavior. These teachers have little patience with any but the most diligent of students. The third group are the administrator's favorites. They send students to the office only as a last resort. When a dean receives a referral from one of these teachers, he knows that all other corrective measures effectively have been exhausted.

It's the first two groups that are open to charges of insensitivity. They are all business and exhibit little patience for individual student concerns. By failing to display willingness to help students overcome problems, these teachers contribute to student feelings of isolation, resentment and low self-esteem. Students interpret the behavior of these teachers as an indication that school has nothing to do with their own worries and concerns. The result: Some students who can't cope act disruptively.

Lack of Data   The general lack of information concerning student behavior contributes to the over-all problem. Nearly one-third of complaints during faculty meetings concerned insufficient information about students and their problems or poor faculty-administration communications. For example, few teachers in the school knew how many students were suspended each year. A strong teacher complaint was that too few teachers knew anything about discipline problems. Teachers said that if they were to contribute to improvements in discipline, then they must know which students were behaving inappropriately. Teachers thus should be told which students display inappropriate behavior and what the behavior is, if teachers are to help with a schoolwide objective of good discipline. Teachers frequently cited these objections when criticizing administrators for a lack of communication.

1 Student warnings   Teachers do not know (or sometimes do not remember) which students have been warned not to disobey a rule again. As a result, some students receive punishment for a first-time offense, while others receive nothing more than numerous warnings.

2   Unscheduled students   Teachers should have a master list of students who are not assigned to any class during a given period. This would help them identify those students who have a legitimate reason for being out of class.

3   Information of referrals   School deans or assistant principals often fail to notify teachers of the disposition of the cases referred to them. Teachers become upset when they discover students that have been sent to the office for punishment have been cleared of charges against them without the slightest teacher consultation.

4   New rules   Administrators sometimes develop new rules unilaterally and don't tell teachers. For example, one dean banned skateboards and frisbees on school grounds, but failed to tell the campus monitors.

5   Follow-up information   Rarely are efforts made to stand back and evaluate how well student discipline strategies are working. At the end of each school year, teachers and administrators should get together to decide how well their discipline procedures have worked, and develop alternative plans where necessary.

Lack of Classroom Management Skills   Few teachers receive any formal training in classroom management, thus, teachers often are justified in disclaiming responsibility for dealing with student misconduct. Strategies such as behavior modification, Teacher Effectiveness Training, or other contemporary approaches adaptable to classroom management were not explored by teachers or the administration at Bay High School. On further investigation teachers indicated that most of the faculty lacked skills in diagnosing behavior problems and prescribing appropriate instructional treatments. Not only were teachers without this training but few nonteaching staff members were exposed to any kind of classroom management technique. Time was not provided by the administration for teachers to meet and discuss ways to help students with behavior problems, and few inschool options were available for troubled students who might be temporarily unable to cope with the regular classroom routine.

Inadequate Administration of Disciplinary Problems   While school administrators often were to blame for failing to communicate with teachers, or notify teachers regarding student referrals, their explanations for these problems varied. One administrator suggested that he was "action oriented"—good at on-the-spot intervention but weak on filling out reports. Another called record keeping her strong suit, but conceded that she has secretarial problems. Other complaints about administrators were more serious. Some teachers doubt that referring students to the deans does any good—so some disruptive students stay in classrooms. And Bay High School administrators did not always obey the law regarding student discipline. In one instance, a dean suspended several students without a hearing. In another case, a student simply was charged with "acting suspiciously" and suspended.

One problem particularly disturbing to students was the selection of school rules that were to be enforced. Inevitably the greatest energy expended by the administration was in enforcing rules related to attendance, smoking, or disrespect for authority. Rarely were discipline problems affecting students—extortion, fighting, name-calling, theft of personal property, and intimidation—attacked with comparable zeal. It's hard for students to believe in a system that tends to regard their own problems as secondary.

The important question: What can be done? Since the cause of many discipline problems seems to originate from administrators and teachers and affect all of the school community, including teachers, what schools may require is a comprehensive, systematic management plan that might include these provisions:

1 Students, teachers and administrators should meet to develop classroom rules, and these rules should be understood by all. These rules should be reassessed and modified, and provisions should be included to handle the problem of inconsistent rule enforcement.

2 Student behavior data should be collected and handed out by one person in the school, and all personnel should be kept informed of student discipline problems.

3 Students and teachers should have a procedure to handle conflicts at the classroom level, and the faculty should meet regularly so that problem students can be identified and helped—parents and people from the community should regularly be contacted to assist in developing plans for aiding troublesome students.

4 Special attention should be given to develop plans to reward students who keep out of trouble, and alternative short-term programs should be developed to help students with behavior problems. The latter should focus on ways to change social behavior.

5 School personnel should be encouraged to develop skills in classroom management, and schoolwide meetings should take place at the end of the year to discuss discipline objectives for the coming year.

ENABLING ACTIVITIES

To aid you to meet the objectives listed in the chapter study guide (page 81), the enabling activities listed below were designed to provide a variety of study directions and exploration activities ranging from the difficult and time-consuming to less complicated, straightforward tasks. It is important that you understand that you do not have to do every enabler listed—choose only those that help you achieve a study guide objective or appeal to one of your specific interests in the chapter topic.

1 Observe a classroom and compare the teacher's techniques for managing surface behavior with those discussed in this chapter.

2 Prepare a paper that outlines the moral and ethical factors a teacher must consider when designing a system of discipline for the classroom.

3 Design a series of simulation incidents that demonstrate the techniques for managing surface behavior discussed in "A differential approach to the management of surface behavior of children in school" by Nicholas Long and R. Newman (*Bulletin of the School of Education*, Indiana University, July 1961, *37*, 47–61) and the punishment variables discussed in "The role of punishment in the classroom" by D. MacMillan, S. Forness, and B. Turnbull (*Exceptional Children*, 1975, *40*(2), 85–96).

4 Summarize the laws of your state regarding corporal punishment.

5 Prepare a 25-minute oral presentation that states your position regarding specific discipline procedures appropriate for a public school classroom. Be sure you state your arguments to support your position.

6 Interview the principal of a school in your community to identify local school policies concerning the disciplining of children.

7 Organize and participate in a panel discussing ethical and moral considerations of classroom discipline.

8 Prepare an oral presentation to be given to teachers that : (a) defines punishment, (b) lists variables that influence the effectiveness of classroom punishment, and (c) offers guidelines for the practical application of punishment.

SELF-TEST

True-False

1 Traditional child-rearing practices deemphasized a child's self-discipline.

2 According to Madsen and Madsen, each individual inherits rambunctious or withdrawn behavior.

3 The definition of discipline includes environmental influences and personal behavior.

4 Values Clarification and Reality Therapy both deal with the importance of relationship and listening techniques.

5 Verbal exchange is an essential characteristic of Transactional Analysis.

6 It is "against the law" to suspend a student.

7 Most discipline problems are resolved through physical punishment.

8 An alternative to suspension might be the Principal's Round Table where students brainstorm ideas about punishment and discipline prevention.

9 Teacher Effectiveness Training, Social Discipline, and Reality Therapy are all teacher-directed models.

10 Comforting/contracting models use a nonpunishing teacher as a comforter and the student as a solution instigator.

11 The largest proportion of suspensions is for truancy.

12 For Values Clarification to be successful, the teacher must clarify the student's internalized values and indoctrinate universal human values.

13 An angry or disruptive student can leave class and seek counseling in the Behavior Clinic.

14 In order for the seven discipline models to be successful, the student must be capable of rational thinking.

15 Teachers who use more than one intervention strategy will observe more success in the long-run.

4

BEHAVIOR MODIFICATION

After reading the selections presented in this chapter and completing the enabling activities, the student should be able to:

1 Differentiate behavior modification from discipline.
2 Develop and defend a definition of behavior modification.
3 Identify the common beliefs about human behavior upon which most behaviorists agree.
4 Differentiate between respondent and operant conditioning.
5 Summarize the basic principles of operant conditioning.
6 Differentiate between punishment, positive and negative reinforcement.
7 Identify and define six consequence schedules.
8 Identify and discuss four ethical issues related to the use of behavior modification.

Behavior Modification

Reid Linn

Behavior modification is a term that has evolved into a "household word" among professionals who deal with children's problems (O'Leary & O'Leary, 1977). It is not only accepted by psychologists and educators, but is used by administrators of hospital and prison programs, group homes, alcohol and drug abuse programs, marital counselors, and smoking and obesity programs. The term elicits responses ranging from rejection to zealous affirmation. Despite common use, weak and inaccurate definitions still exist. In addition, many teachers misunderstand the practical applications of behavior modification.

DEFINITION

Any procedure that promotes a behavior change could be defined as behavior modification. Craighead, Kazdin, and Mahoney (1976, p. 5) point out that "definitions of behavior modification have ranged from the application of the principles of operant conditioning (e.g., Skinner, 1953, 1971) or classical conditioning (Wolpe, 1958) to something called more generally, principles of learning (Ullman and Krasner, 1969) to the more broadly based clinical approaches of Bandura (1969) and Lazarus (1971)." In contrast to these approaches, which refer to underlying principles, Craighead, Kazdin, and Mahoney propose that a definition should be based on rationale and methodology and not a set of principles or theory. This requires an experimental and functionally analytic approach to clinical data which relies on objective and measureable outcomes. Essentially, this would be the behavior analysis approach introduced by Watson in 1913 as methodological behaviorism. Criswell (1981) suggests that behavior modification has taken on a popular meaning much different from its original meaning as defined by Skinner (1953). Examination of the common definitions indicates that the following criteria are stressed most often.

1 Behavior modification has its roots in social and experimental psychology.
2 Behavior modification is a behavior analysis system relying on observable and measurable outcomes.
3 Behavior modification techniques are based on learning principles and/or operant conditioning.

For this chapter, behavior modification is defined as a process in which observable behavior is measurably changed by the systematic application of techniques based on learning theory and experimental research. This definition was adapted from O'Leary and O'Leary (1977). Using this definition, behavior modification does not include procedures such as chemotherapy, psychosurgery, and electroshock therapy.

Behavior modification, then, is systematic analysis of an environment and procedures designed to clearly demonstrate their effect on student behavior. All behavior targeted to be modified must be observable in order to conduct identification, treatment, and evaluation in measurable terms. Behavior modification is not an intervention to alter mood, personality, fear, or self-concept. While these concepts require concern, intervention begins only after they are restated and defined as specific behaviors. For example, out-of-seat behavior and inappropriate verbalization may indicate poor self-concept. It is relatively easy to teach classroom staff members to observe and record the frequency of out-of-seat behavior or the frequency of inappropriate verbalizations which occur during rest period or instructional activity.

Behavior is controlled by observable events which precede behaviors and events which follow behaviors. The preceding events are referred to as "antecedent events" while those following a behavior are referred to as "consequent events." These events are of great importance because they are the determining factors of the frequency, rate, duration, intensity, and pattern of behavior. Therefore, the rationale for emphasizing observable behavior rests with the belief that antecedent and consequent events can be managed which in turn alter behavior.

BEHAVIOR MODELS

While learning theorists propose a variety of models, there are a number of commonly accepted assumptions which provide a basis for the strategies used by all behavior analysts. These assumptions are based on the principles of learning discovered in animal and human experimental research laboratories (Johnston & Pennypacker, 1980). Hilgard and Bower (1966) proposed that learning is the process by which an activity originates or is changed through reacting to an encountered situation, provided that the characteristics of the change in activity cannot be explained on the basis of native response tendencies, maturation, or temporary states of the organism (e.g., fatigue, drugs, hunger). Using this definition, learning is inferred based on the observed changes in activities or behavior. Learning theorists sometimes refer to this change as conditioning. For our purposes, learning will be synonymous with conditioning.

Other theorists (Russ, 1977) focus exclusively on behavior (i.e., performance variables). Learning for them consists of a sequence of behaviors modified by environmental experience (Skinner, 1953). They are not concerned with the unobservable processes which take place between the stimulus, an event, and the response. Our definition of behavior modification is founded primarily on this latter definition of learning.

Russ (1977) lists the following as assumptions made by most learning theorists.

1 Behavior is a basic characteristic of living organisms.
2 Behavior is modifiable, and modification can occur through learning.

3 Most human behavior is learned behavior (Skinner, 1953; Wolpe, 1958). Certainly other processes, such as growth and physical damage (Wolpe, 1958), result in relatively permanent changes in behavior. However, their importance is minimized by learning theorists.

4 The creation, maintenance, and removal of behavior depend on environmental events or stimuli. With changes in events, changes in behavior result. An environmental change can occur as an antecedent or as a consequent event.

5 A lawful, functional relationship exists between behavior and environmental events. (pp. 101–102)

Inappropriate or maladaptive behavior is developed and maintained like any other learned behavior. In theoretical terms, a maladaptive behavior is a conditioned response developed and maintained by antecedent and consequent events. A maladaptive behavior is maladaptive only if labeled as such by someone in authority, and these people become important components in the behavior modification system. Behavior modification techniques are most effective when used by those who want the behavior changed. Where children are concerned, parents and teachers may be the most influential people in the child's environment.

There are major differences among learning theorists. While it is relatively

FIGURE 1
The divisions among connectionist psychologists based on the theorist's approach to the issues of contiguity versus reinforcement concepts. *(Adapted from Russ, 1977.)*

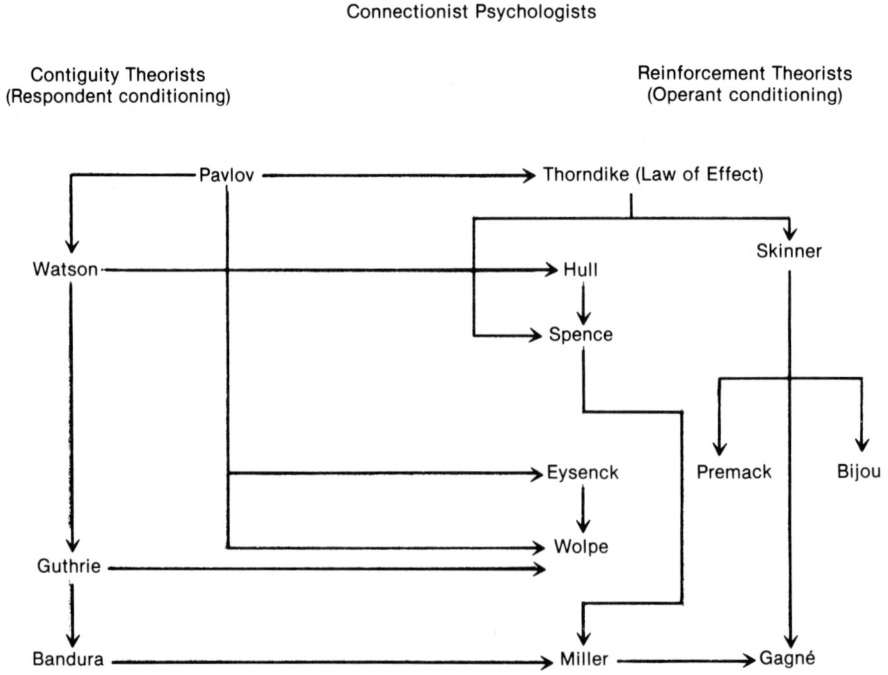

Connectionist Psychologists

Contiguity Theorists
(Respondent conditioning)

Reinforcement Theorists
(Operant conditioning)

easy to group them into a few categories, there exist further divisions within each category. Theorists who view learning as involving a connection between a stimulus and a response have been referred to as connectionists (Hill, 1963; Russ, 1977) and provide most of the support for the behavior modification used in education. Connectionists are divided on two issues. One group has been labeled "contiguity theorists," and they base their theory on the establishment of the learning connection by respondent conditioning. The other group, reinforcement theorists, base their theory on the establishment of the learning connection through operant conditioning. Each can be further divided on individual theoretical concepts (see Figure 1).

Respondent Conditioning

Respondent, or classical, conditioning is concerned with stimuli that automatically elicit reflex responses. A respondent is an innate response, such as a reflex, and is generally thought of as being involuntary. It always follows a specific eliciting stimulus and its frequency of occurrence is determined by the frequency of presentation of the eliciting stimulus. Examples of specific stimuli in the environment are noise, shock, light, or food. Examples of respondents include the constriction of the pupil of the eye when presented with bright light, a startle response to a loud noise, and the reflex action of a muscle recoiling from a source of pain. In respondent conditioning, the stimulus eliciting the respondent is called an unconditioned stimulus (US) and the reflex response is called the unconditioned response (UR). These terms are labeled unconditioned because the relationship between the stimulus and response is automatic or unlearned. Respondent conditioning refers to the process whereby new stimuli gain the power to elicit respondent behavior (Craighead, Kazdin, & Mahoney, 1976). In other words, a neutral stimulus is paired with the unconditioned stimulus and eventually the US develops the power to elicit respondent behavior. The US is called a conditioned stimulus (CS) and the respondent behavior is then called the conditioned response (CR). The respondent conditioning paradigm is presented in Figure 2.

FIGURE 2
(1) represents the natural relationship of an unconditioned stimulus (US) and unconditioned response (UR). (2) represents the pairing, or simultaneous presentation, of the conditioned stimulus (CS) and the unconditioned stimulus (US). After repeated pairings, the conditioned stimulus (CS) can elicit the unconditioned response (UR), which now becomes a conditioned response (CR). *(Adapted from Criswell, 1981.)*

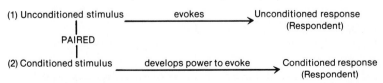

Respondent Conditioning Paradigm

(1) Unconditioned stimulus ——— evokes ——→ Unconditioned response (Respondent)

PAIRED

(2) Conditioned stimulus ——— develops power to evoke ——→ Conditioned response (Respondent)

While Descartes presented the reflex as the basic mechanism of animal behavior, Pavlov gained credit for investigating the conjecture experimentally.
His work centered on the digestive system of dogs. He noticed that meat powder (US) produced salivation (UR) when placed in a dog's mouth. By pairing a
neutral stimulus, such as a bell (CS), with the presentation of the meat powder
several times, the bell would eventually elicit salivation (now the CR) when
presented without the meat powder.

Another example of respondent conditioning was provided by Watson and
Rayner (1920). They demonstrated that a fear response could be conditioned in
young children. Albert, an eleven-month-old boy enjoyed playing with a white
rat without any adverse reaction. As with most young children, Albert dis-
played a fear reaction when a sudden, loud noise was produced. To condition a
fear reaction to the presentation of the rat, a loud noise was produced immediately following the presentation of the animal to Albert. Eventually, the presentation of the rat alone elicited a fear reaction.

The unconditioned response and the conditioned response are not exactly
the same. The conditioned response will continue to occur only if the unconditioned stimulus is presented periodically. If the unconditioned stimulus is not
presented again, the conditioned stimulus loses its power to evoke the conditioned response and extinction gradually occurs. The teacher in the classroom
becomes a conditioned stimulus through the presentation of positive reinforcers. Just the presence of the teacher may be enough eventually to elicit appropriate behaviors from the students. The principal may also become a conditioned stimulus through frequent administration of punishment to students. The
mere presence of the principal may then elicit anxiousness and fear from some
children.

Operant Conditioning

Much behavior is not involuntary or elicited by specific stimuli. The reinforcement theorists propose that behavior is emitted and is maintained by the consequences following it. An operant is a response or behavior that acts on the
environment to produce an effect. Thorndike is Pavlov's counterpart in the
development of reinforcement theory with his work providing much of the
foundation for later investigators.

Operant conditioning can be used to strengthen or increase the frequency of
an existing behavior, or develop and shape a new behavior. When a rat presses
a bar or a pigeon pecks a disc in a laboratory experimental setting, the presentation of food pellets increases the probability that the pressing or pecking behavior will occur with greater frequency in the future. Likewise, when a child
eats all of her/his lunch, the presentation of verbal praise and ice cream may
increase the probability that this desired eating behavior will occur with increased frequency in the future. It is the determination of the types of antecedent and consequent stimuli (events) that modifies responses. The responsibility
of determination and provision of these events rests with the behavior modifier.

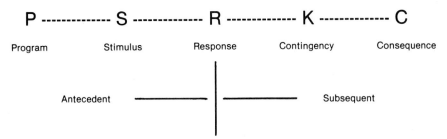

FIGURE 3
Operant paradigm. *(Adapted from Lindsley, 1970.)*

According to Lindsley (1970), the operant paradigm consists of five components: (1) the program, (2) the preceding stimulus, (3) the response, (4) the
contingency, (5) the consequence. One and two are both antecedent events;
four and five are subsequent events, as depicted in Figure 3. Based on this
paradigm, a change made in the program, stimulus, contingency, or consequent
component will result in a modification of the response.

Observational Learning

While respondent or classical conditioning and operant conditioning are the
two most emphasized approaches to learning, Craighead, Kazdin, and Mahoney (1976) recognize and give emphasis to observational learning. This includes
both types of responses—respondents and operants—and is of importance for
inclusion.

Observational or vicarious learning, or modeling (Bandura & Walters, 1963),
suggests that an individual may learn a response by observing a model without
ever actually performing it. Bandura (1965) points out that modeling can also
develop new responses and alter the frequency of previously learned responses.

The requirement of learning through modeling is the observation of a model.
Learning takes place through cognitive or covert coding. Therefore, in order to
determine if learning has actually taken place, the learned response must be
performed. In order to evoke a performance, the response consequences or
incentives associated with that response must be manipulated.

Bandura (1965) studied children who observed a film in which an adult modeled aggressive responses (hitting and kicking a doll). The children were divided into different groups, with some children observing the model's aggression being rewarded; some observing the model's aggression being punished;
and other observing no consequences following the model's aggression. When
the children were given the opportunity to engage in the aggressive behavior,
those who observed the model being punished engaged in less aggressive behavior than the other two groups. When incentives were employed to reinforce
children for modeling the behavior, no differences in aggression were observed

for any of the three groups. While all groups learned the aggressive behaviors, the consequences determined the likelihood that they would be performed.

Behaviorists believe that most behaviors are learned and can be changed by the use of learning principles. Behavior modification attempts to alter observable behaviors or teach and develop new behaviors. Behavior modification does not attempt to alter behaviors with underlying physiological or psychological etiologies.

PRINCIPLES OF OPERANT CONDITIONING

Behavior modification as defined for this chapter relies on principles of learning developed from experimental psychology, with many techniques based on operant conditioning. In fact, the variables essential to a behavior modification program are directly related to the operant paradigm. These can be labeled the ABCs of behavior modification. They include the following: (1) antecedent events; (2) behaviors deemed to be in need of modification; and (3) consequences which will reinforce or punish the behaviors.

The teacher's responsibility is to teach academic and social skills to all students regardless of differences. Not only must the teacher use the commercial programs and instructional techniques to shape the growth of academic behaviors, but must also identify the cues, reinforcers, and punishers necessary to shape the growth of social skills. As a behavior modifier (Haring & Phillips, 1972), the teacher must focus on observable behavior, changing that behavior, study the effect of instructional procedures, and evaluate the total process. They also suggest that to influence behavior directly, the teacher must devise a "plan" that determines: (1) the specific skill and behavior objectives for each child in the class, (2) the specific cues that will evoke responses leading directly to the objectives, (3) the responses to be measured, (4) the reinforcers and punishers to be used, and (5) the consequent contingencies to be tested.

The principles of operant conditioning describe the relationship between a behavior and the environmental events influencing it. Most applications of behavior modification emphasize the consequences that follow a behavior, although antecedent events can also alter behavior. Once specific consequences have been decided, it is important to make these consequences contingent upon performance. This is accomplished by delivering the consequence only after the performance of the target behavior. Examples of commonly occurring consequences are a grade which is dependent upon completion of required coursework and wages contingent upon work.

Reinforcement

Reinforcement is the process of presenting a positive or negative reinforcer following a response. Both of these will increase the frequency or intensity of a response. Negative reinforcement, however, is sometimes confused with punishment. Negative reinforcement is the process of removing an aversive stimulus to increase the frequency or intensity of a behavior. An example of negative reinforcement is the cocktail party boor. When you find this loud, rude lout consistently attending the same parties as you, you begin to refuse invitations from these hosts. Refusal of a specific party host's invitation terminates contact with the boor (negative reinforcer). The probability that you will refuse select party invitations is increased. When a child begins to work after being given the alternatives of working or missing recess, the threat of a negative reinforcer (loss of recess) is removed, which reinforces the appropriate behavior (working).

Positive reinforcement refers to the presentation of a positive stimulus which increases the frequency or intensity of a response. A positive reinforcer is not necessarily a reward—rewards are given in return for service or in recognition of outstanding achievement.

There are two categories of positive reinforcers, primary and secondary. Food, for example, serves as a primary reinforcer because an individual does not have to learn the reinforcing value of it. While food is not always reinforcing (immediately after a large Thanksgiving dinner, for example), when it is used as a reinforcer, its value is automatic. Secondary or conditioned reinforcers are such things as praise, a check for good work, or a golf drive down the middle of the fairway.

Some responses can be used to reinforce other responses. The Premack Principle suggests that the opportunity to engage in a high-frequency behavior can be used as a reinforcer to increase the rate of low-frequency behaviors (Premack, 1959; 1965). In other words, if a child prefers playing records to reading, then playing records can be made contingent upon reading and therefore be used as a reinforcer for reading. "Tokens," which may be points, coins, poker or game chips, stars, or checks can be used as reinforcers. The tokens may be sufficient by themselves; however, the most common practice is to permit the tokens to be exchanged for such things as candy, privileges, records, or cigarettes at some time in the future.

Punishment

Punishment refers to the presentation of an aversive stimulus or event or the removal of a positive event. A punisher decreases the frequency or intensity of a response. Due to the negative connotations usually associated with punishment, it is important to understand the technical definition of this term. Many associate punishment with the infliction of pain, but it does not necessarily involve pain or physical coercion.

There are two kinds of punishment. Type I refers to punishment by application and the use of a punisher or aversive stimulus. Some examples include physical restraint, a sharp command, a special seat, being burned after touching a hot stove, and a spanking. Type II refers to punishment by removal.

Examples include losing tokens or privileges and time-out procedures. Both types are included in the following example (Malott, Ritterby, & Wolf, 1973).

> Due to your fantastic skill as a contingency manager, your parrot now has an active vocabulary that would make a sailor blush. Your wealthy and aging Aunt Minnie, Retired Admiral, U.S. WAVES, will soon be visiting you. Since she is nautical but nice, your parrot will no doubt cause her to blush, be offended, and disinherit you. Oh mercy, what to do? You can use a punishment contingency. Every time the bird says, "hell," you can shake the hell out of it. This is the presentation of a punisher. Being the nonviolent type that you are, you might prefer the termination of a positive reinforcer. Every time the bird offends, you put the night cloth over the cage. You, of course, have no difficulty in assuming that your presence is a positive reinforcer for any man or beast. (pp. 11–2)

Nonlaboratory application of punishment is often difficult due to the conditions influencing the effectiveness of punishment. Guidelines which generally enhance the effects of punishment in nonlaboratory settings include (Craighead, Kazdin, & Mahoney, 1976):

1 Immediate application or removal of the contingent stimulus after the undesired response.
2 Punishment of each and every occurrence of the response.
3 Introduction of the contingent punishing stimulus at maximum intensity, rather than with gradual increases in severity.
4 Removal of motivation for the undesired response.
5 Training of an alternate, acceptable response, especially when the motivation for the undesired response cannot be eliminated.
6 Reinforcement of responses that are incompatible with the punished response.
7 In humans, a description of the punishment contingency given prior to implementation.

Schedules of Consequences

The consequence schedule is critical, because it determines the effect of reinforcement or punishment on a response. A change in the schedule will cause a predictable change in the probability of responses. When reinforcement occurs after each response, the schedule is called "continuous reinforcement." If reinforcement only occurs periodically, the schedule is called "intermittent reinforcement." Continuous reinforcement is deemed to be the most desirable schedule when first developing a response. By reinforcing every response, the behavior modifier hooks the individual into the system. With time, the individual may become bored with the reinforcer and the frequency or rate of responding might taper off. Intermittent reinforcement schedules are used at this point to produce even higher performance rates and increase resistance to extinction. Examples of continuous reinforcement might be turning on the TV or stereo, putting money in vending machines, or going to your favorite restaurant. Examples of intermittent reinforcement would be bowling, shooting a basketball, phoning a friend, or entering a contest. If a vending machine fails to supply soda or candy or your stereo produces smoke and stops playing, rapid extinction of your behavior occurs. However, if you make a strike occasionally or hit two hook shots in a row, you may continue to bowl or play basketball for a long time.

Intermittent reinforcement can be scheduled in a variety of ways. A "ratio schedule" requires that a specific number of responses be made before reinforcement takes place. "Interval schedules" allow for the reinforcement of the first response following a specified time interval. The presentation of reinforcers on either ratio or interval schedules can be fixed (does not change or vary) or variable (constantly changes). Consequence schedules include:

A Continuous consequences
B Intermittent consequences
  1 Fixed ratio (FR)
  2 Variable ratio (VR)
  3 Fixed interval (FI)
  4 Variable interval (VI)

Fixed ratio schedules require that a specified number of responses occur prior to the delivery of the consequence. For example, a fixed ratio schedule of 5 (FR:5) means that every fifth response is reinforced. A variable ratio schedule means that the number of responses prior to reinforcement varies, but reinforcement is based on an "average" number of responses. For example, a variable ratio of 5 (VR:5) means that on the average every fifth response is reinforced. Therefore, if over five trials the required number of responses before reinforcement is 2, 4, 5, 7, and 7, reinforcement occurs on an "average" of every fifth response. On individual trials, though, the organism is not aware of how many responses are required.

A fixed interval schedule requires that a specified time interval must pass before a response is reinforced. For example, given a fixed interval schedule of 2 minutes (FI:2), any number of responses can be made but a reinforcer is presented only after the first response occurring after the 2-minute interval has passed. A variable interval schedule allows the length of intervals to vary around the average. For example, given a variable interval schedule of 2 minutes (VI:2), reinforcers might become available after the following number of minutes: 2, 1, 1, 5, 1, 2, 2 with reinforcement on the "average" of every 2 minutes.

Higher rates of responding are usually achieved with ratio rather than interval schedules. Consistent response patterns tend to be developed by the use of variable schedules rather than fixed schedules. The various intermittent schedules, particularly variable schedules, are important for developing resistance to extinction. The transition from a generous or "dense" schedule of reinforcement to a "lean" schedule must take place gradually to avoid extinction. It is important to emphasize the word "gradual" as it pertains to any shift in procedure, especially the often delicate transition of moving a child from the false schedule of reinforcement, established by the behavior modification program, to the natural schedule of reinforcement found in the real world.

Techniques for Developing New Behaviors

Techniques which are used to develop new behaviors include modeling or observational learning, prompting, shaping, and fading. "Modeling" allows a child to enhance his/her chances of learning by observing a model demonstrate a behavior. It has been demonstrated that important factors in observational learning are: (*a*) the observance of the model receiving positive reinforcement as a consequence of the behavior, and (*b*) the added importance of the model having a higher status and more power than the observer (Bandura, 1965; Mercer & Algozzine, 1977).

"Prompting" involves the use of cues, gestures, models, and examples as antecedent events. These events prompt, or help initiate, a response. Once the response is made, reinforcement can be presented. For some children, physically guiding the response may be a necessary step before mere gestures can be effective. While reinforcement alone might work to develop a behavior, prompting to initiate the response will increase the rate of learning by insuring more rapid approximations of the target behavior or final response.

"Shaping" refers to the reinforcement of small steps or approximations toward a final response. Each response which resembles the final response is reinforced. The important component of the shaping strategy is the development of a response hierarchy by the behavior modifier. Responses that are increasingly similar to the desired final response are reinforced. These increasingly similar responses are referred to as "successive approximations." As the first approximation is performed consistently, the criterion for reinforcement is raised or changed so that the next response more closely resembles the final (goal) response.

"Fading" refers to the procedure for removing the prompts (helpful hints) from the training situation. If prompts are removed too quickly, there may be a breakdown in the learning process so that the response may not occur again. Therefore, fading should be a gradual process until the child finally responds independently. While the prompts are faded, reinforcement of responses made in the absence of prompts should gradually become the rule.

Because these techniques were developed in experimental laboratories with animals, modeling, prompting, shaping, and fading are most apparent in the training of animals to perform various tricks. It would be impractical for the animal trainer to wait until the tricks were performed to present a reinforcer. Likewise it would be impractical for the teacher to wait until the child recited his/her multiplication tables or a parent wait until the child tied his shoes to administer reinforcement. The reinforcer might never be delivered.

Techniques for Altering Existing Behaviors

Reinforcement and punishment were discussed as strategies for changing children's behaviors in an earlier section. To summarize, reinforcement is the presentation of a positive consequence or removal of a negative one after a response to increase the frequency or intensity of that response. Punishment refers to the presentation of an aversive event or the removal of a positive event after a response to decrease the frequency or intensity of that response. Praise and approval are examples of possible reinforcers. A hug, pat on the back, or a smile may be all that is necessary from a teacher to insure continued periods of good work. Warm and positive gestures contingent upon desired behavior can be effective tools in changing or maintaining behavior. Effective punishment methods are soft reprimands, time out from reinforcement, aversive stimuli, response cost (where tokens are lost or fines levied as a result of an inappropriate behavior), and extinction (where ignoring or removal of attention from a behavior results in that behavior ceasing).

There are many other behavior modification techniques which serve to reinforce or punish behavior such as relaxation, desensitization, self-evaluation, satiation, deprivation, and overcorrection, but only the most frequently used have been included for discussion.

Criswell (1981) compiled a list of suggestions from the literature for skill maintenance and behavior alteration. These included:

1 Teach responses that will be reinforced in the subject's natural environment.

2 Train relatives or peers in ways to reinforce the learned responses.

3 Fade the contingencies during training.

4 Train loosely; vary the conditions in the training setting. Use several trainers and several training examples.

5 Use intermittent schedules of reinforcement during training. Conceal the reinforcement contingencies if possible.

6 Teach the subject how to control his/her own behavior. Do this by teaching accurate self-recording and self-reinforcement.

7 Reinforce successive approximations to maintain and generalize responding.

Because people are different, modification of procedures and lists, such as Criswell's suggestions, is necessary in order to develop and implement programs based on the student's functioning level. It is important that the conditions in training approximate as closely as possible conditions that the children will experience after training.

ETHICAL ISSUES

The belief that one's environment can influence his/her behavior is not specific to the behaviorists' approach, but is a basic premise of most therapies. Perhaps it is the knowledge that behavior modification deals primarily with manipulating a person's environment that creates such a strong reaction on the part of its critics. It does appear that the thought of "controlling" another's environment and their social interactions is central to the charges that behavior modification relies on punishment, makes use of bribery, takes away an individual's free will, and does not protect individual rights. London (1971) maintains that, as it expands, the technology of behavior control clearly holds as much promise for serving freedom as it threatens freedom. Technology demands that individual development be maximum and people provided with instruments for self-control.

It is apparent that the most important ethical issue of behavior modification concerns its relationship to freedom—antithesis of control. Some suggest that freedom is an important idea only to people who feel oppressed; and happiness only to those who are miserable. An adherent of individual liberty finds extensive behavior control unacceptable because of the effect on its victims and its gratification for power in its perpetrator. Even in the most free society, some must bear the responsibility for wielding power over others in order to supervise the allocation and distribution of resources, to organize protection and aid for the weak, the ignorant, and the infirm. Some candidates for power will want it because they see its value as an instrument for serving human needs, while others will be intoxicated by it (London, 1971).

Because of the inherent power of behavior modification procedures, some perceive them as dangerous tools. There is truth in these beliefs, for it has the potential for appropriate use or for misuse. Behavioral technology is no more and no less harmful than any other technology such as biochemistry, medicine, electronics, or engineering. Biochemists can produce chemicals to prolong the life of the ill or destroy all life on the planet. Electronics can help us communicate around the world or detonate a nuclear warhead.

Critics have attacked the purposes for which behavior modification might be used and asked if such aims are consistent with the greater welfare of society (Kazdin, 1978). O'Leary and O'Leary (1977) point out that changing a child's specific behavior (e.g., attending or in-seat) is occasionally criticized by education philosophers because the change seems irrelevant to some educational goals (O'Leary, 1972; Winett & Winkler, 1972). While being in one's seat and paying attention are not always inextricably related to learning, the child who is in his seat is more likely to receive effective help from the teacher. In short, having a child sit still and attend is the first step in the progression toward many educational goals.

Aversives, like positive reinforcers, can be listed in a hierarchy which extends from the simple "no" to an extreme such as severe shock. Jimmy is a profoundly retarded adolescent who periodically engages in severe self-abuse. Because of his size he hits himself with such force that he has blinded his right eye and could die should a blow crush his trachea. No antecedent event has been determined to initiate the self-injurious behavior and no intervention has significantly decreased the frequency or intensity of the behavior. As another attempt to alter this behavior, a program of shock therapy is implemented so that Jimmy receives a shock each time he hits himself. His behavior decreases to only one hit during the second month of intervention. Prior to intervention, Jimmy had to be secured in a chair with straps on the average of five times per day to avoid self-abuse. If no other technique has been successful with extreme cases, should we rule out extreme aversives? Endorsement of these techniques should occur in cases that present danger or when undesirable behavior must be decreased before appropriate behavior can be increased.

A common criticism of behavior modification is often stated: "Why should I bribe a student to act like he is supposed to act?" Do behavioral methods equate with bribery? No, because bribery refers to a favor bestowed or promised in order to pervert judgment or corrupt conduct. Kazdin (1978) points out that behavior modification does not dictate goals or purposes. In most applications of behavioral principles, the purpose or goal has been determined in advance. Behavior modification programs in hospitals and institutions, schools, day-care treatment facilities, and prisons have many established goals already endorsed by society; for example, returning the individual to the community, accelerating academic performance, achieving self-help, communication, and social skills, and alleviating bizarre behaviors.

Another issue concerning behavior modification is the often observed clinical nature of the behavior modifier's interaction with the subject. In the educational setting, this refers to the teacher and the student. O'Leary and O'Leary (1977) point out several facets of sensitivity which should concern the teacher. Two of these are (a) the sensitivity necessary to target and train behaviors which will be maintained by the natural environment, and (b) the sensitivity to the actual practices of the child's parents and peers instead of the purported practices of such persons. A third facet of sensitivity concerns a teacher's warmth and emotional responses to a child.

To be a good modifier of behavior one cannot simply dispense attention in a mechanical or machinelike fashion. One must give such attention in a spontaneous, warm manner. Equally important, one must be aware of a child's feelings and desires so that when the child is excited over success the teacher will respond immediately in a sincere fashion. That is, the teacher must have empathy for the child. The most effective teachers are probably those who exhibit a variety of affective behaviors—soft and gentle in one situation but ebullient and ecstatic in another. The teacher will reprimand in a firm manner indicating that unpleasant consequences exist and will be used if certain behaviors do not cease.

In trying to meet society's challenges concerning ethical issues, many education programs have established advisory committees or behavior management committees to help develop, implement, and monitor behavior management procedures. The membership of such a committee is often comprised of teachers, psychologists, medical staff, child advocates, parents, and students.

The committee reviews all procedures and develops strict policies in order to make sure that the behavioral methods used are ethical.

While much appears to have been done to monitor the use of controls for human behavior, new issues will continue to challenge behavior modification. With each new advance comes the potential for misuse. "Technologies do not create or answer moral problems; only men do that. The final issues of their moral intercourse, accordingly, do not depend on how men are able to use their tools, but on how they are willing to use each other" (London, 1971, p. 205).

REFERENCES

Bandura, A. Influence of model's reinforcement contingencies on the acquisition of imitative responses. *Journal of Personality and Social Psychology*, 1965, *1*, 589–595.

Bandura, A. *Principles of Behavior Modification*. New York: Holt, Rinehart, & Winston, 1969.

Bandura, A., & Walters, R. H. *Social Learning and Personality Development*. New York: Holt, Rinehart, & Winston, 1963.

Craighead, W. E., Kazdin, A. E., & Mahoney, M. J. *Behavior Modification: Principles, Issues, and Applications*. Boston: Houghton Mifflin Company, 1976.

Criswell, E. The behavioral perspectives of emotional disturbance. In R. Algozzine, R. Schmid, & C. D. Mercer (Eds.), *Childhood Behavior Disorders: Applied Research and Educational Practice*. Rockville, Maryland: Aspen Systems Corporation, 1981.

Haring, N. G., & Phillips, E. L. *Analysis and Modification of Classroom Behavior*. Englewood Cliffs, N.J.: Prentice-Hall, Inc., 1972.

Hilgard, E., & Bower, G. *Theories of Learning*. New York: Appleton-Century-Crofts, 1966.

Hill, W. F. *Learning: A Survey of Psychological Interpretations*. San Francisco: Chandler, 1963.

Johnston, J. M., & Pennypacker, H. S. *Strategies and Tactics of Human Behavioral Research*. Hillsdale, N.J.: Lawrence Earlbaum Associates, 1980.

Kazdin, A. E. *A History of Behavior Modification: Experimental Foundations of Contemporary Research*. Baltimore: University Park Press, 1978.

Lazarus, A. A. *Behavior Therapy and Beyond*. New York: McGraw-Hill, 1971.

Lindsley, O.R. Procedures in common described by a common language. In C. E. Neuringer & J. Michael (Eds.), *Behavior Modification in Clinical Psychology*. New York: Appleton-Century-Crofts, 1970.

London, P. *Behavior Control*. New York: Harper & Row, 1971.

Mahoney, M. J., Kazdin, A. E., & Lesswing, W. J. Behavior modification: Delusion or deliverance? In C. M. Franks & G. T. Wilson (Eds.), *Annual Review of Behavior Therapy: Theory and Practice*, Vol. 2. New York: Brunner/Mazel, 1974.

Malott, R. W., Ritterby, K., & Wolf, E. L. C. An introduction to behavior modification. Kalamazoo, MI: *Behaviordelia*, 1973, 11–2.

Mercer, C. D., & Algozzine, B. Observational learning and the retarded: Teaching implications. *Education and Training of the Mentally Retarded*, 1977, *12*, 343–353.

O'Leary, K. D., & O'Leary, S. G. *Classroom Management: The Successful Use of Behavior Modification*. New York: Pergamon Press, 1977.

Premack, D. Catching up with common-sense or two sides of generalization: Reinforcement and punishment. In R. Glaser (Ed.), *The Nature of Reinforcement*. New York: Academic Press, 1971.

Premack, D. Toward empirical behavior law: 1. Positive reinforcement. *Psychological Review*, 1959, *66*, 219–233.

Russ, D. F. A review of learning and behavior therapy as it relates to emotional disturbance in children: The behavioral model. In W. C. Morse & M. L. Tracy (Eds.), *A Study of Child Variance: Conceptual Models*, Vol. 2. Ann Arbor: The University of Michigan Press, 1977, 95–179.

Skinner, B. F. *Beyond Freedom and Dignity*. New York: Knopf, 1971.

Skinner, B. F. *Science and Human Behavior*. New York: Macmillan Publishing Company, 1953.

Ullman, L., & Krasner, L. *Psychological Approach to Abnormal Behavior*, Englewood Cliffs, N.J.: Prentice-Hall, 1969.

Watson, J. B., & Rayner, R. Conditioned emotional reactions. *Journal of Experimental Psychology*, 1920, *3*, 1–14.

Winett, R. A., & Winkler, R. C. Current behavior modification in the classroom: Be still, be quiet, be docile. *Journal of Applied Behavior Analysis,* 1972, *5*, 499–504.

Wolpe, J. *Psychotherapy by Reciprocal Inhibition*. Stanford, California: Stanford University Press, 1958.

Effects of Surreptitious Modeling Upon Teacher Classroom Behaviors

David Brown
Daniel Reschly
Howard Wasserman

The effects of observational learning upon subsequent social and intellectual behaviors have been demonstrated amply (Bandura, 1971; Rosenthal & Zimmerman, 1970). This research has revealed the profound influence of models upon a wide variety of behaviors that include aggressiveness, phobic reactions, grammatical structure, rule learning, etc. However, to date little research has been completed that concerns the problem of the possible use of modeling procedures as a means to change teachers' behaviors. The present study is a report of an effort to change a teacher's behavior in a natural classroom setting.

The authors were requested to consult with the teacher of a classroom for emotionally disturbed children as part of a practicum in a graduate class on behavior modification consultation. Briefly, the teacher previously had requested assistance to deal with the "hyperactive" and disruptive behavior of

Brown, David, Reschly, Daniel, and Wasserman, Howard. Effects of surreptitious modeling upon teacher classroom behaviors. *Psychology in the Schools,* 1974, *11*(3), 366–369. Reprinted by permission.

two students. Even though the teacher had requested such assistance, she refused to accept advice offered by the school counselor on one occasion and by the special education consultant on another. Two of the authors were placed in this classroom for the purpose of observing "emotionally disturbed" students and applying behavior modification techniques.

An initial interview with the teacher established her extreme resistance to various behavior modification plans, although she was receptive to the plan of allowing the authors to observe in the classroom and interact with the children. Instead of the behavioral techniques favored by the authors the teacher insisted upon the necessity of psychotherapy in combination with chemotherapy (ritalin) in dealing with the disruptive students. Implicit in her recommendations was the desire to minimize direct teacher involvement in any intervention plan.

Classroom observation established the fact that the two students were definitely not hyperactive, and moreover, led to an intuitive judgment that the teacher maintained a very low rate of positive contacts with individual or groups of students.

Based upon the above observations, two intervention plans were instituted. The first involved the establishment of self-reinforcement contingencies for the two disruptive students. Briefly, this involved stating criteria for reward and allowing the students to decide whether the rewards had been earned. The self-reinforcement plan was successful (see Brown, Reschly, & Wasserman, 1974) even though it was carried out with no teacher assistance.

The second intervention plan, which was the major purpose of the study reported herein, involved an attempt to use modeling procedures as a means to increase the frequency of positive pupil-teacher contacts. Specifically, the frequency of positive contingent social reinforcement was determined before and after such behaviors were modeled by the authors.

METHOD

The authors were in the classroom described above for the purpose of observing the behavior of two disruptive children. This arrangement provided the opportunity to observe carefully the frequency of teacher-initiated positive contingent social reinforcement. The frequency of occurrence of teacher praise and number of times the teacher moved away from the seat at her desk were gathered on five occasions (see Fig. 1): probes 1, 2, and 3 prior to modeling, probe 4 immediately after modeling, and probe 5, 4 weeks after modeling. All data were collected during the first 90 minutes of the school day.

Reliability of observations was obtained, during the second and fifth probes, by comparing the ratings of two observers who operated independently within the classroom. Observations of teacher behavior were made during the first 90 minutes of the school day. Agreements of 100% on probe two and 95% on probe five were obtained.

Modeling out-of-seat behavior and the contingent application of praise was implemented on two occasions, day 31 and day 32. The teacher was not in-

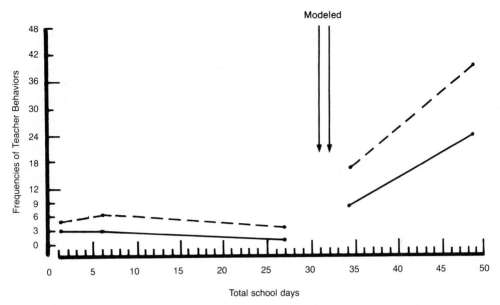

FIGURE 1
Frequency of times teacher came out from behind her desk (●—●) and times teacher positively interacted with students (● – – ●).

formed previously of this intervention procedure, hence she was given no cue to direct her attention toward the model. The teacher remained in the chair behind her desk at all times during the 90 minutes of modeling on both days and seemingly was occupied with class-related work. The model (one of the authors) continuously moved about the classroom and quietly interacted with students. When students attended to their assigned tasks, the model moved closer to the student, occasionally placed a hand on their shoulder, and praised good working behaviors (the model enumerated the positive work behaviors manifested).

RESULTS

As can be seen from Fig. 1 the mean number of times the teacher left her desk and frequency of praise for children prior to modeling were 2.3 and 4.3 respectively. Immediately after modeling intervention the teacher came out from behind her desk 8 times and the incidence of praise increased to 17 during the 90-minute interval. The frequency of these behaviors was 25 and 40 respectively 4 weeks after the initial modeling.

The above results were analyzed statistically through application of the Fisher Exact Method (Walker & Lev, 1953). Frequencies of both teacher praise and number of times she spent away from her desk were found to be significant ($p < .02$).

DISCUSSION

The modeling of interaction with students and praise for student work had a dramatic effect upon the frequency of these behaviors with this particular teacher. While it was impossible to control carefully a number of potentially confounding variables (see Campbell & Stanley, 1963), it seems highly likely that the substantial change in teacher behavior was more than mere coincidence. It is clear from the data reported herein that a set of inappropriate teacher behaviors apparently had existed for a long time (as was substantiated by the principal), and that after modeling conditions considerably more appropriate behaviors were adopted.

Bandura (1971) has demonstrated amply the importance of a number of variables associated with the stimulus value of the model. Factors such as perceived competence, prestige, age, and sex are potential influences upon the effectiveness of a model. However, it should be emphasized that the model in this situation in all likelihood did not possess these important characteristics in any greater degree than the typical consultant to a classroom teacher. The model was rather young (under 30), a graduate student in school psychology, and relatively inexperienced in educational settings. All of these facts were known to the teacher. It seems unlikely that these results were simply due to a model-status factor that exceeds or is beyond that of the typical consultant.

These results seem to have a number of implications for the use of a consultation model by school psychologists, curriculum supervisors, counselors, and others. When overt suggestions for changing teacher behaviors may be excessively threatening, or likely to be rejected for other reasons, some form of covert influence might be attempted. The increasing acceptance of observation and interaction with problem children in the classroom by psychologists and counselors, rather than interacting only on a one-to-one basis outside of the class, provides the opportunity for the kind of covert influence exercised in this study. Even though no directional cues or attention cues were provided, the modeling appeared to have an effect. This procedure avoided a possible confrontation over methods to deal with children and further reduced the "expert-client" relationship that often interferes with effective consultation. On the basis of the above data covert influence, or what we like to call "surreptitious modeling," appears to be a promising procedure for counselors and psychologists in working with classroom teachers.

A caution should be expressed concerning the use of an influence technique such as covert modeling without a prior agreement between the consultant and consultee. In some cases a consultant is requested to help a teacher with problems related to overall professional performance, *e.g.*, discipline in the classroom. In such cases the covert modeling that has been described herein appears to be well within an explicit agreement establishing a helping relationship between the consultant and consultee. However, in cases in which the initial reason for consultation is a third party such as an individual child, consultant modeling for the purpose of influencing the teacher's behavior should be undertaken only when an agreement that specifies possible effects, procedures, etc., is made.

REFERENCES

Bandura, A. *Social learning theory*. New York: General Learning Press, 1971.

Brown, D., Reschly, D., & Wasserman, H. The modification of "hyperactivity" via self-management procedures. Unpublished manuscript, University of Arizona, 1973.

Campbell, D., & Stanley, J. *Experimental and Quasi-Experimental Designs for Research*. Chicago: Rand McNally, 1963.

Rosenthal, T., & Zimmerman, B. Modeling by exemplification and instruction in training conservation. Unpublished manuscript, University of Arizona, 1970.

Walker, H. M., & Lev, J. *Statistical inference*. New York: Holt-Rinehart-Winston, 1953.

A Truce in the "War for the Child"

Howard G. Garner

It is time for those professionals who work with behavior disordered and emotionally disturbed children to give up one of their most cherished, time consuming, and unproductive debates. Should these handicapped children be treated with the effective technology of behavior modification or the sensitivity of feeling oriented therapy? Psychologists, educators, social workers, and psychiatrists encountered this debate over the last two decades and have usually chosen sides with the Skinnerians or the Rogerians. Children with problems have been lured into one camp or the other and subjected to the answer. It is becoming clear that children who receive help from only one of the two camps are being denied the kind of comprehensive treatment and training they must receive if they are to experience their full potential as human beings. It is also becoming clear that behavior modification and affectively oriented treatment are not incompatible. In fact, they can be blended into a powerful and effective program of change and caring.

THE WAR FOR THE CHILD

A few years ago coexistence with the enemy seemed impossible. The basic assumptions of each approach were antithetical and distasteful to the other group. The major clashes between the two positions have centered around the

Garner, H. G. A truce in the "War for the Child." *Exceptional Children*, 1976, *42*(6), 315–320. Reprinted by permission.

issue of internal versus external control of behavior. The psychodynamic proponents, with their early roots in the Freudian tradition, view emotional and behavioral problems as being caused by internal conflicts. Low self image, unexpressed anger, "not OK" feelings, and anxiety are just a few of the concepts used to explain the abnormal behavior of maladjusted children. The feeling oriented therapists believe that changes in observable behavior occur when the internal conflicts have been brought to the surface and "worked through." On the other side, the behaviorists believe that behavior is primarily under the control of external events in the life of the individual. Children are seen to repeat behaviors that are followed by enjoyable events and to stop behaviors that are not reinforced by pleasure. Therapy for children with problems consists of carefully retraining the child to exhibit positive behavior by providing pleasurable experiences in small amounts immediately following small changes in observable behavior. One group focuses almost exclusively on forces inside the child while the other group concentrates on the effects of observable events in the child's daily life.

The battles in the war have included debates between the titular protagonists Skinner and Rogers. However, many who have listened to the tape recordings of those debates have expressed disappointment and surprise that they could not identify which scholar belonged to which voice on the tape. It seems the ideas of these two leaders were not as far apart and incompatible as expected. Followers of these men, however, have engaged in skirmishes that were fiery and explosive. For example, debates raged over the relative merits of the terms "emotional disturbance" and "behavior disorders." Each camp claimed their label was the preferred flag to fly over these children's problems. The psychodynamic camp preferred the term "emotional disturbance" since it implied that the emotions of the child needed working through. The behaviorists used the more general label "behavior disorders" which focused on observable behavior and not on internal emotional states. These semantic squabbles have hurt no one and have given the academicians something to talk about. The hurting came when treatment programs for children restricted their interventions to the exclusive techniques of one camp or the other.

The Strategies of Each Side

Programs based on the behaviorist model have included the engineered classroom (Hewett, 1968), structured classroom learning (Haring & Phillips, 1962), desensitization therapy (Wolpe, 1958), precision teaching (Kunzelmann, 1970), contingency contracting (Homme, 1970), and various innovative applications of learning theory to classroom behavior (Whelan & Haring, 1966; Valett, 1966; Ullmann & Krasner, 1965). These programs share the assumption that the events which follow a child's behavior are the most important variables affecting the child's future actions. In the behavioral approach a careful analysis is made of the events which are pleasurable to the individual child, and these events (candy, free time, attention, praise, and special privileges) are provided in small amounts contingent on prescribed changes in the child's behavior. Careful attention is given to providing appropriate stimuli that increase the probability of positive behavior that can then be rewarded. There are numerous reports showing the effectiveness of these programs in achieving significant changes in the behavior of children who were previously disturbing and disruptive.

The psychodynamic or feeling oriented approach to these children has also developed a variety of treatment techniques. Bettelheim's Orthogenic School (1950), play therapy (Axline, 1947), psychodrama (Moreno, 1946), group therapy (Lifton & Smolen, 1966), transactional analysis (Harris, 1967), and milieu therapy (Redl, 1966) share the assumption that children's disturbing behaviors are symbolic of deep seated internal conflicts. Feelings of inadequacy, fear, aggression, rejection, impotence are seen as the motivators pushing the child to act out his frustrations and confusion. Therapy for these children consists of providing an accepting and sometimes permissive environment in which the child can bring to the surface and resolve internal emotional conflicts. The proponents of these therapies believe that disturbing behavior will change to positive and adaptive relationships with others when the child's damaged ego is allowed to express feelings and to gain insight into the dynamics of his problems. A positive self concept is developed through the relationship between the child and therapist, and thereafter, the child is said to become more self directed and socially adaptive. The effectiveness of these therapies has also been reported in the literature with dramatic changes occurring in children's attitudes, values, and behaviors.

Neither Strategy Is Sufficient

It is clear that both approaches have been beneficial to some children. What has not been obvious until recently is the fact that these two approaches can be combined to provide a comprehensive treatment program for disturbed and disordered children. Not only is it possible to combine these two systems, but it also may be necessary in order to accomplish the difficult goals of treatment. The number of complex needs of emotionally disturbed and behavior disordered children involve variables which are the focus of each strategy. 1) These handicapped children do suffer from internal emotional conflicts: They have also been reinforced in strange ways to exhibit deviant behaviors. 2) They lack skills for building deep and trusting interpersonal relationships with others: They have not learned to read and write and add because no one ever broke those skills down into their component parts and rewarded the mastery of each sequential element. 3) They do not know how to distinguish their feelings of anger and frustration nor how to express them without hurting someone else: They have learned to enjoy emotionally charged conflicts with others and sometimes these conflicts serve as positive reinforcers for disruptive and dangerous behaviors. 4) They are deeply moved by the suffering of a small animal but coldly indifferent to the personal agony of a classmate: They are impulsive and do not anticipate the consequences of their actions. 5) They need a time and place to explore the scary world of their internal fears and self doubt: They need external structure to help them maintain control of their behavior. In short, emotionally disturbed and behavior disordered children need both behavior modification and feeling oriented therapy. The professionals who serve them must discover ways of meeting each need even if they must suffer the compromise of long held theoretical positions.

A NEW ORIENTATION: A TRUCE FOR THE CHILDREN

First we need to acknowledge that the behaviors of all children and adults are affected by the rewarding events that occur in their lives. At the same time we must acknowledge that all children and adults have feelings, self concepts, and attitudes that also influence their behavior. Interventions that focus on either observable behaviors or internal feeling states will have an effect on the other. For example, if we develop a powerful reinforcement system to increase the rate of a child's attention to reading tasks, his attitudes toward himself are going to change as his reading skills improve. Likewise, if through a therapeutic relationship a child gains insight into the causes behind his feelings of frustration and anger, his aggressive behavior toward his peers is going to be affected. We know from our experience with these children that behavior influences feelings and that feelings influence behavior. We do not have to decide which comes first.

Interpersonal Relationships and Tokens

Once the interdependent relationship between feelings and behavior has been accepted, we can begin to design programs that blend affectively oriented experiences with systematic external reinforcers. Most behavior disordered and emotionally disturbed children lack adequate internal controls over their own behavior. Therefore, the early stages of treatment may need to include a carefully planned, individualized system of external controls. Positive reinforcers are discovered for each individual as a result of an intensive examination of the child's feelings for activities, material goods, and people. This examination is successful only if the behavior manager establishes a trusting relationship with the child.

The adult child relationship is also important in the selection of the behaviors which are to be reinforced. In Homme's contingency contracting approach (1970), he suggested a series of planning sessions with the child to select the behaviors to be "targeted" during each sequential phase of the reinforcement plan. Disturbed and disordered children frequently set their expectations for their own behaviors at unreasonable heights while more devious youth will attempt to minimize the demands on their behavior. The quality of the interpersonal relationship between the behavior manager and the child is the most important variable in handling either extreme.

The importance of the interpersonal relationship between the behavior manager and the child was dramatically demonstrated in a training program for teaching-parents in foster homes for delinquent youth (Phillips, Phillips, et al., 1973). In the first replication of a home called Achievement Place, the researchers found that although the token economy being used was exactly the same as in the successful model, the result of the second foster home was a "disconcerting failure." A close examination of all the variables showed these behaviorists that the differences between the two homes centered on the quality of the interpersonal interactions between the teaching-parents and the youngsters. They summarized their learning by writing. "Many clinical colleagues have told us all along that the 'relationship' is an essential component of any therapy. We are now convinced they are right. However, we are finding that the 'relationship' can be broken into measurable and teachable behavioral terms" (p. 79).

Another behaviorist, Rosenberg (Gray, 1974), also discovered that the elements of a successful relationship could be taught. Instead of training teachers to develop positive interpersonal relationships, Rosenberg trained modification techniques in building positive relationships with their teachers. Rosenberg believes this creative innovation is "kind of a Rogerian use of behavior modification" (p. 42). It seems Rogers and Skinner are united at last.

Record/keeping and Feelings

All behavior modification approaches contain a careful record-keeping system of the children's behaviors. Graphs and charts abound in classrooms using token economies. This record keeping activity provides an excellent opportunity to allow the children to focus on personal feelings of pride, success, disappointment, or frustration. Small group discussions can be held in which each child is allowed to report his daily accomplishments and to identify the feelings he or she has about that day's successes compared with previous days. Many writers have described these handicapped children as lacking the skills of understanding the cause and effect relationship between behavior, feelings, and consequences. The data from the behavior mod program provides a daily, common experience which all of the children can relate to and understand. As trust and openness increase in the group, the children can learn to give each other feedback regarding the behaviors which resulted in the earning or the failure to earn checkmarks. On different days the teacher can lead discussions on topics such as "What behavior did you see in another person today that you liked?"; "What did you do today that made you feel good?"; or even "What are the positive qualities you see in a particular child?" The Human Development Program by Bessell and Palomares (1967), provides an excellent guide for daily group experiences in the affective domain. These small group discussions build awareness of self and others, social interaction skills, and self concept mastery skills. "Magic circle" activities or "feelings classes" can be combined with or used separately from the discussion of the results of the external checkmark system.

Moving from External to Internal Control

Behavior modifiers have been criticized for building dependence on external reinforcers and decreasing internal control or self discipline. When this occurs, the behaviorists argue that the schedule of reinforcement was not properly "thinned," i.e., the rewards were not gradually decreased in frequency until the success experience alone was reinforcing. Another related problem was uncovered in recent research by Greene and Lepper (1974). They found the pairing of external reinforcers with behaviors that are already under internal control actually decreased the frequency of the behaviors when the reinforcers were removed. These negative side effects are crucial issues in the use of behavioral technology, and psychodynamic interventions can be helpful in avoiding these potential pitfalls.

When children become dependent on external reinforcers, they have feelings about that dependency. It may make them angry at themselves for needing it or at the behavior modifier for exerting control over their lives. When children are offered rewards for behaviors they are already internally motivated to perform, other feelings are generated—perhaps feelings of being demeaned by the system. These feelings are important for the growth of the child's internal controls, and he or she needs help in understanding and expressing those feelings. The life space interview (Redl & Wineman, 1952) is a psychodynamic method of dealing with life events "on the spot" in order to provide ego support or to use the child's life experience for some specific treatment gain. The use of this technique within a token economy system allowed one child to admit, "I don't need these points anymore. I can control myself." This insight along with other communications allowed him to move from the point system to a more informal system of positive reinforcers. We continued to reinforce his progress with praise and adult attention for having outgrown the point system. The daily use of this close, interpersonal communication system allows the behavior manager to alter the reinforcement system in response to growing ego strength and the child's ability to exercise internal control. The growth of a positive self concept, the awareness of new social and academic skills, and the experience of internal reinforcers and good feelings are essential to the transfer of the new behavioral repertoire to a regular classroom where the external reinforcers are less structured and systematic.

Working with Parents

Both behavior modifiers and psychodynamic therapists have shown concern for the role parents play in the remediation of their children's problems. Parents have been trained by the behavior mod people in the use of operant techniques while family therapy is the psychodynamic vehicle for improving intrafamily communication of feelings. Little has been done to combine the power of both approaches. Ronald E. Brown, the principal of Bryant elementary school in Kansas City, Kansas, has used positive reinforcement with parents in an innovative way. Instead of using telephone calls to discuss problem behaviors, Brown calls to praise parents for the child's improved attendance, promptness, or academic achievements (Goodall, 1972). The Learning Center in Anne Arundel County, Maryland, has employed a highly structured contingency system involving parents as significant reinforcers for children's positive behavior (Brown, Cohen & Turner, 1972). Frequent meetings with parents and children are held to modify goals, alter reinforcers, and facilitate communication within the family unit. The N Street School in Richmond, Virginia, is an experimental school within a school directed by Burwell Robinson of Virginia Commonwealth University. This program has blended the behavior mod aspects of the Anne Arundel County school with a peer group approach to develop leadership skills in middle school youth. Daily group meetings in groups of nine students have as their purpose the solving of one's own personal problems through helping and caring for others. The intense caring that has resulted led one group to invite the mother of a truant group member to come to one of their meetings with her daughter in order to work on the student's attendance problem. This program for potential drop outs is a creative example of the attempt to blend the strengths of behavior modification, humanistic caring for others, and work with parents into a cohesive, effective life experience for youth with problems.

MOVING BEYOND THE TRUCE

It is likely that there are other programs across the country integrating the powerful interventions from both theoretical models. In the past these efforts have not been adequately reported in the literature—possibly because of anticipated attacks from both camps where accommodation with the enemy is sometimes viewed as undesirable or impossible. But the time has come to acknowledge honestly that neither behavior modification nor psychodynamic approaches has the answer. They both have a handle on important factors that affect children's lives, and those of us in the business of helping children with behavioral and emotional problems need every handle we can grasp and employ. Step one in moving beyond the "truce" is a greater willingness and courage to share our efforts to blend these traditional antagonists even though we may be subjecting ourselves to the harsh criticism of the purists.

Step two will require continued research to clarify which treatment approaches are most effective in remediating various types of academic, social, and personal disabilities. The diagnostic tests that are currently being used too often provide the practitioners with descriptive statements about the child's problems rather than prescriptions for individualized treatment. More research is needed to establish which diagnostic tests most effectively combine to form an effective battery without overwhelming the child with hours of frustration and failure.

The third step beyond the truce is to modify our training programs for the professionals who serve these children. Universities continue to departmentalize the social workers, psychologists, special educators, and psychiatrists with each group receiving indoctrination in a particular treatment model. No wonder the attempts "out in the field" to unite these professional groups in a working "treatment team" so often result in a battle ground instead of cooperative planning. The training programs for the various specialists must find new ways of sharing their expertise with each other. The students in these programs need training in how to use the insights and techniques of other professional groups.

Finally, this combination of approaches must include more than behavior modification and psychodynamic treatment. The ecological approach to understanding and intervening in disordered behavior must be incorporated in order to avoid focusing solely on the child who is the victim of ineffective family and community interactions. Biogenetic factors are clearly present in certain types of disorders such as autism and childhood schizophrenia, and chemotherapy may be necessary with severe behavior disorders.

More than a reconciliation of two old enemies is our pressing need. Hopefully, when the history of the treatment of maladjusted children is written, the 1970s will be noted as the time when the warring professional factions declared a truce in the "war for the child" and began integrating their knowledge in a new spirit of cooperation and helping.

REFERENCES

Axline, V. *Play therapy.* Boston: Houghton Mifflin, 1947.
Bessell, H. & Palomares, U. *The human development program.* La Mesa CA: Human Development Training Institute, 1967.
Bettelheim, B. *Love is not enough.* Glencoe IL: Free Press, 1950.
Brown, W., Cohen, S., & Turner, P. Behavioral education: An optimistic approach with school ejected students. In J. J. Campbell (Ed.), *Reading: A matter of value.* College Park MD: College of Education, University of Maryland, 1972.
Goodall, K. Shapers at work. *Psychology Today.* 1972, *6*, 53–63.
Gray, F. Little brother is changing you. *Psychology Today,* 1974, *17*, 42–46.
Greene, D. & Lepper, M. Intrinsic motivation: How to turn play into work. *Psychology Today,* 1974, *8*, 49–54.
Haring, N. & Phillips, E. L. *Educating emotionally disturbed children.* New York: McGraw-Hill, 1962.
Harris, T. *I'm ok-you're ok.* New York: Harper & Row, 1967.
Hewett, F. *The emotionally disturbed child in the classroom.* Boston: Allyn & Bacon, 1968.
Homme, I., *How to use contingency contracting in the classroom.* Champaign IL: Research Press Company, 1970.
Kunzelmann, H. (Ed.) *Precision teaching: An initial training sequence.* Seattle WA: Special Child Publications, Inc., 1970.
Lifton, N. & Smolen, E. Group psychotherapy with schizophrenic children. *International Journal of Psychotherapy,* 1966, *16*, 23–41.
Moreno, J. *Psychodrama.* New York: Beacon House, 1946.
Phillips, E. L., Phillips, E. A., Fixsen, D. & Wolf, M. Behavior shaping works for delinquents. *Psychology Today,* 1973, *7*, 75–79.
Redl, F. *When we deal with children.* New York: Free Press, 1966.

Redl, F. & Wineman, D. *Controls from within*. New York: Free Press, 1952.

Skinner, B. F. *Science and human behavior*. New York: Macmillan Company, 1953.

Ullmann, L. & Krasner, L. Case studies in behavior modification. New York: Holt, Rinehart, & Winston, 1965.

Valett, R. E. *The remediation of learning disabilities: A handbook of psychoeducational resource programs*. Belmont CA: Fearon Publishers, 1966.

Whelan, R. & Haring, N. Modification and maintenance of behavior through systematic application of consequences. *Exceptional Children*, 1966, *32*, 281–289.

Wolpe, J. *Psychotherapy by reciprocal inhibition*. Stanford CA: Stanford University Press, 1958.

ENABLING ACTIVITIES

To aid you to meet the objectives listed in the chapter study guide (page 117) the enabling activities listed below were designed to provide a variety of study directions and exploration activities ranging from the difficult and time-consuming to less complicated, straightforward tasks. It is important that you understand that you do not have to do every enabler listed—choose only those that help you achieve a study guide objective or appeal to one of your specific interests in the chapter topic.

1 Review the reports on applied behavior modification by Williams, Koegel, and Egel and Brown, Reschly, and Wasserman and identify all the elements of behavior modification described by Linn.

2 List each element of behavior modification described by Linn and its frequency that you observe during a normal day.

3 Prepare a 20-minute presentation for parents explaining what behavior modification is and how it works.

4 Go to your library and collect five articles whose authors disapprove of behavior modification. Summarize their arguments.

5 Prepare a "position paper" defending behavior modification techniques.

6 Interview five parents, five teachers, and five school administrators for their position regarding the use of behavior modification.

7 Identify and list five alternative strategies to behavior modification.

8 Using the principles of behavior modification, eliminate an existing behavior or develop a new behavior in someone else.

9 Organize and participate in a debate on the question "Resolved: Behavior modification is an unethical practice and should be banned in public schools."

SELF-TEST

True-False

1 If you alter an individual's antecedent event, you will be able to change their behavior.

2 Albert's initial reaction to the loud noise is called a conditioned response.

3 Extinction will occur when the unconditioned stimulus is not intermittently reintroduced with the conditioned stimulus.

4 Reinforcement is the major behavior modifier in operant conditioning.

5 A teacher, to be a successful behavior modifier, must identify specific reinforcers and punishers which will be used.

6 Positive reinforcers must be tangible items in order to be of value.

7 Punishment must be painful to be effective.

8 Behavior should be taught in the same location to keep conditions stable.

9 Criswell suggests that teachers train relatives and peers to reinforce the student's learned responses.

10 Prompting can be used to develop and maintain behavior.

11 It is imperative that a teacher be consistent in her/his emotions, either always cheery or aloof, to be a successful behavior modifier.

12 Behavior modification can be used as a technique to control a student's behavior so that educational objectives can be reached.

Multiple Choice

13 One criterion necessary for behavior modification is:
(a) observable behavior
(b) systematic techniques for analyzing behavior
(c) both of the above
(d) subject and reinforcer

14 According to behaviorists, why do children develop maladaptive behavior?
(a) history of being reinforced for that type of behavior
(b) stimuli in the environment caused disturbed responses
(c) became a learned behavior
(d) all of the above

15 In the respondent conditioning process, a pairing is made between the:
(a) CR and CS
(b) CR and UR
(c) CS and US
(d) CR and US

16 Which of the following is an example of negative reinforcement?
(a) Carole wears her thongs so she won't get burned from the hot sidewalk.
(b) Mother slapped little Bobby's hand when he reached for the pan on the stove.
(c) All of Rosalie's team members thumped her on the back when she made the touchdown.
(d) David doesn't cook dinner anymore because June teased him about the "rocklike" quiche he made.

17 Which is an example of the Premack Principle?
(a) Leila gives Karen a sticker so she'll do her language workbook.
(b) Russell and Penny work together so they can tutor each other.
(c) Maryellen will do her statistics so she can work at the computer.
(d) Miss Sue's class plays their favorite game before settling down to academics.

18 If you wanted a student to continue to respond at a high rate, what kind of schedule of reinforcement would you put him on?
(a) fixed
(b) intermittent
(c) continuous
(d) response-dependent

19 You get paid every two weeks. What kind of schedule in reinforcement are you on?

(a) fixed-ratio

(b) fixed-interval

(c) variable-ratio

(d) variable-interval

20 The best way initially to train your dog to roll over is:

(a) shaping

(b) punishment

(c) modeling

(d) prompting

5

AFFECTIVE EDUCATION

CHAPTER STUDY GUIDE

After reading the selections presented in this chapter and completing the enabling activities, the student should be able to:

1 Differentiate affective education from discipline.
2 Prepare and defend a definition of affective education.
3 Identify and describe five existing affective education programs.
4 Discuss the effectiveness of affective education based on the findings reported in the literature.
5 Justify a pro or con position on the question, "Should affective education be taught in the schools?"

Affective Education

Charlie Hughes

Hidden away in a dusty file or hanging on a wall in the central office is a document. This document exists in every school system but is seldom seen. It is the local system's written philosophy of education. In it are the guiding tenets and values of what is considered a "good" and complete education. In most is a section which mentions the school's responsibility for the social and emotional growth of students. Some go so far as to include self-worth, self-acceptance, self-concept, and the acquisition of socially appropriate values. What is being referred to is affect, and the method for attaining these goals is affective education.

Historically, proponents of affective education have suggested that it should be seen as curriculum and given equal status with other more traditional academic curriculum. As early as the mid-1800s, educators such as John Dewey and Horace Mann wrote that schools should be involved in the affective growth of students. In the late 1950s and throughout the 1960s the terms "humanism," "humanistic," and "humanistic education" became popular and were used to describe a growing emphasis on the affective development of the individual. The proponents of this emerging movement included psychologists such as Abraham Maslow, Carl Rogers, and Erich Fromm. Others took the principles outlined by the early theorists and designed methods and approaches aimed at helping school-aged children (as well as adults) realize full emotional potential. Hiam Ginott, William Glasser, Thomas Gordon, and Sidney Simon and his associates helped entrench affective education in the schools. In 1964 a taxonomy of educational goals relating to the affective domain was published (Krathwohl, Bloom, & Masia, 1964) to classify affective objectives in a precise and organized manner so that inferences could be made about student behaviors. The effect of this publication was to further establish affect as a goal of education.

Gallup polls of attitude toward education (Burton, Hunt, & Wildman, 1980) have indicated that the public feels the schools should be responsible, at least in part, for the moral and affective development of students. Morse, Ardizzone, MacDonald, and Pasick (1980) suggest that affective education is a growing public concern and a critical issue for several reasons. They state that personal and social values are in a crisis, that new values are in conflict with the old, and in many instances socialization does not take place in the home. Clearly, public attitude, humanistic concerns, and rapid social change are intertwined and have given rise to the promotion of affective education in the schools.

AFFECTIVE EDUCATION AND EXCEPTIONAL STUDENTS

If one accepts the premise that a "normal" student needs an affective curriculum to promote self-acceptance, self-concept, development of values, and an awareness of interactive relationships with others, then it should be used with exceptional students. Boersma, Chapman, and Maguire (1979), and Larsen, Parker, and Jorjorian (1973) found that learning disabled students had lower self-concept than regular students. Garner (1974) stated that behaviorally disordered students showed deficits in communication skills, appropriate expression of emotions, self-concept, and trust of self and others. A national institute for developing competencies for teachers of emotionally disturbed students (Wood, 1979) included teacher skills to help develop intra- and interpersonal competencies for this population of students. Gresham (1981) listed several studies which showed that mentally retarded students have difficulty interacting with normal peers and are not readily accepted. Included in Gresham's review is research that indicates the same situation exists for the learning disabled and behaviorally handicapped. Another study (O'Such, Havertape, & Pierce, 1979) showed that children in all three categories of exceptionality (EMR, LD, and BD) scored significantly lower on a self-concept scale than did normal and gifted students.

DEFINITION AND GOALS

Webster's Third New International Dictionary (1976) described "affect" as "feeling, emotion . . . subjective aspect of an emotion considered apart from bodily changes." "Affective" is seen as "relating to, arising from or influencing feelings or emotion . . ."

Ringess is quoted by Burton, Hunt, and Wildman (1980) as defining affective learning as dealing "with the emotional aspects of one's behavior—the influences on our choice of goals, and the means we choose for attaining them . . ." (p. 315). Popham (1975) wrote, "affective learner behaviors are those that reflect one's attitudes, interests and values" (p. 170).

From these definitions it can be assumed that the affective part of affective education refers to a person's underlying emotions, which influence perceptions of self and surroundings. Behaviorism aside, affective education is an attempt to modify the internal perceptions and feelings of an individual in such areas as self-esteem and self-concept in a manner that will, it is hoped, cause changes in social and, in some cases, academic behavior.

Morse et al. (1980) break down the goals of affective education into personal and qualitative dimensions. The former is concerned with assisting the student to develop a positive self-concept combined with high self-esteem. The latter refers to an observable outcome—an individual who can effectively cope with the developmental tasks appropriate to his or her age level. They go on to say that a major goal of affective education for exceptional students is to assist them to assess realistically what they can do as opposed to what they would like to do.

Baskin and Hess (1980) summarized seven affective education programs and grouped the major goals of these approaches into three categories: (1) internal-emotional, which deals with feelings, emotions, and self-esteem; (2) cognitive, which promotes understanding of social causation and the ability to generate verbally alternative ways to behave in various social situations; and (3) overt-behavioral, which focuses on producing observable, positive, interactive behavior. Examples of the more commonly used programs include the following:

1 Human Development Program (Bessell & Palomares, 1970)   Known as "magic circle," this approach takes the form of a discussion group that sits in a circle. The discussion focuses on a selected topic about which each child may share feelings and experiences if he or she chooses. The students' responses are accepted in a nonjudgmental manner during a 10- to 30-minute session. The teacher assumes a leadership role by clarifying thoughts and feelings and using reflective listening techniques. The discussions can occur at one or all of three "levels" which reflect specific goals of the program. These levels are self-awareness, mastery, and social interaction. Self-awareness topics are geared toward helping students understand similarities and differences regarding themselves and others. Mastery topics are intended to aid the students to view themselves as capable individuals through discussion of abilities and their use. Social interaction topics are used to facilitate discussion of how the students affect others during social interaction and how they themselves are affected by others. Materials included in the "magic circle" program are activity texts through grade six, a theory manual, and information regarding implementation. Inservice or training in the Human Development Program is generally recommended for teachers using this approach.

2 Developing Understanding of Self and Others (DUSO)   Developed by Dinkmeyer (1970), DUSO has two levels: DUSO D-1 for students 5 to 8 years and DUSO D-2 aimed at students age 7 to 10. Activities are provided to stress a particular unit such as self-acceptance and include stories with an object lesson, discussion, role play, and the use of puppets to encourage participation. The teacher, as in the "magic circle," acts as a discussion leader and facilitator while also structuring the experience. Some prime objectives of DUSO are helping students develop an "emotional vocabulary" to help them identify and communicate feelings and to aid them in understanding that emotions and behavior are interrelated.

3 Toward Affective Development (TAD)   The goals of TAD (Dupont, Garner, & Brody, 1974) are similar to the two preceding programs, with its emphasis on awareness of feelings and their effects on self and others. Other goals unique to TAD involve openness to experiences and the facilitation of cooperation among peers. The teacher's role is essentially the same as with the other programs, although teacher participation in activities is encouraged. There are numerous lessons, which are broken down into five main sections or unifying themes. TAD is aimed at students in grades 3 through 6 and the commercial package includes a manual and various instructional aids such as discussion pictures, filmstrips, cassettes, and posters.

4 Values Clarification   Differing from other programs in that it is not a commercial package and stresses a different aspect of affect, Values Clarification is nonetheless an affective procedure widely used in schools. Procedures and activities are included in handbooks which the teacher uses with the students. Development of original ideas and lessons by teachers is encouraged. The theory behind this approach is outlined by Raths, Harmin, and Simon (1966) and subsequent teaching strategies are found in publications such as *Values Clarification: A Handbook of Practical Strategies for Teachers and Students* (Simon, Howe, & Kirschenbaum, 1972). The primary goal of Values Clarification is to help students discover and build their own values. Presumably, an effect of following this procedure is the development of positive self-esteem and self-concept. The teacher, as in most affective curricula, maintains the role of nonevaluative facilitator.

It is important to note that all of these programs were developed, and in some cases field tested, for "normal" school-aged children with no affective curriculum designed specifically for exceptional children. Morse, Ardizzone, MacDonald, and Pasick (1980) point out a lack of adopted affective programs to meet the needs of exceptional children. These needs include such areas as physical impairment, developmental lag, and emotional problems. There have been attempts to adapt affective curriculum to special education populations. *Developing Values with Exceptional Children* (Simon & O'Rourke, 1977) attempts to deal with this issue and some mention is given to using the Human Development Program (HDP) with behavior-problem students.

Again, if one accepts the necessity of helping exceptional students develop in the affective realm, there must be some effort to adapt or develop programs. This is not to say that adaptations are not being made. These and other materials are being used, new approaches are developed and to some extent field tested, but this is done on a school district level or in individual classrooms. Information on such techniques must be disseminated on a wider basis.

EFFICACY OF AFFECTIVE EDUCATION

A selected review of published studies using experimental procedures to evaluate the efficacy of affective techniques was conducted. Predictive studies of popular affective programs are summarized in Table 1. Baskin and Hess (1980) and Medway and Smith (1978) reviewed the findings of ten studies using the HDP as the independent variable and eleven studies using the DUSO program. In addition, they reviewed one evaluation of the effects of TAD on affective measures. Both Baskin and Hess (1980) and Medway and Smith (1978) report mixed findings for the HDP on self-concept, self-awareness, and self-image. Their general conclusion is that the stated goals of the HDP and the usefulness of the program in reaching these goals is not strongly supported by the literature. The same situation exists for the DUSO program.

Medway and Smith (1978) reported TAD as being effective in helping 6th grade students generate alternative solutions to hypothetical problem situations. Another author (Hudgins, 1979) found no significant differences between

TABLE 1
EFFICACY OF AFFECTIVE EDUCATION

Author	Population	Independent variable	Dependent variable	Instruments used	Results
Garner, 1974	Students in 3rd & 4th grades, identified as behaviorally disordered. 2:1 ratio, male to female.	Small-group sessions utilizing activities and materials from various affective programs.	Classroom behavior, self-concept, and peer status.	*Fla. Affective Categories Scale *Devereaux Elem. Beh. Rating Scale *Piers-Harris Children's Self-concept Scale	Experimental group showed significant gains in self-concept and behavior rating by teachers.
Lockwood, 1978 (Review of 13 studies)	School-aged students in elementary and secondary regular education programs.	Values Clarification techniques.	Self-concept, self-esteem, values development, and classroom behavior.	*17 different assessment devices.	Summarized results indicate no significant effects on self-concept, self-esteem, or values. Positive effects were indicated on classroom behavior as perceived by teachers.
Medway and Smith, 1978 (Review of 7 studies using the HDP)	Elementary school students in regular education programs.	HDP. Five studies used teachers as facilitators and two used counselors.	Self-concept, self-image, and attitudes toward school.	*Coopersmith Self Esteem Inventory *HDP Developmental Profile	Summarized results indicate little support of HDP's positive effects on affect. Some evidence that affective experiences have some effect on self-concept but HDP was no more effective than others.
Medway and Smith, 1978 (Review of 8 studies using DUSO program)	Elementary school students in regular education programs.	DUSO. Five studies used teachers as facilitators and two used counselors.	Self-concept, self-awareness, self-esteem.	*Coopersmith *Piers-Harris *DUSO Affective Device	For every study showing positive effect of DUSO on affectivity, another shows little difference between experimental and control group.

154

Study	Sample	Program	Dependent Variables	Instruments	Results
Medway and Smith, 1978 (Review of 1 study using TAD program.)	Students in 6th grade regular education classes.	TAD program.	Social problem-solving skills.	Discussion pictures of problem situations.	Experimental group verbally generated more alternatives to the situations.
Hudgins, 1979	4th grade regular education students; 52% male, 46% female.	TAD program.	Social adjustment, self-concept.	*California Test of Personality *Piers-Harris	No significant results were found between the control and experimental group.
Baskin and Hess, 1980 (Review of 3 studies using the HDP)	Elementary school students, 2nd–4th grades, in regular education programs.	HDP	Self-esteem, self-concept.	*"Self-esteem indices" *Sears Self Concept Instrument	Two of the studies reported no significant changes in posttests. One study showed significant changes in gain score scores.
Baskin and Hess, 1980 (Review of 3 studies using DUSO)	Elementary school students, 1st–3rd grades, in regular education programs.	DUSO	Self-esteem, self-reliance, self-concept	*California Test of Personality *DUSO Affectivity Device *Piers-Harris	In one study no change was reported in self-esteem, while in another self-reliance was reported to be increased. Another reported no significant change in posttest scores except for the DUSO Affectivity Device.
Locke and Gerler, 1981	Visually impaired students at a special school, grades K–3.	HDP and DUSO. One group used HDP, one DUSO, and one control group.	Self-image, attitude toward school, classroom behavior.	*Self Appraisal Inventory *School Sentiment Index *Pupil Behavior Rating Scale	Some increase in self-appraisal for the experimental groups, the other two dependent variables had no pretest data.

a control group involved in art projects and an experimental group that was exposed to activities from the TAD program.

Lockwood (1978) summarized thirteen investigations and indicated that there is not strong support for claims that Values Clarification promotes positive self-esteem, self-concept, or the development of values. There were, however, indications of positive effects on perceived classroom behavior.

On the other hand, Garner (1974) and Locke and Gerler (1981), working with handicapped populations, report positive findings indicating growth in affective areas as a result of student exposure to affective programs. Garner used a combination of approaches, HDP included, to examine the effects of small-group experiences on behaviorally disordered students in the 3rd and 4th grades. The variables examined included classroom behavior, self-concept, and peer status. Both self-concept and teacher ratings of behavior were reported as being positively affected by the small-group experience. Locke and Gerler reported that experimental groups of visually impaired students benefited in the area of self-image when exposed to the HDP and DUSO programs.

Based on the literature available, the efficacy of affective education techniques is unclear. It appears that the initial problem in evaluating affective programs, as well as comparing the results of predictive research in this area, is defining the outcome goals. Medway and Smith (1978) noted that while self-concept is the most often used outcome goal in studies of this type, it is defined and evaluated differently in each study. Lockwood's (1978) comment that thirteen studies on the effectiveness of Values Clarification used seventeen different outcome measures illustrates this point clearly. Some critics feel that it is not just a problem of defining or agreeing on outcome measures, but as Divoky (1975) stated, "the field is amorphous, the goals and objectives unmeasurable, and the rhetoric often incomprehensible" (p. 22). While this may be an overly harsh criticism of affective education, the issue of measurability needs to be addressed before one can make sense of the data available. As Baskin and Hess (1980) point out, if you use a different measure, you get different results.

The need for measurability is given special emphasis in the area of exceptional students. Special education teachers must establish measureable goals and objectives for their students, and this difficult task is compounded in the area of affect.

Another problem is who is to implement these programs and what are their qualifications. The question is difficult to assess in many studies, because the qualifications or the extent of training these individuals have is not stated. Hudgins (1979), for example, concluded that the significant variable in studies showing consistent gain was a high degree of training for the facilitators. In addition, personality appears to affect the results of affective procedures. Therefore, the use of different facilitators within and between studies makes it difficult to analyze program effectiveness.

A last, confounding variable is time. Most evaluations used a treatment period of no more than 3 or 4 months. It is doubtful that even the most ardent supporter or harshest critic of affective education would consider this long enough to evaluate techniques dealing with so complex a problem.

OTHER ISSUES

1 Should Affective Education be Taught in the Schools? This issue is emotional in nature. Proponents and opponents take firm stances and on occasion the dialogue becomes fierce. Traditionally, the teaching of ethics, morals, and values has been the responsibility of the church and family. The issue of who should be charged with teaching values has been given increased attention with the resurgence of "fundamentalist" religion. Spokespersons, through the public media, denounce secular attempts to develop personal value systems with students. Proponents of affective curriculum, more specifically individuals involved with the values clarification techniques, state they are not teaching values but rather are providing students opportunities to discover what their values are. This line of reasoning is based on the assumption that many people, students and adults alike, are not aware of the personal value systems which guide much of their behavior. Once a value is understood, a decision can be made as to whether or not it is "working" for the individual.

A similar objection to affective education in the schools is raised by those who feel the home is responsible for forming the child's values and promoting his or her emotional well-being. This often reflects the attitude that it is the family's right to pick and choose what values should be taught and what methods should be used to instill self-esteem and self-concept. This issue, among others, has been a catalyst for parents removing their children from public schools and enrolling them into private schools—both secular and religious.

Privacy is another concern that has been voiced—privacy for both the family and the child. Attributed to affective curriculum is a picture of the child discussing his or her problems and feelings about the family. Misgivings about others knowing their business elicits protests from parents when their child is involved in affective education. Arguments that the child's right to privacy is often violated are usually generated by concern for the child's well-being. It is pointed out that some children may be uncomfortable in exposing their thoughts and feelings in front of others. Most educators who use affective techniques, and the developers of commercial programs, respond to this charge by pointing out that the student does not have to participate or share unwillingly. The question could be asked, however, "Do all teachers follow this 'rule'?" What about subtle nonverbal cues from the teacher such as approving nods for students who participate and none for the abstaining child?

2 Teacher Preparation Another criticism of affective education centers on teachers who are not trained or qualified, but are using affective techniques. As mentioned earlier, Hudgins (1979) pointed out that a key to the effectiveness of affective curriculum may lie in the amount of training of the facilitator. An untrained teacher may produce undesired results. Picture a teacher ridiculing a student for sharing an idea or allowing the rest of the class to "put down" a student for expressing a feeling. Morse et al. (1980) describe an untrained teacher shouting at the students to "shut up" because it was time for the circle. Schwartz (1980) and Delattre (1980) both caution against teachers trying affective techniques without adequate training. Schwartz goes on to say that one reason teachers are often poorly prepared is that the trainers are just as equally unprepared to train. Added to this is the way inservice is provided in many school districts. Inadequate time is provided to obtain the needed skills and there is little or no follow-up built into the training.

Warger (1979) warns against the assumption that any teacher has the qualities necessary to use affective curriculum effectively. She attempts to describe what types of persons are interested and are effective in implementing these programs. She concludes that not all teachers are suited to work with their students on this level.

3   Use of Prepackaged Curriculum   A fear held by some observers of the affective "movement" is that using prepackaged programs serves as a substitute for preparation and skill knowledge. Programs such as the HDP, DUSO and TAD include manuals that contain lessons, objectives, and in some cases the sequence in which these activities should be presented. The concern is that teachers will use these manuals as "cookbooks," to be followed without preplanning for individual or group needs. Further, it is felt that if a teacher does not have facilitative skills such as reflective listening, the use of "I–messages," and ways of communicating respect and empathy, following a lesson plan in a manual will be of little use or even damaging to those taking part. In short, this issue of prepackaging is not a criticism of programs themselves, but reflects a fear that if they are used without prerequisite skills and adequate thought, misuse may occur.

SUMMARY

The issues and concerns discussed in this chapter regarding affective education can be broken into three areas: (1) problems in evaluating program efficacy, (2) the question whether it should be included as a curriculum in public school, and (3) concerns about the conditions surrounding its actual implementation.

The first issue, efficacy, is clouded by problems in research, ranging from lack of clearly defined, measurable outcome goals, the qualifications of those persons implementing the programs, and the lack of information on long-term use of the various approaches. The dearth of reported follow-up to these predictive studies further complicates the situation.

The question of whether or not affective growth and the development of values should be in the schools is not likely to be resolved. Due to the subjective and emotional nature of this issue, it is unlikely that any amount of objective information will produce a compromise. The intuitive appeal of affective techniques combined with the perceived need of many children in this area, will most likely keep the interest of many educators. The personal beliefs and values of individuals holding the opposing opinion will, in all probability, remain the same.

Concerns about implementation centered around teacher preparation, potential abuse of prepackaged materials, and whether all teachers can effectively use affective curriculum. There appears to be some evidence that the amount of training a teacher receives affects the outcome of affective treatment. It would be hoped that adequate preservice and/or inservice would address this problem along with the problem of "cookbook" use of prepackaged materials.

It is a relatively easy task to point out shortcomings, problems, and mistakes. The solutions to these imperfections are not as easy. An obvious recommendation regarding the examination of affective education is that more predictive research be carried out with regular and special education students. Just doing more research may not provide an adequate solution. Long-term studies appear to be necessary to discern effects of the various approaches. Information on the training and experience of the facilitators needs to be included in these reports, and it would be helpful to objectify the stated goals of affective programs. "Humanists" may need to borrow from the "behaviorists" and use observable, measurable behaviors in order to test the efficacy of affective education.

In reviewing the literature on affective education, the issues are addressed in global terms. Thoresen (1969) represents a more focused query by asking "what treatment?", "by whom?", "for whom?", and "with what problem?" Identifying these variables on an individual level may prove to be the most difficult and the most productive task addressing the issues surrounding affective education.

REFERENCES

Baskin, E. J., & Hess, R. D. Does affective education work? A review of seven programs. *Journal of School Psychology*, 1980, *18*, 40–50.

Bessell, H., & Palomares, U. *Methods in Human Development, Theory Manual and Curriculum Activity Guide*. San Diego: Human Development Training Institute, 1980.

Boersma, F. J., Chapman, J. W., & Maguire, T. O. The "students perception of ability scale": An instrument for measuring academic self concept in elementary school children. *Educational and Psychological Measurement*, 1979, *39*, 1035–1041.

Burton, J. K., Hunt, T. C., & Wildman, T. M. Who transmits values? The public schools. *Educational Leadership*, 1980, *37*, 314–318.

Delattre, E. J. Moral education: A response to Burton, Hunt, and Wildman. *Educational Leadership,* 1980, *37*, 319–320.

Dinkmeyer, D. *Developing Understanding of Self and Others*. Circle Pines, MN: American Guidance Service, 1970.

Divoky, D. Affective education—Are we going too far? *Learning*, 1975, *4*, 20–27.

Dupont, H., Gardner, O., & Brody, D. *Toward Affective Development*. Circle Pines, MN: American Guidance Service, 1974.

Garner, H. G. Mental health benefits of small group experiences in the affective domain. *The Journal of School Health*, 1974, *44*, 314–318.

Gresham, F. M. Misguided mainstreaming: The case for social skills training with handicapped children. *Exceptional Children*, 1982, *48*, 422–433.

Hudgins, E. W. Examining the effectiveness of affective education. *Psychology in the Schools*, 1979, *16*, 581–585.

Krathwohl, D. R., Bloom, B. S., & Masia, B. B. *Taxonomy of Educational Objectives. The Classification of Educational Goals Handbook II: Affective Domain.* New York: David McKay Co., Inc., 1964.

Larsen, S. C., Parker, R., & Jorjorian, R. Differences in self concept of normal and learning disabled children. *Perceptual and Motor Skills*, 1973, *37*, 510.

Locke, D. C., & Gerler, E. R. Affective education for visually impaired children. *The Humanist Educator*, 1981, *20*, 11–20.

Lockwood, A. L. The effects of values clarification and moral development curricula on school-aged subjects: A critical review of recent research. *Review of Educational Research*, 1978, *48*, 325–364.

Medway, F. J., & Smith, R. C., Jr. An examination of contemporary elementary school affective education programs. *Psychology in the Schools*, 1978, *15*, 260–269.

Morse, W. C., Ardizzone, J., MacDonald, C., & Pasick, P. *Affective Education for Special Children and Youth: What Research and Experience Say to the Teacher.* Reston, VA, C.E.C., 1980.

O'Such, T. G., Havertape, J. H., & Pierce, K. A. Group differences in self concept among handicapped, normal, and gifted learners. *The Humanist Educator*, 1979, *18*, 15–22.

Popham, W. J. *Educational Evaluation.* Englewood Cliffs, NJ: Prentice-Hall Inc., 1975.

Raths, L. E., Harmin, H., & Simon, S. B. *Values and Teaching.* Indianapolis: Charles E. Merrill, 1966.

Ringess, T. A. *The Affective Domain in Education.* Boston: Little, Brown and Co., 1975.

Schwartz, L. Z. Affective education: Scourge or triumph? *Teacher*, 1980, *97*, 22–24.

Simon, S. B., Howe, L. W., & Kirschenbaum, H. *Values Clarification: A Handbook of Practical Strategies for Teachers and Students.* New York: Hart Publishing Co., 1972.

Simon, S. B., & O'Rourke, R. D. *Developing Values with Exceptional Children.* Englewood Cliffs, NJ: Prentice-Hall Inc., 1977.

Thoresen, C. E. Relevance and research in counseling. *Review of Educational Research*, 1969, *39*, 263–281.

Warger, C. L. What kind of people are interested in using affective methods? *Education*, 1979, *100*, 117–130.

Webster's Third New International Dictionary of the English Language Unabridged. Boston: G. & C. Merriam Co., 1976.

Wood, F. (Ed.) *Teachers for Secondary School Students with Serious Emotional Disturbance Content for Training.* Advanced Institute for Trainers of Teachers for Seriously Emotionally Disturbed Children and Youth, Department of Psychoeducation, University of Minnesota, 1979.

The Place of Affective Education in Special Education

William C. Morse

THESE TIMES

Matters of affect and school mental health are in general suspension these days. When we envisioned higher self-actualization in the decade just passed, we hardly thought we were going to end up with burnout as a major theme. At a time when schools are drawing back from affective education, teachers know, by contrast, that the need is actually increasing.

Fortunately, teaching is still largely a "king of the hill" profession: so much of what really happens in schools remains the province of the individual teacher who conducts the minutes, hours, and days on into years within the confines of the classroom domain. Teachers respond to the reality of children's lives as they spend all those hours together with them. Who knows better than class-room teachers the problems which youngsters face these days?

The fact of the matter is, there is still considerable discretion in the hands of the teacher for the experiences a pupil has in school. The exciting thing about this special issue of TEC is that affective education is too important to leave to the mental health experts. The teachers who have written these articles are testimony to the concern and the methodology required to make affective edu-cation intrinsic to special education curricula.

Has there been a time in recent memory when affective education was more needed in the schools? A society in flux is a high-risk society for growing up. The number of one-parent families, the economic press on so many primary family groups, and a reduction in many community support systems leaves the schools holding the obligation to provide stability and support for more and more youngsters. A recent report indicated that we still hold to our myth of the typical family in America when in truth only 5% of families have mother at home, father working, and two children under 18, while 50% of American fami-lies move every five years. A teacher recently told me: "There are so many with no place to turn for help. I listen a lot." If one has neglected to study the full impact of social change on children, Segal and Yarhaes' book (1979) entitled *A Child's Journey* is an excellent if depressing account.

Even as this is a high-risk culture for growing youngsters in general, growing up "exceptional" in any dimension of special education adds to the risk for achieving emotional integration and social skills. The practices of special edu-cation—even of the behaviorally disordered!—have not always recognized the emotional side of our task. In our concern for making the youngster able to

Morse, William, C. The place of affective education in special education. *Teaching Exceptional Children*, 1982, *14*(6), 209–211. Reprinted by permission.

compete in the mainstream whenever we possibly can, we have concentrated on academic parity.

Our pupils are often behind. There is so much knowledge they should have and so many academic skills they must be taught in order to survive. For those with most severe limitations we feel obligated to maximize the mechanics of self-care and self-maintenance. In many classrooms the time spent on such goals is considered primary and leaves little if any time for a pause from these formal tasks to work for affective goals. As a matter of fact, there are those who would admonish or exhort their pupils "to behave" rather than teach them how to relate positively to each other. Seldom would we admonish a pupil to read in place of teaching the necessary skills; the same should hold true for affective matters.

Thus it is that full-fledged engagement of teachers in affective education is not just another of the school's periodic epiphenomena which have their temporary day in the curriculum. Rather, this engagement is a recognition that the cognitive and affective spheres (an artificial separation, to be sure) are both the responsibility of special education. But it takes courage and skill to maintain the concern for mental health attributes in the current constriction.

THE SCHOOL MENTAL HEALTH LEGACY

Affective education is the inheritance of the school mental health movement. The inheritance was hardly a legacy. In the first place, the school mental health movement never developed a well formulated program which was intrinsic to the ongoing school process. Also, just as with special education, help was considered the responsibility of experts, not the regular classroom teacher. Children with mental health problems were referred to the experts—school social workers, psychologists, or guidance workers. Specialist skills were to be applied, usually on a one-to-one basis. Those who acted out were referred to the principals.

What true affective education represents is "class streaming" emotional support. There are two reasons for this. The first is that traditional expertise in mental health had a low permeation index for the life of the school. It took place on the edge of the basic school curriculum. Even if that expertise were to be applied in a group setting, the group was created as a special association rather than having the group worker come in and work with the classroom teacher, where the problem originated. We know, especially now when they are in short supply, how great a proportion of school youngsters need these specialized services to work on their personal problems whether they originate in home or in school. Specialized mental health services, both individual and group, are an essential part of school mental health. We need more, not less.

In addition to the need for traditional services for extreme cases, we know equally well that all youngsters need to pay organized attention to mental health problems as they grow up. It is increasingly difficult today for children to grow up strong and stable without conscious attention to what is happening to them. Children need to do this as part of their regular school experiences. They can well use life situations in classrooms, as well as cognitive and affective planned experiences, to focus their attention in the affective domain.

Of course, it cannot all be done in the classroom island. One neglected area, as we move from extrinsic to intrinsic mental health programming in schools, is attention to the total school climate. Since the classroom is not an island, what goes on there is linked to school processes which are in turn interfaced with other community systems. If we teach a youngster reasonable social skills while school authorities, peers, or other teachers operate on a more primitive basis, those skills have no place to go once the pupil exits our classroom door.

Most of the articles in this TEC issue deal with classroom applications. The larger school complex must be considered as well, if we are to get a return for our efforts (Berlin, 1975). Just as schools are known for their academic climate, there is also an emotional climate which supports or suppresses. This climate can be assessed by such devices as Moos (1979) scales.

RANDOM VS. PLANNED AFFECTIVE EDUCATION

Confronted with an added "responsibility" for affective education, many teachers are inclined to throw up their hands. Enough already, and now something for which my training never prepared me! Where do we get the time? And how will parents respond? These and many other resistances are real. They deserve a detailed examination which is not possible here but is available in the CEC publication, *Affective Education for Special Children and Youth* (Morse, Ardizzone, Macdonald, & Pasick, 1980).

Yet teachers are also keenly aware of the struggle of special children to put it all together so that they have the confidence and ego strength to deal with their special reality. Many special children have social relationship problems, as well as self-esteem concerns. And who needs the buoyancy of a quota of joyous experience more than these youngsters?

It may be a source of relief for the teacher to remember that we are not proposing more; we are proposing a conversion of the affective effort that is already taking place. We already spend time motivating the uninvolved, resolving peer conflicts, encouraging a reluctant student to join in the group, trying to enliven a depressed child, and recognizing that special kids need to keep a stiff upper lip as they confront their reality. What is proposed in the articles in this issue of TEC is to get on with the perennial business of planned teaching in the affective area. Jersild (1952) said it long ago: The function of the school is to enhance the child's self-concept.

There is one caution in reading these articles. It lies in anticipating instant success. The strategies portrayed may produce an immediate return, but that is not likely. Changes in fundamental affective dispositions are made over time, as new concepts become embedded in the self. New ways have to be practiced, tested, and adopted by the individual child, and there are relapses. Dramatic changes are less likely than gradually emerging new behaviors which must be supported in day-to-day living situations.

Affective education requires consciously directing our affective interventions and not leaving the matter to happenstance or haphazard efforts. Goals are very complicated and intertwined but, for convenience, we can conceptualize them as follows: Through activities such as those reported in these articles we seek to enhance relevant, positive self-concept/self-esteem, to encourage positive socialization, and to help the child find an adequate response to the myriad of affective feelings one has, including those that are sad, anxious, pleasurable, and so on.

These affective experiences are not something that, once accomplished, will remain with us for all time. While it is true that individual successes at any age bode well for the youngster's future accomplishment, the human dilemma gives no surcease. Maintaining one's mental health is an endless and progressive quest throughout life. Those of us who teach have our own personal agendas of unfinished business in affective competency. We can use our own life experiences as one source of empathic feeling for children and adolescents, as we remember what it was like to be a child. We can identify with the struggle toward maturity, since it was and is our own struggle as well. A few of the articles in this issue propose methods of collecting direct first-hand information from our pupils. There is a tendency in the field to forget this advice and impose programs that fit adult perceptions rather than pupil perceptions.

In this selection of articles, the role of the teacher as a person is clearly recognized. "Know thyself" is the advice you will find, as well as "know thy pupils." To extend this a bit further, many of the authors recognize the critical relationship between the teacher and individual pupils, but point out as well that the teacher relationship applies to the class as a group in affective education. When a film mental health series was used recently for classroom affective education, for example, what transpired in a given classroom was more a consequence of the particular teacher-pupil relationship than the materials themselves.

When we get at the core of affective education, we begin to appreciate the fact that helping another human being to feel worthwhile and adequately monitoring affective dispositions is anything but easy. In the process of "helping" we may diminish the sense of self-adequacy because our concern generates sympathy for the child rather than empathy with the youngster in his or her efforts. We may be cultivating what has been termed "learned helplessness" rather than coping capacity. This is, of course, always a special problem in helping children—constantly judging at any given point in time how much they can do for themselves. Several of our authors point out how certain handicaps call forth overprotectiveness in parents and in teachers. Some teachers came into the field as missionaries to the destitute, and certain special children come to school with deft ways of doing less for themselves than they might. Acceptance of limitations has to be balanced with acceptance of one's own potentials.

But the special child has more to grapple with in this regard than would be expected for a normal child.

Given the fact that special education youngsters face additional general risk, are there certain particular configurations of risk for given categories of children? And, are there specific affective methodologies which are therefore to be employed with particular types of children? Or are the individual differences *within* a category greater than *between* categories? In this regard, there seem to be two underlying considerations reflected in the content of these articles. One is age relevance, meaning the use of procedures which are suited to the developmental state of the child rather than chronological age. The second is the use of processes which only require responses available in the children's repertoire, whatever their disability.

CONCLUSION

Affective education provides an excellent example of the difficulty of practicing psychoeducation. Such a blend of psychological conceptualization and classroom practice is hard to achieve. Teachers are pressed to find useful, goal directed activity for a group of children every hour of every school day. Sometimes this includes recess and the noon hour.

School goals are multiple, and sometimes diffuse. On the conceptual side, we would prefer to be specific, approaching a given psychological dimension with a single targeted intervention fitted to a psychological theory. To create a symbiosis of the layers of practice and theory is always a challenge. Since children are so individual in their growing up, each to his or her own pattern, communication with each one and a knowledge of each one is essential but taxing. Certain of the articles address these issues and suggest what teachers can do above and beyond specific methodologies. For example, role taking is described and the reasons for its importance clarified. Then the procedures are described in detail.

When we ask what it was like to be a child, we usually indulge in adult anthropomorphic attributions to children. We have all been children, but we forget and study our psychology texts in a vain effort to rediscover what we were. But some of the authors point out a better way through direct communication with children in the classroom.

The essential challenge in quality affective education is not to expect miracles. If we wish to change self-concept and sometimes even identity factors in a youngster, it will not be enough to depend upon the methods or procedures described in these articles except as illustrations. Several articles provide a nice balance of a procedure described with the psychological conditions that will maximize effectiveness. It is interesting that the injection of interpretation, clarification, and specific management suggestions for the child is found more with young children. Such ad hoc episodes around real life happenings in class are also appropriate for adolescents, though much more difficult to do.

Some of us have experienced an easy time with our own socialization, self-concept evolution, and emotional modulation; to others it has been a struggle. Most of us had the assistance of many persons. A teacher can certainly help but cannot expect to accomplish all the change alone, especially if other life factors are negative for the child. Of course, teachers are in a continuous stream of doing things with youngsters, interacting in a variety of ways. A teacher can apply the test, "While doing these appropriate things, am I demonstrating in my interchanges what the affective lesson is supposed to teach?"

This issue of *TEACHING Exceptional Children* contains a lively series of classroom curricula which have been tested by our teacher peers, and found useful. As critical as these what-to-do-Monday examples are, they are also vehicles for conveying fundamental human relationships. When using an affective methodology, one has to ask, "Am I also modeling the essence of what I hope the children will learn?"

REFERENCES

Berlin, J. N. *Advocacy for child mental health*. New York: Brunner/Mazel, 1975.
Jersild, A. T. *In search of self*. New York: Columbia University, 1952.
Moos, R. *Evaluating educational environments*. San Francisco: Jossey-Bass, 1979.
Morse, W. C., Ardizzone, J., Macdonald, C., & Pasick, P. *Affective education for special children and youth*. Reston VA: The Council for Exceptional Children, 1980.
Segal, J., & Yahraes, H. *A child's journey*. New York: McGraw-Hill, 1979.

Children's Attitudes toward the Magic Circle

Robert W. Day
Robert E. Griffin

The literature of the 1970s in counseling, education, and psychology has given much attention to programs of developmental guidance and psychological education (Aubrey, 1975; Ivey & Alschuler, 1973; Martorella, 1975; McCurdy, Ciucevich, & Walker, 1977; Sprinthall, 1975; Vicary, Swisher, & Campbell, 1977). Initially, the literature was concerned with defining and describing psychological education, establishing the legitimacy of these programs in educational and other human services institutions, and delineating goals, methodology, and resources. Recent emphasis, however, has focused on program implementation and outcome research designed to assess the nature and extent of the impact of developmental guidance and psychological education.

One program that has been widely used and has been the focus of research and evaluation efforts (Gerler & Pepperman, 1976; Halpin, Halpin, & Hartley,

Day, Robert W., and Griffin, Robert E. Children's attitudes toward the magic circle. *Elementary School Guidance and Counseling*, 1980, *15*, 136–146. Reprinted by permission.

1972; Harris, 1976; Hess, Peer, & Porter, 1978) has been the Human Development Program (Ball, 1974a; Bessell & Palomares, 1973), commonly known as Magic Circle or HDP. Magic Circle is a comprehensive, sequential, developmentally based, affective education curriculum designed for use with the general classroom population. Sessions are focused on basic themes of awareness, mastery, and social interaction. Gerler and Pepperman (1976) surveyed the attitudes of 400 rural Pennsylvania students in grades two through six after two years of twice-per-week participation in Magic Circle sessions. In the following study several items were added to the questionnaire used in the Gerler and Pepperman study, and the results of student response to that survey are the focus of this report.

TREATMENT PROGRAM

Sample

Participants of the study ($N = 187$) were students of the second, fourth, and sixth grades of two rural Alabama elementary schools. Each grade at both schools consisted of two self-contained classes; all classes were approximately equal in size and of similar composition. The second grade consisted of 11 white and 17 Black males and 12 white and 16 Black females for a total of 56 students. The fourth grade was composed of 61 students: 14 white and 22 Black males; 11 white and 15 Black females. The sixth grade contained 16 white and 12 Black males, 20 white and 22 Black females for a total of 70.

Group Leaders

Magic Circles were led by the classroom teachers; each participated in an intensive three-day didactic and experiential training program (Bessell & Palomares, 1973; Doverspike, 1970; Fearn, McCabe, & Ball, 1975; Gerler, 1973; Nadler, 1973) immediately preceding the school term and were provided supervision and consultation on a regular schedule from the initiation through the conclusion of the project.

Program

Throughout the entire school year students were involved in daily Magic Circle sessions following the prescribed curriculum for their respective grade levels (Ball, 1974b; Bessell, 1972a, 1972b).

INSTRUMENTATION AND DATA COLLECTION

The attitude questionnaire used by Gerler and Pepperman (1976) was used to assess student attitudes regarding their participation in the Magic Circle. Although the questionnaire was modified by the addition of five items, original items of the survey were unaltered, and the four basic categories of questions—enthusiasm, learning, expression of feeling, and listening—were retained. Questions were presented orally to student participants along with a printed copy of the questionnaire on which responses were marked. The survey was labeled "Questions About the Magic Circle" and was administered by one of the researchers to students of each class in the absence of the group leaders. The survey was administered two weeks before the conclusion of the school year and one week before the conclusion of the project.

RESULTS AND DISCUSSION

Table 1 presents results of student responses to the questionnaire by grade and total sample. The total results of the Magic Circle survey are placed next to the Gerler and Pepperman (1976) survey results of items in which commonality between the surveys appeared.

Enthusiasm for Magic Circles

More than three-fourths of the survey's respondents indicated that they liked being in Magic Circles, but only about 60% indicated a belief that other children liked participation in Magic Circle. More than half the students expressed a desire for further participation in Magic Circle on a daily basis, and more than half said that they hoped to be involved in Magic Circles the following school year. When asked if school was more fun on days when Magic Circle was held, the majority (62.6%) responded in the affirmative, but a substantial number (23.5%) responded negatively and some (13.9%) remained undecided.

Although most researchers (albeit through primarily informal and nonquantitative means) have tended to find a high degree of enthusiasm among children toward the Magic Circle, empirical results of this study revealed less enthusiasm for the program than is typically reported. Lack of enthusiasm was particularly noticeable in response to items in which students were asked about subsequent participation in the program. In addition, the trend of enthusiasm (or lack thereof) seemed to be age- and grade-related, with children in the upper grades endorsing Magic Circle activities to a lesser extent than their younger counterparts. Results indicate consistent enthusiasm on the part of second graders, while sixth graders were consistently unenthusiastic and fourth graders somewhat ambivalent. The origin of these attitudes would seem to merit further examination, as would questions concerning: (a) whether these opinions persist after more lengthy exposure to the program and (b) whether responses would be different at these levels if the program were initiated at earlier or later points in the school careers of these students.

In general, the participants of the present study exhibited less enthusiasm for Magic Circle than did participants of the Gerler and Pepperman (1976) study. But the present research participants had participated in daily sessions of HDP for one year duration, whereas participants in the Gerler and Pepperman research had been involved in activities on a two-day per-week schedule for two years. The extent to which duration and frequency of participation were variables of impact in student attitude is not known but is believed to have been influential. If such is the case, then a serious question is raised as to whether there might be an optimal level of exposure (saturation point) to the program.

Students involved in the Gerler and Pepperman (1976) survey were more affirmative of school being more fun on the days when Magic Circle was conducted than were the students involved in this research. It is difficult to explain the reasons for this difference. One explanation may be that on special activities days, such as assemblies and field trips, HDP did not occur. Such events might be expected to be viewed by elementary students in a more positive manner than the daily school routine that included Magic Circle. Although there is no report of alternative activities for participants in the Gerler and Pepperman research, it may be that days during which Magic Circle was not scheduled were more typical school days composed of the usual school curriculum and events, and that neither days involving nor excluding the program were inherently more or less attractive. Taken together, such situations could have contributed to the relative difference in reaction of the two groups to this item because of different standards of comparison being employed. It may also be that more children of the Gerler and Pepperman study simply viewed Magic Circle as fun because of the sessions themselves or participants involved.

One item was added to this section of the Gerler and Pepperman (1976) questionnaire: Should classes at other schools use Magic Circles? Two-thirds (67.4%) of HDP participants agreed that classes at other schools should be involved in Magic Circles, 13.4% did not believe that children at other schools should participate in Magic Circles, and 19.3% were undecided. Some students seemed to be sufficiently displeased with the Magic Circle program to withhold recommending this program to others. Approximately one third of the students withheld recommending the program to their peers in other schools.

Learning in the Magic Circle

The authors of the Human Development Program suggest that students who are exposed to the program develop a greater degree of understanding and insight into their own feelings and into the feelings of others. The data from this study seem to substantiate this belief but with some interesting side effects. Although 81% of the students felt that they had learned more about themselves and 86% felt that they had learned more about their peers, less than half (40.1%) considered these learnings to be as important (44% responded that Magic Circle was *not* as important) as other school activities, and only 61% saw Magic Circle as helpful in school. Responses regarding personal learning and the importance of that learning were less positive for fourth and sixth graders than for students of the second grade.

Although many factors might account for these reactions by students, per-

TABLE 1
CHILDREN'S ATTITUDES TOWARD THE MAGIC CIRCLE

Question	2nd (n = 56)			4th (n = 61)			6th (n = 70)			2nd (N = 187)			G&P Study (N = 400)		
	Yes	NO	?	YES	No	?	Yes	No	?	Yes	No	?	Yes	No	?
Enthusiasm for Magic Circles															
1. Do you like being in Magic Circles?	82.1	7.1	10.7	80.3	6.6	13.1	72.9	20.0	7.1	78.1	11.8	10.2	83.5	5.3	11.2
2. Do you think other kids like being in Magic Circles?	73.2	7.1	19.6	57.4	4.9	37.7	51.4	12.9	35.7	59.9	8.6	31.6	50.3	5.7	44.0
3. Do you wish you could be in Magic Circles every school day?	73.2	19.6	7.1	47.5	41.0	11.5	40.0	50.0	10.0	52.4	38.0	9.6	72.0	19.3	8.7
4. Do you hope to be in Magic Circles next year?	76.8	7.1	16.1	63.9	14.8	21.3	34.3	47.1	18.6	55.1	26.2	18.7	77.6	8.1	14.3
5. Is school more fun on days you have Magic Circles?	67.9	21.4	10.7	60.7	27.9	11.5	45.7	35.7	18.6	62.6	23.5	13.9	73.0	10.2	16.8
[a]6. Should classes at other schools use Magic Circles?	73.2	14.3	12.5	75.4	6.6	18.0	55.7	18.6	25.7	67.4	13.4	19.3	—	—	—
Learning in Magic Circles															
7. Do you learn things about yourself in Magic Circles?	81.5	10.7	1.8	90.2	4.9	4.9	67.1	27.1	5.7	81.3	15.0	4.3	51.0	25.8	23.2
8. Do you learn things about other kids in Magic Circles?	83.9	8.9	7.1	88.5	4.9	6.6	87.1	8.6	4.3	86.1	8.0	5.9	91.5	2.8	5.7
[a]9. Do you learn things about your teacher in Magic Circles?	82.1	7.1	10.7	90.2	4.9	4.9	84.3	15.7	0.0	85.6	9.6	4.8	—	—	—
[a]10. Do other kids and your teacher learn things about you in Magic Circles?	80.4	7.1	12.5	80.3	8.2	11.5	70.0	17.1	12.9	76.5	11.2	12.3	—	—	—

Question															
11. Are Magic Cirlces as important as the other things you learn in school?	60.7	26.8	12.5	31.1	50.8	18.0	31.4	52.9	15.7	40.1	44.4	15.3	40.0	22.7	37.3
12. Do Magic Circles help you in school?	71.4	12.5	16.1	60.7	21.3	18.0	52.9	31.4	15.7	61.0	22.5	16.6	60.0	15.0	25.0
Expressing Feelings in Magic Circles															
a13. Do you feel comfortable participating in Magic Circles?	75.0	12.5	12.5	68.9	19.7	11.5	58.6	25.7	15.7	69.5	17.1	13.4	—	—	—
14. Do other kids make fun of you when you talk in Magic Circles?	26.8	67.9	5.4	13.1	77.0	9.8	22.9	67.1	10.0	20.9	70.6	8.6	12.5	72.0	15.5
a15. Do other kids feel comfortable participating in Magic Circles?	44.6	23.2	32.1	44.3	6.6	49.2	30.0	18.6	51.4	38.0	16.0	46.0	—	—	—
16. Do you make fun of other kids when they talk in Magic Circles?	17.9	82.1	0.0	13.1	82.0	4.9	28.6	68.6	2.9	20.8	77.0	2.7	6.3	88.2	5.5
17. Are you afraid to say things in Magic Circles?	25.0	73.2	1.8	23.0	68.9	8.2	30.0	58.6	11.4	26.2	66.3	7.5	15.8	73.0	11.2
Listening in Magic Circles															
18. Do you listen when other kids talk in Magic Circles?	89.3	10.7	0.0	88.5	6.6	4.9	84.3	14.3	1.4	87.2	10.7	2.1	87.5	3.8	8.7
19. Do other kids listen to you when you talk in Magic Circles?	71.4	12.5	16.1	68.9	9.8	21.3	45.7	18.6	35.7	61.0	13.9	25.1	43.2	7.3	49.5
20. Does the leader listen to you when you talk in Magic Circles?	82.1	12.5	5.4	86.9	8.2	4.9	78.6	5.7	15.7	82.4	8.6	9.1	94.0	1.0	5.0

Note: Percentage endorses response category.
aQuestions not asked by Gerler and Pepperman.

haps the attitude of teachers toward HDP is an important factor. That is, the HDP is often perceived by teachers as a frill, or, at best, an activity that has comparatively less validity than the academic curriculum. It is conceivable that ambivalent, cautious, lax, or rejecting attitudes of teachers/leaders toward the program are communicated to students in subtle as well as overt ways and that these communications, in turn, have a detrimental effect upon the success of the program in the classroom. It may be that existing cultural restrictions on affectivity are sufficiently powerful to lower the value of affective education in the eyes of students.

With the exception of Item 7, the present findings are almost identical with those of the Gerler and Pepperman (1976) study and provide further support for their contention that affective education programs are often misunderstood, underemphasized, and pursued haphazardly.

Two additional questions, nine and ten, were inserted in this section (see Table 1).

A large number of students seemed to believe that they became better known to their peers and teacher (76.5%) and that they obtained interpersonal knowledge about their teacher (85.6%) through participation in Magic Circle. These results further support the conclusion that special learning occurs during Magic Circle sessions. Although it has not been proposed by program authors or investigated by researchers, it may be that obtaining personal knowledge about the teacher is one of the most attractive and effective features of the Magic Circle.

Expressing Feelings in the Magic Circle

One out of five participants in this study indicated that peers ridiculed him or her during Magic Circle sessions; in turn almost an equal number of participants professed that they made fun of others. More than one-fourth responded that they were afraid to make verbal contributions to Magic Circle discussions. These results may cast some doubt upon the receptivity of all students to Magic Circle participation.

Making fun of others is a violation in spirit, if not in letter, of the rule that put-downs of and negative remarks about fellow members are not to occur. Furthermore, if being made fun of is viewed as psychologically harmful, then required participation in the Human Development Program could have negative results. Two questions naturally arise from such an eventuality: Can psychological education be required of all students if the possibility of detrimental effects is as distinct as these results suggest? Is it probable that all teachers/leaders can become sufficiently competent to provide a cooperative group climate solely by reading HDP literature and participating in brief training programs designed to develop skill in using Magic Circle?

Students in this study were more prone to express reservations about discussing feelings in the Magic Circle than were participants in Gerler and Pepperman's (1976) research. Such a finding seems to support that how the program is conducted (context and conditions) is as important as the content of the program itself in determining the outcome of HDP.

In addition to the three items of the Gerler and Pepperman survey, students were asked if they and their peers were comfortable participating in Magic Circles. Nearly 70% of the participants responded feeling comfortable participating in Magic Circles, but only 38% believed their peers were comfortable during the sessions.

Listening in Magic Circles

Most participants indicated that they (87.2%) and their leader (82.4%) listened during Magic Circles; however, only 61% believed that their peers listened. It seems that one of the primary conditions necessary to the success of the Magic Circle process was questioned by a sizeable number of students; namely, that everyone listens when someone is talking.

In comparison to students surveyed by Gerler and Pepperman (1976), a similar percentage of students in this study were inclined to assert that they attended to others, a slightly smaller percentage believed that their teacher/leader listened, and a substantially larger percentage believed that their peers listened. Differential response of the two groups to the survey instrument suggests that further exploration of student attitude toward Magic Circle would be fruitful.

CONCLUSION

It seems that although the general attitude of most participants toward Magic Circle was positive, there was sufficient general and specific dissatisfaction by students with the Human Development Program to question the appropriateness of the program for all students in all cases. The factors that undergird student attitude might constitute an appropriate focus for further research regarding Magic Circle, particularly multivariate designs involving student attitudes, as well as other variables.

Differential response to the questionnaire by age/grade would certainly be another fruitful area of research. This study found the fourth grade typically to be a pivotal group in regards to attitudes, sometimes responding similarly to second-grade students and at other times expressing opinions in close alignment with students in the sixth grade. Second grade students were generally positive in their attitudes toward Magic Circle, while the overall opinion of sixth graders was characterized as primarily negative. Questions raised earlier about the stability of these attitudes and the interaction of such factors as program design and developmental level of participants would seem to be quite appropriate for further research.

The responsibility of the leader to provide a threat-free environment, encourage listening, and communicate the importance of learning in Magic Circle sessions is further accented by the results presented in this study. That is, the importance of the facilitator/leader role is markedly underscored by the realization that (a) the areas identified by this study as those involving negative student attitudes may be areas of concern in other situations in which Magic Circle is used, and (b) these areas are within the domain of influence and the realm of responsibility of the group leader.

Finally, results of this study in association with the results of the Gerler and Pepperman (1976) research raise an important philosophical issue as to whether all children should be unquestioningly exposed to developmental guidance or psychological education. Such concerns are not intended to imply a challenge to the overall concept of psychological education but rather to suggest that student attitudes, interests, and motivations can play a major role in the success or failure of these activities and, as the developmental point of view suggests, these attitudes must be taken into consideration when implementing programs.

REFERENCES

Aubrey, R. F. Issues and criteria in developing psychological education programs for elementary schools. *Counselor Education and Supervision,* 1975, *14,* 268–276.

Ball, G. (Ed.). *An overview of the human development program.* La Mesa, Calif.: Human Development Training Institute, 1974. (a)

Ball, G. *Human development program level vi activity guide.* La Mesa, Calif.: Human Development Training Institute, 1974. (b)

Bessell, H. *Human development program level ii activity guide.* La Mesa, Calif.: Human Development Training Institute, 1972. (a)

Bessell, H. *Human development level iv activity guide.* La Mesa, Calif.: Human Development Training Institute, 1972. (b)

Bessell, H., & Palomares, U. *Methods in human development: Magic circle theory manual* (Rev. ed.). La Mesa, Calif.: Human Development Training Institute, 1973.

Doverspike, J. E. Counseling with younger children: Four fundamentals. *Elementary School Guidance and Counseling,* 1970, *5,* 53–58.

Fearn, L.; McCabe, R. E.; & Ball, G. *Human development program supplemental idea guide.* La Mesa, Calif.: Human Development Training Institute, 1975.

Gerler, E. R. The magic circle program: How to involve teachers. *Elementary School Guidance and Counseling,* 1973, *8,* 86–91.

Gerler, E. R., Jr., & Pepperman, C. W. Children's reactions to small group psychological education. *Together,* 1976, *1,* 40–47.

Halpin, W. G.: Halpin, G. M.; & Hartley, D. L. The effects of classroom guidance programs on sociometric status of second grade pupils. *Elementary School Guidance and Counseling,* 1972, *6,* 227–232.

Harris, S. R. Rational-emotive education and the human development program: A guidance study. *Elementary School Guidance and Counseling,* 1976, *11,* 113–122.

Hess, R. J.; Peer, G. G.; & Porter, M. A. The human development program and pupil self-concept. *Humanist Educator,* 1978, *7,* 15–22.

Ivey, A. E., & Alschuler, A. S. (Eds.). Psychological education: A prime function of the counselor. *Personnel and Guidance Journal,* 1973, *51,* 586–691.

Martorella, P. H. Selected early childhood affective learning programs: An analysis of theories, structure and consistency. *Young Children,* 1975, *30,* 289–301.

McCurdy, B; Ciucevich, M. T.; & Walker, B. A. Human-relations training with seventh-grade boys identified as behavior problems. *School Counselor,* 1977, *24*, 248–252.

Nadler, D. Affecting the learning climate through magic circles. *Elementary School Guidance and Counseling,* 1973, *8*, 107–111.

Sprinthall, N. A. (Ed.). Special theme issue: Personal development through schooling. *Counselor Education and Supervision,* 1975, *14*, 244–322.

Vicary, J. R.; Swisher, J. C.; & Campbell, R. C. One school's approach to planning for affective education. *Humanist Educator,* 1977, *15*, 193–202.

ENABLING ACTIVITIES

To aid you to meet the objectives listed in the chapter study guide (page 149), the enabling activities listed below were designed to provide a variety of study directions and exploration activities ranging from the difficult and time-consuming to less complicated straightforward tasks. It is important that you understand that you do not have to do every enabler listed—choose only those that help you achieve a study guide objective or appeal to one of your specific interests in the chapter topic.

1 Observe a teacher using affective education techniques.
2 Prepare a 20-minute presentation for parents explaining what affective education is and how it works.
3 Go to your library and collect five articles whose authors disapprove of affective education. Summarize their arguments.
4 Prepare a "position paper" defending affective education techniques.
5 Interview five parents, five teachers, and five school administrators for their position regarding the use of affective education.
6 Identify and list five alternative strategies to affective education.
7 Differentiate the objectives of affective education with those of behavior modification.
8 Prepare and demonstrate one lesson in a series to enhance self-concept.
9 Go to your library and prepare a list of all the books available dealing with affective education.

SELF-TEST

True-False

1 Historically, affective education was recognized by the curriculum but not actively dealt with.
2 Public opinion states that schools should concentrate on academic skills such as the three R's.
3 Affective education is especially important for the positive development of exceptional children's self-concept.
4 Affective education considers the individual emotions and how these interact with behavior to form personality.
5 The qualitative goal of affective education is to assist the individual in enhancing his or her self-concept and self-esteem.

6 To be a successful facilitator of the Magic Circle, no previous experience is necessary except having a warm, caring attitude.

7 The goal of the cognitive approach is to emphasize understanding and intellectualization for behavior.

8 In DUSO, activities to develop an emotional vocabulary include role playing, the use of puppets, and listening to stories with an object lesson.

9 TAD and Values Clarification are similar because both approaches stress peer involvement and verbalization of internal emotions.

10 Affective education was originally designed to handle both normal and exceptional populations.

11 DUSO and TAD were found to improve participants' self-concepts sooner than other programs.

12 Handicapped populations benefited from affective education, especially when using a small-group experience.

13 There is no standard assessment for self-concept.

14 Family responsibility and privacy are two major criticisms for removing affective education from the curriculum.

15 Most teachers with college degrees in education can successfully implement affective programs.

6

SECONDARY PROGRAMS FOR HANDICAPPED STUDENTS

After reading the selections presented in this chapter and completing the enabling activities, the student should be able to:

1 Define eight "learning tasks" of adolescence.
2 Differentiate normal adolescence and deviant behavior.
3 List and describe eight characteristics of adolescent programs for handicapped individuals.
4 List and describe five approaches to developing a secondary program.
5 Discuss the issues related to the education of LD adolescents and other handicapped individuals.
6 List and discuss the program alternatives available for handicapped adolescents.

Secondary Programs for Handicapped Students

William Evans
Susan Evans

Education for the exceptional adolescent is in a period of metamorphosis. Until recently (Kett, 1977) few programs existed for educating handicapped adolescents. Many factors have contributed to the current interest in the creation and extension of secondary programs.

Compulsory attendance laws increased the number of adolescents attending public schools and reflected the belief that education is necessary for future success in an increasingly sophisticated society (Marsh & Price, 1980). Many adolescents with behavior and/or learning problems, however, were simply excluded or eventually dropped out of school. These students constituted an excluded minority, which prompted litigation to secure their right to receive an education. This litigation resulted in laws such as PL 94-142, PL 93-380, and PL 93-112, which provided the legal bedrock for special educational and vocational programs in public school settings (Razeghi & Davis, 1979).

Concurrent with this litigation, the National Advisory Committee for the Handicapped in 1976 noted that the emotionally handicapped in secondary schools were less likely to receive special education services than elementary aged students (McDowell & Brown, 1978). This problem also existed in programs for learning disabled adolescents (Alley & Deshler, 1979; Cullinan & Epstein, 1979; Goodman & Mann, 1976). This resulted in part from a belief that educational interventions are more effective if started when the child is young (Alley & Deshler, 1979). As a result, programs for the handicapped in secondary schools were given a low priority. A third contributing factor was that the handicapped students who had been provided special education in the elementary schools had not yet progressed into secondary schools.

At the beginning of the 1980s a strong interest in the handicapped adolescent was noted among educators (Cullinan & Epstein, 1979; Marsh & Price, 1980). Funded research projects, textbooks, journal articles, conference presentations, and the creation of the Child Service Demonstration Centers are examples of the expanded interest in this area (Wiederholt, 1978).

DEFINITIONS

In comparison to younger children, the behavior of adolescents may be far more complicated. Many problems such as school nonattendance, academic inability, psychopathology, school violence and vandalism, vocational problems, drug abuse, and sex-related problems make education for the adolescent a difficult challenge (Epstein & Cullinan, 1979).

The adolescent period is characterized by new experiences and expectations. Havighurst (1972) suggests that eight tasks are prerequisite to healthy adolescence: *(a)* to achieve more mature relations with male and female peers; *(b)* to achieve a masculine or feminine social role; *(c)* to accept one's own physique and be able to use the body effectively; *(d)* to achieve emotional independence from parents and other adults; *(e)* to prepare for marriage and family life; *(f)* to prepare for an economic career; *(g)* to acquire systems of values, ethics, and other principles needed to guide behavior; and, *(h)* to develop socially responsible behavior.

During the adolescent period, some individuals indicate they cannot meet these expectations. These indicators may fall into two broad categories: socio-emotional characteristics and academic-cognitive characteristics (Goodman, 1979). Socio-emotional problems such as social adjustments, social perception, self-concept difficulties, inadequate motivation, and juvenile delinquency may accompany academic difficulties. Examples of academic-cognitive characteristics that adolescents might exhibit are underachievement, chronicity or a long-standing history of behavior problems, language problems, and reading difficulties.

There are problems in defining the "typical" or "ideal" adolescent and the "deviant" adolescent (Clarizio, 1979). Much of what is ordinarily considered deviant behavior may be experimentation that normally occurs during adolescence. Though there is little agreement on definition and incidence figures (Goodman & Mann, 1976), deviancy among mildly handicapped adolescents may be categorized into four areas: learning disabilities, emotional disturbance, juvenile delinquency, and mild retardation (Clarizio, 1979).

There are varying definitions for the learning disabled adolescent. Many have developmental disabilities (i.e., students who have not learned specific prerequisite skills, Wiederholt & McNutt, 1979). Other frequently mentioned characteristics are hyperactivity and severe, chronic reading disabilities (Clarizio, 1979). It is difficult to describe clearly "the" adolescent learning disabled student. The decision to label a student as learning disabled may be arbitrary and based on the general definition which is more applicable to the elementary-aged student (Goodman & Mann, 1976).

Attempts to categorize emotionally disturbed adolescents are also difficult (McDowell & Brown, 1978). As with learning disabilities, many definitions of emotional disturbance were written with the elementary student in mind. This problem is compounded by the "normal" behavior deviations of adolescence. The behavior of the emotionally disturbed adolescent may be quite resistant to change, although this also varies from condition to condition (Clarizio, 1979). In addition, a distinction may be made between an individual with a mild behavior problem who is in need of assistance through the regular education program and an individual with a moderate problem who is in need of a self-contained special program (McDowell & Brown, 1978).

The category of juvenile delinquency, a label stemming from the legal process, is an age-bound phenomenon (Clarizio, 1979). The incidence of juvenile delinquency peaks at age 17. Prognosis is dependent upon anti-social activity; whether it is individual, gang, or psychopathic.

The last category, mild retardation, is unique in that these individuals are often not considered retarded after leaving school (Clarizio, 1979). To one degree or another, they may become self-supporting after high school.

STATE OF THE ART

Unique problems occur in the education of handicapped secondary school students. As a result, assessment and curriculum must be tailored to reflect the needs of these students.

Characteristics of Secondary Programs

Until 1979 little descriptive data had been collected and reported to document existing secondary programs. Two national surveys have since been reported that provide specific information about these programs. From a survey of 741 high school LD teachers, Schmid, Algozzine, Wells, and Stoller (1980) report the following:

1 A total of 74 percent were female teachers.

2 The most common teacher age ranges were 22–26 years (26.4 percent), 27–31 years (31.5 percent), and 32–36 years (14.6 percent).

3 Of the respondents working with LD adolescents, 73 percent are certified in learning disabilities by their state (66.2 percent had K-12 certification).

4 There was an average of 1½ LD teachers and ½ an aide per school.

5 Most teachers were trained in a college program oriented toward remediation of academic or process deficits and are presently using a teaching style that reflects these orientations.

6 A total of 78 percent of the respondents worked in a resource room and 85 percent were employed full-time in one school.

7 Nearly half of all LD adolescents served were in grades 9 and 10.

8 Of seven role components, ability to remediate academic skills was ranked as most important (see Table 1).

9 Of fifteen areas of teaching activity, remediation of basic skills was ranked first in amount of time spent during the day (see Table 2).

TABLE 1
ROLE COMPONENTS RANKED FROM MOST TO LEAST IMPORTANT

Role component	Mean rank
Remediation of academic skills	2.06
Development of appropriate behavior	3.45
Tutoring to pass academic subject	3.76
Development of career and vocational	4.21
Development of values and personality	4.28
Screening and diagnostic testing	4.32
Consulting with general educators	4.74

TABLE 2
TIME SPENT ON TEACHING ACTIVITIES RANKED FROM MOST TO LEAST TIME SPENT

Activity	Mean rank
Remediation of basic skills	2.11
Direct academic instruction to aid students in passing subject	3.75
Planning	4.44
Modifying inappropriate behavior	5.05
Remediating process skills	5.15
Counseling students	5.21
Development of social skills	5.74
Individualized education plans	6.13
Development of intact personality	6.56
Administration of diagnostic tests	6.64
Nonteaching duties	6.61
Development of appropriate values	6.68
Development of career and vocational goals	7.04
Consulting with general educators	7.22
Staff meetings	8.16

Deshler, Lowrey, and Alley (1979) identify five program options being used to provide service to LD adolescents. These options include the following:

1 The basic skills remediation model provides developmental or remedial instruction for basic academic skill deficits. Reading and math are employed with approaches, objectives, and materials similar to those of the elementary school resource room program. A total of 51 percent of the respondents reported using this model.

2 The functional curriculum model emphasizes preparing students to function in society. Instruction focuses on consumer information, completion of applications and forms, banking and money skills, and self-care. The general school curriculum is considered inappropriate; thus, the LD teacher is responsible for developing and delivering a substitute. This model was used in 17 percent of cases and operated from a "self-contained" setting.

3 The work-study model emphasizes instruction in job- and career-related skills and on-the-job experience. Students spend part of the day at a job site and the remainder in school. This model was used in 5 percent of the cases responding and was generally based in a "self-contained" setting.

4 The tutorial model provides specific instruction in areas in which the student is experiencing failure or difficulty. The teacher's responsibility is to help the student succeed in the mainstream. This model is associated with a resource room setting and used in 24 percent of the cases reported.

5 The learning strategies model is designed to teach students how to learn rather than focus on a specific course content. The model is used primarily with moderate to mild LD students in a resource room setting. Of the respondents, 4 percent reported using this model.

Deshler, Lowrey, and Alley also report that only 11 percent of the secondary LD population fall into the severe category. This finding, if validated, has many implications for program content.

Problems

The assessment of an individual is often difficult due to the volume of reports and records in the student's cumulative file. These reports are often contradictory. They may reflect changes in school or teacher orientation, program direction, and teacher preference. Martin (1979) states that the initial assessment of secondary school students may be a conclusion of past reports rather than an examination of current difficulties.

Factors such as aggressive behavior may lead to either exclusion from school or dropping out and present unique diagnostic problems. While aggressive behavior may be forgiven at the elementary school level, it is rarely tolerated at the high school level. As a result, it is important to obtain an accurate evaluation in order to provide appropriate interventions and avoid unnecessary conflicts with school behavior codes.

Overriding this, of course, is the realization that only a limited amount of school time is available to remediate the student's problems. Interventions become much more complex when only one or two school years remain for the student. Career education and the role of the student as an adult become increasingly important curriculum considerations. Therefore, the secondary curriculum must focus on the unique needs and problems of adolescents.

Alley and Deshler (1979) state that a content curriculum, while appropriate at an elementary level, may not be suitable for secondary handicapped students. Exceptional adolescents do not have the prerequisite skills to compete equally in subject-oriented classes. This presents serious programming difficulties in that the majority of classes at the secondary level are content oriented (Marsh & Price, 1980). The special education teacher can alleviate many of these difficulties by adapting materials and serving as a resource to the regular classroom teacher. These changes and adaptations, however, should serve to facilitate learning, not reinforce the notion of differences between student abilities.

Approaches

Scranton and Downs (1975) note a need for an increased number of special education programs at the secondary level. In addition to this, more appropriate classroom materials and state financial support is necessary if handicapped secondary students are to be fully served.

Curriculum for secondary special education students should present an array of choices. While academics are an integral part of the high school curriculum, social skills and vocational training must be included in the educational programs of all students.

Programs need to be made available that are free of traditional content restraints (Knoblock, 1979). Curriculum, if it is to be relevant, must be an integrated and active entity. Alley and Deshler (1979) point out that far too often the secondary learning disabilities and emotionally handicapped student receives a curriculum that has been developed for the mildly retarded student. As a result, all exceptionalities are grouped under the rubric of "handicapped" with one all-encompassing curriculum that separates these students from their more normal peers.

While a totally integrated curriculum might be desirable, a variety of curriculum models have been presented for educating the handicapped adolescent (Goodman & Mann, 1976). There appears to be agreement among the proponents of these various approaches that academic remediation is a necessary component of secondary programming. Functional literacy should be the minimum goal achieved through identifying specific academic weaknesses and then adapting regular class materials for student use.

A second area of agreement concerns the implementation of vocational programs. Public Law 91-142 and Section 504 of the Rehabilitation Act of 1973 provide a legal impetus for vocational education. As a result, vocational funds are assured for the handicapped as well as eliminating any legal basis for job discrimination. The school curriculum should allow for vocational training as well as a broad diversity of work experiences. Career exploration, vocational assessment, job training, job-seeking skills, and work habits are components which should be included in a vocational curriculum (Brolin & Brolin, 1979). Williamson (1974), however, points out that participation in vocational education programs can be stigmatizing. In the past, failing students have been removed from subject area classes and placed in vocational programs. A program that has a balance of content and vocational training may resolve this problem.

A broader view of vocational and social skill training is offered in a career education curriculum. Career education offers a more extensive concept of vocational training with the emphasis placed on teaching values that allow for the integration of the working individual into the community. Social skills, the use of leisure time, and the value of work are stressed (Brolin & D'Alonzo, 1979; Williamson, 1974). Providing a knowledge of the role that the individual plays as a consumer, producer, and member of society reinforces the teaching of job and academic skills.

There are a number of conclusions that can be stated concerning the education of exceptional adolescents.

1 The role of secondary education is unclear. The curriculum that is offered in many schools may not be suitable for many students (McDowell & Brown, 1978).

2 There are little data about the nature of secondary students or programs. Programs have proliferated, but little empirical data are present that would indicate the efficacy of any one method (Alley & Deshler, 1978; Goodman & Mann, 1976).

3 The problems posed by secondary handicapped students may be highly resistant to remediation. Many problems have been reinforced for years and as a result have become a part of the behavioral repertoire of the student (Deshler, 1978).

4 Most techniques that are currently used with secondary special education students are an adaptation of elementary school methods. Research is needed to develop materials and methods that are pertinent to the unique needs of adolescent handicapped students (Goodman & Mann, 1976; McDowell & Brown, 1978).

5 Secondary schools may mask the problems of the mild and moderately handicapped by offering more flexible programs and more chances for social success through athletics and clubs. As a result, many of the limitations of the handicapped are obscured (Goodman & Mann, 1976; Marsh & Price, 1980).

SUMMARY

There is a need for additional information in the area of secondary education for exceptional students. More commitment to research is needed at this level—particularly in the areas of definition, identification, and incidence (Knoblock, 1979; Scranton & Downs, 1975; Wiederholt, 1978). Goodman (1979) notes that to provide a data base for sound program development, there is a critical need for research concerning high school records, incidence of various handicapping conditions at the secondary level, and further assessment and follow-up after high school.

There is also a lack of research in the area of curriculum development and program implementation (Wiederholt, 1978; Williamson, 1974). Clarizio (1979) observes that there are few organized programs of study intended for deviant adolescents. According to Wiederholt (1978), several issues must be addressed: *(a)* tests and materials need to be developed or reevaluated; *(b)* curriculum components need to be defined and implemented; and *(c)* a range of services needs to be developed.

Because of the various different types of handicaps at the secondary level, the curriculum needs to be flexible and more suitable to the needs of the student in the future. For example, the effectiveness of career education for learning disabled adolescents needs to be examined. Questions to be answered include the age to begin career education, the types of programs to offer, persons responsible for implementation, and suggestions for follow-up after high school (Williamson, 1974). Students of all handicapping conditions should be allowed to investigate human service vocations as well as highly industrialized technological jobs. The possibility of college should also be an option for the mildly handicapped adolescent.

To fully implement programs, it is necessary to recognize all provisions of PL 94-142. In particular, regular educators and special educators should be partners in educating the handicapped adolescent. Goodman (1979) notes that greater coordination is also necessary in the in-depth preparation of Individualized Education Plans because of all the resources and personnel involved in secondary education.

A concern expressed by many researchers is the need for more extensive teacher preparation in secondary special education (McDowell & Brown, 1978; Wiederholt, 1978). Particularly in the area of vocational education, a commitment is needed for inservice training programs (Brolin & Brolin, 1979; Sabatino, 1979). Most professionals in the field of vocational education are not trained adequately to meet the needs of all handicapped adolescents.

Community resources play an important role in the education of the handicapped adolescent. Education of secondary handicapped students can be facilitated in the future if there is an awareness of the appropriate use of community resources and increased cooperation and information sharing among agencies (McDowell & Brown, 1978; Sabatino, 1979).

To meet these needs, a greater commitment to funding secondary special education programs is necessary. In particular, Williamson (1974) expresses a need for more funding for learning disabilities specialists to design and field test different programs.

With mildly handicapped adolescents, it seems that an ideology of special education has failed to evolve (Sabatino, 1979). Much work and additional research is needed in this neglected area. Commitment is needed to provide a data base for sound program development suitable to the needs of all handicapped adolescents. Provisions of PL 94-142 must be recognized and followed. More extensive teacher preparation is necessary at this level. Community resources must be effectively used, and finally, a greater commitment to funding is needed.

In spite of all the issues that must be faced in the future, there are encouraging signs of progress (Epstein & Cullinan, 1979). Professional groups acknowledge concern and organizations have been developed which concentrate on this area of education. Title VI-G has helped fund 50 Child Service Demonstration Centers, 23 of which include adolescents. These changes and trends may signal the beginning of a new era in which research and field experimentation will lead to new methods, materials, and program delivery models for handicapped adolescents.

REFERENCES

Alley, G., & Deshler, D. *Teaching the Learning Disabled Adolescent: Strategies and Methods.* Denver, CO: Love Publishing Company, 1979.

Brolin, J. C., & Brolin, D. E. Vocational education for special students. In D. Cullinan & M. H. Epstein (Eds.), *Special Education for Adolescents. Issues and Perspectives.* Columbus, OH: Charles E. Merrill, 1979.

Brolin, D. E., & D'Alonso, B. J. Critical issues in career education for handicapped students. *Exceptional Children*, 1979, *45*, 246–253.

Clarizio, H. F. Adolescent development and deviance. In D. Cullinan & M. H. Epstein (Eds.), *Special Education for Adolescents. Issues and Perspectives*. Columbus, OH: Charles E. Merrill, 1979.

Cullinan, D., & Epstein, M. H. (Eds.), *Special Education for Adolescents. Issues and Perspectives*. Columbus, OH: Charles E. Merrill, 1979.

Deshler, D. D. Issues related to the education of learning disabled adolescents. *Learning Disability Quarterly*, 1978, *1*, 1–10.

Deshler, D. D., Lowrey, N., & Alley G. R. Programming alternatives for L. D. adolescents: A nationwide survey, *Academic Therapy*, 1979, *14*, 389–395.

Epstein, M. H., & Cullinan, D. Education of handicapped adolescents: an overview. In D. Cullinan & M. H. Epstein (Eds.), *Special Education for Adolescents. Issues and Perspectives*. Columbus, OH: Charles E. Merrill, 1979.

Goodman, L., & Mann, L. *Learning Disabilities in the Secondary School: Issues and Practices*. New York: Grune and Stratton, 1976.

Goodman, L. Programming for academic disabilities. In D. Cullinan & M. H. Epstein (Eds.), *Special Education for Adolescents. Issues and Perspectives*. Columbus, OH: Charles E. Merrill, 1979.

Havighurst, R. J. *Developmental Tasks and Education*. New York: David McKay, 1972.

Kett, J.F. *Rites of passage*. New York: Basic Books, 1977.

Knoblock, P. Educational alternatives for adolescents labeled emotionally disturbed. In D. Cullinan & M. H. Epstein (Eds.), *Special Education for Adolescents. Issues and Perspectives*. Columbus, OH: Charles E. Merrill, 1979.

Marsh, G. E., & Price, B. J. Methods for teaching the mildly handicapped adolescent. St. Louis, MO: C. V. Mosby, 1980.

Martin, R. Legal issues in special education. In D. Cullinan & M. H. Epstein (Eds.), *Special Education for Adolescents. Issues and Perspectives*. Columbus, OH: Charles E. Merrill, 1979.

McDowell, R. L., & Brown, G. B. The emotionally disturbed adolescent: Development of program alternatives in secondary education. *Focus on Exceptional Children*. 1978, *10*, 1–15.

Razeghi, J. A., & Davis, S. Federal mandates for the handicapped: Vocational education opportunity and employment. *Exceptional Children*, 1979, *45*, 353–359.

Sabatino, D. A. Obstacles to educating handicapped adolescents. In D. Cullinan & M. H. Epstein (Eds.), *Special Education for Adolescents. Issues and Perspectives*. Columbus, OH: Charles E. Merrill, 1979.

Schmid, R., Algozzine, B., Wells, D., & Stoller, L. *Final Report: The National Secondary School Survey*. Unpublished manuscript, University of Florida, 1980.

Scranton, T. R., & Downs, M. L. Elementary and secondary learning disabilities programs in the U.S.: A survey. *Journal of Learning Disabilities*, 1975, *8*, 61–66.

Wiederholt, J. L. In L. Mann, L. Goodman, & J. L. Wiederholt (Eds.), *Teaching the Learning Disabled Adolescent*. Boston: Houghton Mifflin, 1978.

Wiederholt, J. L., & McNutt, G. Assessment and instructional planning: A conceptual framework. In D. Cullinan & M. H. Epstein (Eds.), *Special Education for Adolescents. Issues and Perspectives*. Columbus, OH: Charles E. Merrill, 1979.

Williamson, A. P. Career education: Implications for secondary L.D. students. *Academic Therapy*, 1974, *10*, 193–199.11

Issues Related to the Education of Learning Disabled Adolescents

Donald D. Deshler

During the past ten years educational programs for children identified as learning disabled have evolved as major educational options at the elementary level. The rate of growth of such programs has far exceeded similar special education alternatives for other groups of handicapped children. While professionals have been unable to universally agree on the learning and behavioral characteristics of the learning disabled, appropriate and efficient procedures for identification and effective instructional interventions, the public schools have responded to the concerns of parents and teachers by moving ahead and assigning large numbers of children to programs for the learning disabled.

As children identified as learning disabled in the elementary grades have progressed through the programs provided them, it has become apparent that the impact of their learning disabilities has not been substantially altered and that, consequently, they enter secondary schools still hampered by their disability. This observation suggests a) that the nature of learning disabilities, however defined, is highly resistant to remediation; or b) that the interventions employed lack the power required to eliminate the condition or to minimize its consequences. Case studies and anecdotal reportings suggest that learning disabilities obtain at maturity and prevail as a major inhibitor of developing human resources. Operating on the assumption that learning disabilities have historically been a significant contributor to the subpopulation of problem learners, the existence of a subpopulation of adults can also be assumed whose life styles have been substantially altered by the presence of learning disabilities. An examination of data on individuals who are unemployed, underemployed, adjudicated, and dependent confirms the impact of characteristics such as those ascribed to learning disabilities. However, in contrast to the public school programming there has been no comparable investment in the design of interventions or compensatory provisions to enhance the performance of learning disabled adolescents or adults. As adults, these individuals appear to be neither identified nor treated as learning disabled. Their needs have been ignored and the consequences of their disabilities allowed to manifest themselves as social

Deshler, Donald D. Issues relating to the education of learning disabled adolescents. *Learning Disability Quarterly*, 1978, *1*(1), 2–10. Reprinted by permission.

and economic disadvantages. Only recently has society begun to recognize the personal and societal loss resulting from not responding to the needs of this group.

Because learning disabled adults are more likely to be underemployed than unemployed and socially competent than incompetent, their identity is frequently obscured by their membership in larger subpopulations of individuals experiencing similar problems for other reasons. This situation coupled with the relatively short time during which schools have been treating them as a group with special needs has complicated the process of researching the status of learning disabled adults.

It is not only timely, but essential, that a major investment be made in studying the impact of learning disabilities in adolescence and the prevailing conditions which surround its presence as inhibitor of human potential in adulthood. The remainder of this paper will delineate some of the major issues that professionals need to address if the unique needs of learning disabled adolescents and young adults are to be understood and met.

ESTABLISHING AN EPIDEMIOLOGY BASE

The state of the art pertaining to learning disabilities among adolescents and young adults is such that an initiation of programmatic research and development efforts without the benefit of an epidemiology data base on the population would be to risk perpetuating unfounded assumptions. Speaking of the learning disability field, Cruickshank (1977) has charged that "there are absolutely no adequate data of either an epidemiological or demographic nature to provide a base for adequate programming" (p. 61). Larsen (1978) has discussed the problems resulting from an unclear specification of which students should be included in the category of learning disabilities:

> In some instances, school systems, and in fact, entire states seem to view the category of learning disabilities as a convenient avenue by which the vast majority of their underachieving may be provided special assistance. This tendency to label anywhere from 5–10 percent of a given school population as learning disabled (i.e., handicapped) is indeed indicative of gross misconceptions of what actually constitutes learning disabilities and detracts from the provision of service to pupils who exhibit severe problems in achievement and/or language (p. 7).

Larsen's concern is particularly warranted at the secondary level in light of increasing reports of underachievement among secondary pupils due to a lack of motivation, poor teaching, etc. (Martin, 1976). A failure to clearly differentiate between the large number of students who are underachieving for the above reasons and those who have specific learning disabilities will result in the provision of special services to nonhandicapped pupils at the expense of those who are truly learning disabled. Therefore, an issue of primary importance for professionals in learning disabilities is to clearly delineate those learning and behavioral characteristics which define the condition of learning disabilities in adolescents and young adults.

The Study of Learner Characteristics

Investigations of characteristics associated with young learning disabled groups have not established that adolescents share the same attributes. In contrast, considerable anecdotal evidence suggests that learning disabilities are qualitatively different as manifested by the adolescent (Siegal, 1974; Deshler, 1978). The question of how a disability may vary as a function of age is critical. Thus, Mercer, Forgone, and Wolking (1976) have noted that "the emphasis on both early identification and secondary programming might establish age as crucial to a functional definition of L.D." The implication that a single definition may not apply to both elementary and secondary students is a challenging one.

As characteristics are studied in relation to age it is important to keep the following factors in mind. First, since secondary education (grades 7–12) covers at least six years it may be inappropriate, in a general sense, to refer to the characteristics of secondary LD youth. Just as significant differences may exist between a first and a sixth grader, there may be a similar degree of variance between LD adolescents in early junior high school and those in high school or post-high school settings. As LD adolescents progress through various developmental stages during their secondary education or encounter different curricular or environmental demands from junior to senior high school, learning disability characteristics may be manifested in different ways. Second, consideration should be given to predictive factors within younger age groups of LD students and their relationship to LD in adolescents. Strategies for studying LD adolescent characteristics should include (a) an examination of characteristics of adolescents who, prior to junior high school, were identified as LD; (b) an identification of adolescents who currently meet the criteria for specific learning diabilities but have not previously been diagnosed; (c) a specification of the characteristics of LD adolescents who succeed in traditional secondary settings; and (d) a specification of the characteristics of LD adolescents who do not succeed or maintain themselves in the secondary schools.

At present many school programs for LD adolescents define these students primarily in terms of academic deficits manifested in reading, math, and spelling. In light of the demands of a secondary curriculum requiring competency in listening, written expression, oral expression, and thinking (e.g., problem solving), such definitions seem unnecessarily narrow. Even if attention is directed to performance in each of these areas, an analysis of the LD adolescent's characteristics must also consider disorders in basic psychological processes. Goodman and Price's article found elsewhere in this issue addresses this question directly:

Yet without attention to the process component of the definition, we are left with merely an underachievement model. However, underachievement alone is an insufficient substantiation of the diagnosis of learning disability even though it constitutes one criterion for the identification of the learning disabled individual. The identification of process disorders becomes increasingly important at the secondary level as the proportion of 'underachievers' to the total school population increases with the transition from elementary to secondary school.

The difficulties associated with the measurement of process deficits are not to be minimized, but the field should recognize resolution of this problematic area as one of its major challenges.

Finally, few professionals have emphasized areas of strength in LD adolescents. Most students are defined in terms of characteristics that specify their weaknesses. Superior functioning in terms of higher-order cognitive skills, compensatory strategies, or nonacademic talent should be identified as strengths to be enhanced toward achieving maximum human potential for LD adolescents. The study of characteristics should therefore consider integrities as well as deficits within students.

Nonlearner Characteristics

While the condition of learning disabilities has traditionally been defined in terms of learning and behavioral characteristics intrinsic to the individual, it is also important to consider the degree to which contextual factors contribute to a disability experienced by an LD adolescent. Some contexts or settings, such as the larger comprehensive high school, tend to precipitate or accentuate disabilities while others serve to conceal or minimize them. To the extent that such factors impact the LD adolescent they should be analyzed as carefully as characteristics intrinsic to the learner. Thus, Hardin (1978), for example, has acknowledged the need for assessing interactions among conditions surrounding the learner, and the interface between learner characteristics, the task at hand, and other environmental factors.

TRENDS IN SECONDARY EDUCATION

As special educators totally immerse themselves in the design and implementation of programs or research on LD adolescents they often tend to ignore current trends and issues in secondary education as a whole. Since learning diabilities are largely an educational phenomenon and problem (Larsen, 1978), special educators must be keenly aware of events in secondary schools in general and make programming and research decisions within that context. While current trends and issues in general education should not dictate decisions made for the handicapped, an unawareness of these factors could result in decision making that is counterproductive for handicapped youth. The paragraphs below outline some of the issues and trends that special educators should be familiar with. While this listing is by no means exhaustive, it is indicative of the types of factors that can have significant impact on programming and research efforts for LD adolescents.

Structural Changes in Secondary Education

In 1972 the USOE appointed a national panel to study the education of adolescents in the United States (Martin, 1976). The panel was charged with the task of preparing an analytical report describing the current status of secondary education in the U.S. As a result of its work the panel presented a set of observations and recommendations. Several of these recommendations have the potential for influencing education for LD adolescents. They are presented below.

1 That as an institution and as a social concept the American high school remains the keystone of this nation's educational system. However, it requires orderly reform.

2 That the inadequate concept of the comprehensive high school be replaced with the more practical goal of providing comprehensive education through a variety of means including the schools.

3 That educational programs be inaugurated for the joint participation of adolescents and other interested and qualified adults in the community.

4 That small, flexible short-term, part-time schools be established and made available.

5 That compulsory daily attendance be reduced from all-day sessions to an academic day of 2-4 hours.

6 That the basic role of the high school as society's only universal institution for education of the intellect be reemphasized.

Arguing that the confines of one building are no longer sufficient enough to contain all the valuable and necessary experiences for today's youth, a dominant theme of the panel's report is the value of shifting the emphasis away from the comprehensive school to comprehensive education. The panel highlights the importance of more actively involving the family, community, and other nonschool resources in the educational process. Certainly, programming considerations for LD adolescents must extend beyond the traditional school concept. Since a significant number of LD youth may be among those adolescents who are school dropouts, interventions must be designed which are preventative in nature as well as being comprehensive enough to meet the needs of those who are no longer in school settings.

The panel's recommendation regarding community participation in the educational process has direct implications for high school LD programs. Many of these are designed and operated as if they represent the final educational opportunity for LD adolescents. As a result, educational plans for students become "last ditch efforts" and educational objectives are written totally from a survival perspective. By systematically creating linkages between the high school and other educational programs and resources in the community that would be available for the adolescent who is past high school age, programming efforts for LD adolescents can be extended past the traditional four-year high school. Such planning would allow those responsible for providing education to LD adolescents in high school settings to design programs which are a part of a total educational system rather than ones that represent a student's last educational opportunity.

Academic Concerns

According to the results of a recent Gallup poll (Gallup, 1977), many adults feel that the general quality of education throughout the nation has deteriorated. Adults were asked to grade the schools on a continuum of "A" to "F"; only 37% gave the schools an "A" or a "B" rating, compared with 42% in 1976. These concerns may in part be caused by information suggesting a decline in test scores and grade inflation and may account for such trends as "back-to-basics" movements and competency-based testing.

Many states have adopted competency testing requirements as a means of determining if a student should graduate from high school. The merit of such testing is surrounded by much controversy. Proponents feel that the adoption of minimum competency standards offers a means of upgrading academic performance and raising national test performance. Opponents, on the other hand, stress that such exams measure competency in a narrow sense and fail to assess such attributes as good judgment, creativity, or self-confidence. The implications of such testing for LD adolescents are far reaching. Not all of the states which have adopted minimum competency testing have specified differential standards and assessment procedures for handicapped youth. Thus, LD adolescents with minimal reading skills may be unable to demonstrate their competence of content items due to the reading level of the exam. Furthermore, if competency testing of secondary populations reveals a significant number of regular students with deficient skills, the teaching focus of secondary schools may change so that more teachers may emphasize those skills that are tapped in the examination. On the other hand, special services within schools may come under increased pressure to provide assistance to nonhandicapped students who fail the exam.

Concern over declining test scores in addition to feedback from teachers, parents, and employers concerning decreasing literacy among today's students has also given momentum to the "back-to-basics" movement, a loosely defined movement with a diversity of adherents. Some of the most conservative supporters of basic education advocate a very standard, rigid presentation of subject matter (Brodinsky, 1977) which seems to conflict with the current trend, both in regular and special education, toward individualization of instruction. Other advocates, however, view "back-to-basics" as a movement emphasizing basic skills, but not excluding individualization and provision for expanded curricular opportunities. Because of the ambiguous nature of the movement, its effect on learning disabled students is not yet clear; however, forces within the movement may cause a perpetuation of unfounded assumptions pertaining to learning disabled adolescents.

A broad range of other trends and issues in secondary education could be discussed. Among them are alternative education option, educational accountability, educational finance, occupational education, curriculum relevancy, and individualization within the secondary schools. A similar array of issues in society as a whole also have the potential to impact educational programming and decision making on behalf of LD adolescents. Among these are development of mass media, rate of change within society, changes in family structure, employment and labor trends, leisure time, and access to jobs.

In summary, it is imperative that programs and instructional objectives for LD adolescents be designed in light of trends and issues both in schools and society in general. Planning without an awareness of these factors runs the risk of creating programs that will have minimal and short-lived impact on students.

INTERVENTION

A State of the Art

Over the past few years the development of programs for LD students at the secondary level has received a significant amount of attention. Much of this attention has been the direct result of PL 94-142. Thus, this period of program development has largely been one of probing and experimentation. However, a review of programming efforts for LD adolescents (Deshler, Lowrey, & Alley, in press) suggests that some recognizable trends have surfaced regarding available options for service delivery to LD adolescents. Three major programming options are: programs with a remediation emphasis, programs with a compensatory emphasis, and programs built around an alternative curriculum emphasis. A general description of each is given below.

Briefly, a remedial program focuses on instruction of deficits primarily in the areas of reading, spelling, and mathematics and is largely an extension of special education efforts for LD students at the elementary level. Since these students at the secondary level still lack many of the basic skills, programming efforts are directed toward mastery of minimal competencies in the above areas. For the most part, programs which follow a remedial model attempt to keep students mainstreamed as much as possible and thus provide services out of a resource room.

A compensation-based program is designed to give students strategies or procedures for acquiring information through nontraditional modes or methods. For example, students may be taught how to compensate for a reading deficit by relying on taped materials, peer tutors, and visual aids. A major thrust of the intervention efforts of this approach is to modify the instructional variables as much as the student himself/herself. For example, regular class teachers may be asked to modify their lecture techniques to match the learning style of the LD student. As with the remedial program, students are kept in the mainstream as much as possible and, thus, compensatory programs provide services through a resource model.

Finally, an alternative curriculum program is designed to afford LD adolescents exposure to a different curriculum than the one offered by the high school. In many cases the existing curriculum is seen as too difficult, irrelevant, or inappropriate for the LD adolescent. In most cases, the alternative curriculum emphasizes functional, life-adjustment skills that are designed to prepare the LD adolescent for postschool living. This approach is often operated within a self-contained model.

When these major programming trends began to emerge a few years ago, professionals initially viewed them as mutually exclusive and matters of "either-or" decisions. However, as these programming options are observed in operation, professionals are beginning to acknowledge that each approach may have potential value with certain youngsters and under certain conditions. At this point in time, there are no data available to justify the application of any of these approaches nor do existing data allow a comparison between their relative effectiveness. Therefore, the field of secondary LD could benefit greatly from descriptive information from existing service delivery approaches for LD adolescents. Specifically, each of the above approaches needs to be carefully described in terms of the type of youngster it serves (i.e., age, IQ, achievement, learning, and behavioral characteristics, educational history, etc.), major underlying assumptions and rationale, staff support, training, and capabilities. At present, this information is not available on the existing service approaches. Its availability would allow the field to operationally define each approach and to identify others. Also, such data may indicate that the various service approaches are relatively compatible and may, in fact, represent a range or continuum of services for LD adolescents at different ages and with different disabilities.

While the need for research data to guide educational decision making is ever present, the need in secondary LD is particularly great. Research efforts are just beginning on the LD adolescent population (Meyen & Deshler, 1978). In the interim, professionals can do much to shed light on and refine intervention and programming efforts. Specifically, existing programs should regularly be subjected to hard, probing questions by those responsible for the day-to-day operation of these programs as well as by outside professionals. Probing questions should be raised regarding underlying assumptions, time allocation to instructional activities, content of instructional objectives, degree to which the target behaviors generalize and are maintained, etc. The inquiry of existing practices can do much to refine programming efforts and can greatly enhance the interpretation of data gathered through formal research efforts.

Needs and Challenges

The complexity of the task of designing appropriate educational services for LD adolescents should not be minimized. Practitioners must resist the temptation of too quickly embracing an apparent programming solution for LD adolescents. All answers should be viewed as temporary at best and better alternatives should continually be sought. Current attempts at service delivery for LD adolescents stand in need of refinement and modification. In addition, new models must be developed that take into account a linkage between community and school resources both during and after high school. In its early years, the learning disability field had the experience of too quickly embracing apparent solutions only to learn at a later point in time that the solution was limited in its effectiveness. Hopefully, we have learned from those experiences so that our progress in designing interventions for LD adolescents will not be impeded by similar mistakes.

There are several issues and questions related to intervention efforts for LD adolescents. Some of these are briefly discussed below.

First, workable options for delivering special education services at the secondary level need to be developed. Common barriers to effective service delivery include scheduling conflicts which prevent cooperative planning between special and regular educators, and time limitations which prevent providing LD adolescents intensive intervention and at the same time allow them to remain abreast of their core curriculum classes. In order significantly to impact LD adolescents it will be necessary to consider options which alter traditional school practices. For example, creating school days on which some classes are available before or after regular school hours, allowing LD adolescents more than four years to complete high school, utilizing time during the summer months for intensive intervention or for the opportunity to earn credit. In short, it is unreasonable to expect LD adolescents to meet the same graduation requirements within the same four-year time period as nonhandicapped youth while at the same time receiving a significant amount of LD services. Something must be sacrificed. Unfortunately, LD adolescents often compromise in both areas by reducing their experience and exposure in the regular classroom as well as in the time spent in the LD service.

Second, interventions must be designed to promote generalization and maintenance of behaviors. The impact of interventions applied in special education are typically not analyzed from a long-term perspective; rather, their effectiveness is usually measured only during the time the student is in the special services setting. A more meaningful measure of the effectiveness of special educational intervention is to determine the extent to which it will be generalized and maintained across settings, tasks, and time. Interventions designed and implemented with LD adolescents must be examined to determine their effectiveness in this regard.

Third, instructional goals and objectives of intervention programs must be clearly articulated and justified. Instructional emphasis should be given to those areas which are most likely to yield success and to impact LD adolescents. Many programs for LD adolescents, for example, have been designed to include specific components for affective education. While the logic of including such components seems obvious, practitioners must carefully assess (a) their ability to deliver these competencies to LD adolescents, (b) the actual impact of such intervention attempts, and (c) the value of taking time away from instruction focusing on cognitive deficits to intervene in affective areas.

REFERENCES

Brodinsky, B. Back to the basics: The movement and its meaning. *Phi Delta Kappan*, 1977, *58*, 522–527.

Cruickshank, W. M. Myths and realities in learning disabilities. *Journal of Learning Disabilities*, 1977, *10*, 58–65.

Deshler, D. D. Psychoeducational aspects of learning disabled adolescents. In L. Goodman, L. Mann & J. L. Wiederholt (Eds.), *Teaching the learning disabled adolescent*. Boston: Houghton-Mifflin, 1978.

Deshler, D. D., Lowrey, N., & Alley, G. R. Programming alternatives for learning disabled adolescents: A nationwide survey. *Academic Therapy*, in press.

Gallup, G. H. Ninth annual Gallup poll of the public's attitude toward the public schools. *Phi Delta Kappan*, 1977, *59*, 33–48.

Hardin, V. B. Ecological assessment and intervention for learning disabled students. *Learning Disability Quarterly*, 1978, *2*, 15–20.

Larsen, S. Learning disabilities and the professional educator. *Learning Disability Quarterly*, 1978, *1*, 5–12.

Martin, J. H. *The education of adolescents; the final report and recommendations of the national panel on high school and adolescent education*. Washington, D.C.: USOE, 1976.

Mercer, C. D., Forgnone, C., & Wolking, W. D. Definitions of learning disabilities used in the United States. *Journal of Learning Disabilities*, 1976, *9*, 376–386.

Meyen, E. L., & Deshler, D. D. The Kansas Research Institute in Learning Disabilities. *Learning Disability Quarterly*, 1978, *1*, 73–75.

Siegel, E. *The exceptional child grows up*. New York: E. P. Dutton and Co., Inc., 1974.

The Emotionally Disturbed Adolescent: Development of Program Alternatives in Secondary Education

Richard L. McDowell
Gweneth Balcklock Brown

A major dilemma confronting public education today is how to provide an appropriate education for adolescents who exhibit a variety of behavior disorders. The Education for All Handicapped Children Act (Public Law 94-142) has the potential to dramatically change the educational prospects of this previously neglected secondary level group. University personnel, state directors of special education, public school administrators, and teachers have begun to direct attention toward discovering and developing educational procedures that will be effective with disturbed and troubled youth. The time when these youth can be rejected by or expelled from the public schools is passing.

Although the law states that all children must be served by the public schools, the "how to's" of an appropriate education for secondary age handicapped youth are in the beginning stages of development and, in all likelihood, will take many more years to evolve. In the meantime, educators charged with the responsibility of developing and establishing programs for adolescents with behavior disorders need to take stock of where the field has been and what is currently known. Until more relevant research is forthcoming, sharing of information pertaining to successful programming strategies is critical if the full potential of the law is to be realized.

Throughout most of man's history, individuals with physical or behavioral differences were systematically abused, neglected, and excluded from important segments of society. Efforts to provide services for what we now term exceptional or handicapped persons began in Europe approximately 150 years ago. The first real efforts in the United States to educate exceptional persons occurred in the latter half of the nineteenth century with the establishment of residential schools. A majority of these schools, however, did not address the needs of emotionally or behaviorally disordered children.

By the late 1960s and early 1970s, public educational services for select categories and age groups of handicapped children were provided in most local community schools but, unfortunately, children and youth with emotional and behavioral disorders all too frequently were still neglected by the schools. Expulsion was the most commonly used practice in dealing with the emotionally or behaviorally disordered child—especially youth at the secondary school level. As late as 1976, the National Advisory Committee for the Handicapped

McDowell, Richard, and Brown, Gweneth B. The emotionally disturbed adolescent: Development of program alternatives in secondary education. *Focus on Exceptional Children.* 1978, *10* (4), 1–15. Reprinted by permission.

estimated that 81 percent of the nation's emotionally disturbed children were not being served by the nation's public schools. Of those served, most fell in the mild to moderate range, and almost all were of elementary age.

With so few schools providing adequate educational programs for emotionally or behaviorally disordered youth, college and university special educational personnel interested in children with behavior disorders began to focus their attention and energies on the mild to moderately disturbed elementary age child. Nelson and Kauffman (1977) found a paucity of published information on the secondary level student. Similarly, in a review of the Bureau of Education for the Handicapped's personnel preparation programs in emotional disturbance, Brown and Palmer (1977) found that only 10 of the 118 projects, in their request for funds, demonstrated an attempt to provide teachers with the skills and competencies necessary for working with the secondary level student. Even among the 10 projects providing some experiences at the secondary level, most focused on the elementary child and paid only limited attention to the secondary level.

In their review, Brown and Palmer (1977) state that "of all the age groups, the education of the secondary level emotionally disturbed child appears to be the most neglected by special education. Programs focused on the skills and competencies necessary for setting up quality educational programs at the secondary level simply do not exist in most areas of the country" (p. 173). It is no wonder, then, with so little published information available and with so few teachers having received educational experiences related to teaching this population, that school administrators find it difficult to locate and hire teachers with the skills and "know how" to appropriately educate the disordered secondary level student. Until systematic programming and research efforts can be conducted at the secondary level, much of what gets implemented will be adapted from techniques found to be successful with students at the elementary level.

THE POPULATION

Identification and Classification

Every teacher, when given the task of identifying emotional or behavioral disorders in children, can think immediately of some child they taught whom they believed to have been behaviorally disordered. If pressed to elaborate on what caused them to believe that a child was behaviorally disordered, many would identify aggressive behavior, others might indicate the child's inappropriate verbalization, and still others might point to withdrawing behavior. The point is that emotional or behavioral disorders come in many forms. Attempts to classify or categorize emotional or behavioral disorders have been of little value in developing educational programs. Classification has implied that there is a preferred or prescribed method of treatment for specific categories—but, this has not been the case. Those who have worked with disordered children know from experience that each case must be studied individually and that a treatment plan must be designed to meet the child's specific needs without regard to the assigned classification. Classification, however, does allow us to make generalizations with regard to the similarities found in certain groupings, as well as to provide us with a rather standardized method of communication.

Some professionals believe that some type of homogeneous grouping is necessary when designing educational programs; others advocate some type of heterogeneous grouping so that, for example, you don't end up with eight highly aggressive, acting out boys in one classroom. There are pros and cons for each view. Before accepting either position, three questions should be considered:

1 How will such placement affect the child?
2 How will the behavior of the identified child affect the other children in the program?
3 How will the behavior of this child affect the teacher's interactions with all the children in the program?

These three factors are listed in order of priority. The major concern always should be the effect upon the individual child being considered for placement. Placement in a special program should be made with the primary purpose of benefiting the individual child—not simply to provide convenience for the teacher or the school system.

Definitions and Descriptions

Defining the emotionally or behaviorally disordered child is a difficult task that becomes even more difficult and complex when applied to an adolescent population. The problem of definition is compounded by normal deviations in behavior during the period referred to as adolescence. Typical crises, for example, might be the stress that occurs when the adolescent attempts to establish autonomy or when relationships with the opposite sex are redefined. These crises are experienced by everyone. How they are handled determines the comfort or stress the individual feels when confronted with situations that require resolution of the issues involved.

Some individuals handle adolescent crises easily and are able to resolve such issues with limited effort. For these individuals, adolescence is largely an enjoyable experience. For others who have more difficulty in dealing with and finding solutions to their crisis situations, adolescence is a time of stress and pain. The behavior they exhibit in their attempt to resolve issues often exceeds that limits society has established for behavior variability. Depending upon the extent to which the behavior exceeds the limits, the behavior may be excused as being normal adolescent behavior or punished, if it infringes upon adult society. *Any definition of behavior disorders that is to be applied to an adolescent population must approach the fine line separating accepted behavior variance and behavior viewed as being deviant.*

Definitions presently in use by educators were written with the elementary age child in mind. The easiest of these definitions to adapt to the secondary age child is the classical list of characteristics developed by Bower (1960) for use in identifying the emotionally disturbed child. Bower believed that, to be considered emotionally disturbed, a child was to exhibit one or more of the following characteristics, either to a marked extent or over a period of time.

> **1** An inability to learn which cannot be explained by intellectual, sensory, or health factors.
> **2** An inability to build or maintain satisfactory interpersonal relationships with peers and teachers.
> **3** Inappropriate types of behavior or feelings under normal conditions.
> **4** A general, pervasive mood of unhappiness or depression.
> **5** A tendency to develop physical symptoms, pains or fears associated with personal or school problems (pp. 9–10).

Another definition that begins to recognize not only degrees of severity but differences in educational programming was developed by Kauffman (1977). It was written for educators, and apparently with the elementary age child in mind. With a little effort, however, the reader should be able to adjust it for an adolescent population.

> Children with behavior disorders are those who chronically and markedly respond to their environment in socially unacceptable and/or personally unsatisfying ways but who can be taught more socially acceptable and personally gratifying behavior. Children with mild and moderate behavior disorders can be taught effectively with their normal peers (if their teachers receive appropriate consultive help) or in special resource or self-contained classes with reasonable hope of quiet reintegration with their normal peers. Children with severe and profound behavior disorders require intensive and prolonged intervention and must be taught at home or in special classes, special schools, or residential institutions (p. 23).

The commonalities between Bower's definition and Kauffman's, as well as others (Pate, 1963; Hewett, 1968; McDowell, 1975), seem to rest on two major points: (1) the inability to establish appropriate satisfying relationships with others; and (2) demonstration of behavior which either fails to meet or exceeds the expectations of those with whom the individual comes in contact.

Given the earlier statement pertaining to normal adolescent crises, great care must be taken in determining whether the behavior being considered is within a normal development pattern and is progressing toward a satisfying solution, or whether it is a behavior pattern resulting in conflict and stress and is making little or no progress toward more acceptable and rewarding ways of behaving. If, in fact, definitions do establish the parameter for conducting identification, screening, and diagnostic procedures, care must be taken, on an individual basis, to assure that special services are indeed a necessary step in assisting the adolescent's development. Then, if such a program is warranted, the public schools have a responsibility to provide it.

Continuum of Behavior Disorders   Kauffman (1977), in his definition of behaviorally disordered children, suggests a continuum of behavior disorders ranging from mild to profound. He appears to divide this continuum into two major segments—mild-to-moderate and severe-to-profound. Admittedly, to separate mild disorders from moderate disorders and severe disorders from profound disorders is often difficult. For program purposes, however, more of a distinction can be made between mild and moderate. The child or adolescent with a mild disorder can in all likelihood be provided assistance and remain within the regular educational program. Mild disorders tend to be more transient in nature than do the other levels of the continuum.

Moderate disorders tend to last longer and usually require some type of special placement. Length of placement, however, tends to reflect school policy rather than the condition of the child (McDowell, 1969). Schools have a tendency to think in terms of school year with regard to placement. In fact, within a majority of public school programs, the appraisal and review procedure is designed to function within that time framework. It appears to be an accepted belief, and practice, that movement of a child from one program to another is easier on the child and everyone else concerned if that movement takes place at the end of the nine-month term. In reality, of course, behavior disorder is not designed around the school year. With appropriate intervention, and many times without any intervention, the behavior may change or improve in a much shorter time period, such as in the case of an acute situational stress. The child or adolescent may need only to be shown an alternative method or behavior for dealing with the stress even though at the time the stress was introduced, the individual's behavior was disturbed to the extent that special services were required.

The distinction between moderate disorders and severe disorders usually is made on the basis of the amout of contact with reality maintained by the individual. Children or adolescents in the moderate category tend to have problem behaviors but retain relatively intact contact with reality and, with the exception of the specific problem area, are able to function fairly well. (We, of course, recognize that behavior problems can generalize and interfere to a great extent with the individual's ability to function in many aspects of living.) The moderately disordered individual usually will require some type of special intervention program. To date, these individuals have been served through either the resource room or the self-contained classroom.

The severely disordered child or adolescent, because of the exaggerated state of his or her behavior, has required a special self-contained class. A majority of these children have yet to be served by the public schools. Instead, they are found in residential schools, institutions, or at home. A distinction is not made here between the severely disordered and the profoundly disordered in that both require essentially the same type of placement and services. To many professionals in the field, the two terms are used interchangeably, although a case can be made for separating the two groups. Present technology, however, does not make it expedient to do so.

Juvenile Offenders   Another type of behavior disorder overlaps to a certain extent with the above described continuum but, at the same time, is treated as if it were a separate entity. The label given to this problem is *juvenile delinquency* or a *juvenile offender*. Since such labels are attached through a legal process rather than through a diagnostic process, educators have attempted to ignore this problem, for the most part. If the individual so labeled creates problems for the school, he or she usually is passed back to the juvenile justice system to resolve the problem.

In a majority of these cases, the school problem is truancy—a situation many schools choose to ignore. The typical comment pertaining to such a situation is that to do anything other than ignore it would be more trouble than it's worth. Schools are having to face the fact, nevertheless, that state laws dictate the age at which students can terminate their school experience. Also, the juvenile justice system is emphasizing, as part of its conditions for probation or parole, that youth return to school. This gives the school another population of students who, because of their behavior, have been identified as being "different" and, as such, may require special attention and/or special programs.

Children and adolescents from each of the described categories exist and can be found in every school district. Public Law 94-142 has mandated that appropriate educational programs be provided for them. Each state education agency is responsible for developing programs at the local level for these needs.

THE ROLE OF EDUCATION

The role of secondary education in America today is somewhat unclear because of the generalized expectations placed upon it by the community. Secondary education is expected to produce graduates who are capable of entering the world of work or of continuing their education at a higher level, as well as becoming responsible members of society. Limitations as to how this is to be accomplished have been imposed under the guise of economic prudence; and the result of such a stance has been the development of large high schools which appear incapable of keeping track of their students on a daily basis, much less on a period-to-period basis. An agency or system that is unable to determine where its clients are at a given time is not able to enforce effective management procedures or provide effective leadership.

An increase in student population decreases the probability that its members will have a feeling of involvement with the program. If experience has taught us anything, it is that for optimal learning to occur, the student must have a feeling of belonging and involvement. Without these conditions, pride and accomplishment are lacking. Many of the students who are experiencing this lack merely go through the motions of learning. The relevancy of the available curriculum also may contribute to this lack of involvement. A curriculum presented in a format that does not allow for generalization to the students' everyday environment runs the risk of being perceived as not relevant and not worthy of the time or investment of self on the part of students to acquire that particular piece of knowledge. Certain areas within a curriculum do not lend themselves to immediate application to the individual student's environment but, hopefully, a majority of students are able to experience relevancy in most of what they study and to develop self control that allows them to handle nonrelevant material in an appropriate manner.

For a growing percentage of the student population, the traditional curriculum does not appear to be relevant or even appropriate. For years, America's secondary education was geared to produce graduates who were expected to enter college. This emphasis led to development of the college preparatory curriculum to the point that it became almost the only way a student could earn a high school diploma. Educators closed their eyes to alternatives to the college preparatory curriculum. Anything less was looked upon as having little value. This was a time when the high school diploma was viewed as a prerequisite for a successful career. Next, it was the college degree. Today, even the college degree does not guarantee its holder a job, much less any success. Is the next step or basic requirement a graduate degree? Such a proposal would not be realistically possible nor even reasonable.

The obvious alternative to the questions posed here is reassessment of the secondary curriculum to determine alternative routes a student may choose to reach graduation. Because of court rulings pertaining to the tracking of secondary students, it would be necessary to devise a mechanism whereby students would be able to shift from one route to another should they change their mind with regard to the desired outcome. The point of entry into an alternative would have to be established. Core areas common to all alternatives would need to be identified. Desired competencies for each alternative also would need to be identified, along with establishment of criteria for determining attainment of those competencies. This would be a massive undertaking, not only in redesigning the curriculum but in convincing many educators and a large segment of the general population that such an endeavor would be worthwhile and beneficial. The flexibility that such a program could allow, nevertheless, would permit the development of individualized educational planning. Such planning is necessary if we are to provide for the individual needs of students. Only through such flexibility can we approach the concept of an "appropriate education" as proposed in Public Law 94-142.

In the past, special education programs for the emotionally or behaviorally disordered adolescent have been tied to the traditional curriculum. Educators didn't necessarily want to prepare this student for college, but if the student was to earn a high school diploma rather than a certificate of attendance, he or she must do it in the traditional manner. That meant accumulating an established number of units of credit in various academic areas. Some educators operated from the position that these units could be earned only in the regular classroom—which had the effect of excluding the special education student who for any reason was unable to function in the regular classroom, regardless of whether or not he or she could demonstrate the competencies being taught. Other educators interpreted the regulations pertaining to these units of credit to mean that if the student could demonstrate the required competencies of an academic area, whether in the special classroom or in the regular classroom, the student earned the credit toward graduation and the high school diploma. This matter of administrative interpretation is an issue that should be resolved. A resolution supporting the concept of competency demonstration would not cheapen the high school diploma but, rather, could serve to strengthen it for all students. The diploma would represent acquired skills rather than attendance and minimal performance.

Acquiring a high school diploma may not be an appropriate goal for some adolescents with emotional or behavioral disorders. Goals or objectives may need to be varied depending upon the severity of the disorder and the way in which it manifests itself. Students with mild disorders probably would be able to complete the requirements for an academic diploma in the regular program if that were the direction or alternative they chose to pursue. Decisions pertaining to terminal outcomes or goals should be made on a case-by-case basis and should be flexible enough that, should the adolescent's disorder improve or deteriorate, the individual plan could be revised so as to be appropriate.

Alternatives available to the educator for working with the emotionally or behaviorally disordered adolescent should range from (1) a self-help program that might include motor training, language training, social skills, and survival skills, to (2) a vocational program that might include training in survival academics as they apply to vocational areas, social skills, vocational skills, on-the-job training and workstudy activities, to (3) an academic program. Program alternatives should not operate in isolation from each other but should serve to support each other, each an integral part of the total education program.

PROGRAM DEVELOPMENT

Successful implementation of any new program is contingent upon the thoroughness with which its designers develop the total plan for operation. Such planning should begin with establishment of a number of statements or principles that reflect the population to be served, the purpose of the program, and the philosophical base upon which the program is to be built. A secondary public school program for emotionally or behaviorally disordered adolescents has the purpose of assisting students in their academic and social growth in a way that will allow them to function successfully within their environment. This statement encompasses the belief that every child or adolescent, regardless of the severity of any disorder, is capable of learning something; and that, through learning, positive change can occur within the individual. Also included in this statement is the belief that each student should have the opportunity to develop his or her potentials to the best ability.

Given appropriate curriculum alternatives, the development of an individual educational plan provides the student the best chance to accomplish this. Here, the educational environment is seen as supportive to the adolescent. Success on assigned tasks assists in developing a positive self-concept. Disordered behavior is viewed as the result of faulty learning experiences. The educational environment is structured so as to support the introduction of order and consistency into the student's daily life. Through the use of order and consistency, the student learns what to expect from the environment and to develop self-control. The ability to appropriately exercise self-control is a major goal of this program.

Program planners should recognize the importance of administrative support in the operation of any project. Administrative support for a program should be obtained prior to introducing the program within the system. Too many special educators have learned the hard way that special classes cannot be operated in the manner in which they were designed if the administrator of the facility in which they are located is not supportive of the program. Further, such a program can be damaged even if the administrator does not take a position with regard to it; simply by allowing it to exist with no active involvement either way is perceived by many as lack of support. The administrator does set the model which a majority of employees will follow. An informed administrator is usually a supportive administrator—this should be taken as a cue to involve the selected building administrator in early stages of planning. If the administrator is unable to take an active role in the planning process, he or she should be kept informed of its progress, preferably through direct communication. If this is not possible, his or her appointed representative should be included, with periodic direct contacts to help determine if the administrator is receiving the correct information.

At the appropriate time, the entire building staff should be included in the planning process. The more staff members know about a program and what it is trying to accomplish, the greater the likelihood that they will become actively involved in it. Carefully planned inservice meetings pertaining to the special program can facilitate establishment of cooperative arrangements between regular programs and the special program. Once a special program has been implemented, some type of continuing dialogue should be established with the regular program. One method of doing this is through formation of an advisory committee to the program. One of the functions of the program advisory committee should be to involve the community and maintain contact. In many instances, state and community resources can be called upon to provide some program funding, as well as to provide outside expertise pertaining to various aspects of the program.

Environmental Arrangement

The educational environment is designed to provide support to the students as they work with assigned tasks. The amount of structure is determined, for the most part, by the severity of the student's disorder. One way of conceptualizing this is to consider the student and his or her relationship to these three dimensions (see Figure 1).

The first dimension is the extent of *environmental structure* required to

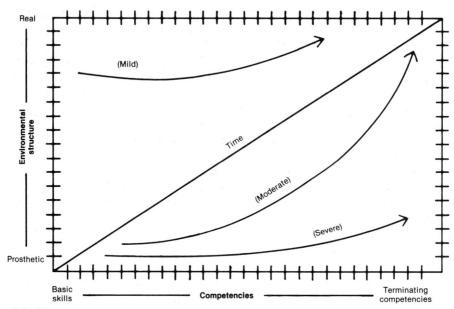

FIGURE 1
The relationship between environmental structure and acquisition of competencies across time.

provide the optimum learning environment. For moderately and severely disordered students, this represents a high degree of structure. The educational environment may be regarded as a prosthetic environment in that it contains controls not usually found in the classroom. As the student gains in self-control, the prosthetic environment is gradually faded so that the classroom structure approximates that found in the regular classroom.

The second dimension pertains to acquisition of desired *competencies*. Basic skills in a given area may need to be taught before entering other areas. As the student progresses, he or she moves closer and closer to the terminating competencies established.

The third dimension is *time*. As the student moves from the prosthetic environment and gains in the successful acquisition of competencies, time in the program becomes a factor. Time represents the interval necessary for the student to acquire the ability to function within the real environment, and at the same time move toward the acquisition of terminating competencies. These two processes are not separated for treatment purposes. They work in harmony, but not necessarily at the same rate.

The lines in Figure 1 marked "mild," "moderate," and "severe" are approximations of how each of those categories might be represented as the student progresses across the three dimensions. These dimensions serve as the underlying organization of educational environment.

At least four environmental arrangements are appropriate for use in secondary level programs within the school. Selection of program for placement purposes usually is determined by severity of the disorder.

1 *Regular Class Placement*   This option is used when the disorder is considered to be mild and when the regular class teacher is provided supportive assistance in working with the child's problem. Multiple teachers at the secondary level can create some problems with this approach. The strong point in favor of this option is that the student remains with his or her peers.

2 *Resource Room Model*   In this option the student goes to the resource room or teacher for limited periods each day. The rest of the school day is spent in regular classes. This approach is recommended primarily for students with mild behavior disorders and has the advantage, like the first option, of integrating the student with peers.

3 *Special Class Placement*   This option is usually a self-contained classroom where the student may remain with one teacher for most, if not all, of the school day. An advantage with this type of arrangement is that it allows the teacher to control the amount of structure necessary for each student. This is the traditional type of program that has been used extensively in the past. It has been used primarily with students who are in the moderate to severe categories. Students in this program are integrated into the regular program whenever such a move is deemed feasible and desirable; unfortunately, though, such integration has met with only limited support from regular class teachers. A major limitation to this type of arrangement at the secondary level is that it inhibits certain types of movement on the part of the students. Movement from one classroom to another between periods is the normal state of affairs in secondary programs, and lack of this type of movement many times is seen by the special student as something that makes him or her different from the rest of the student body. If possible, some form of comparable movement should be built into the special student's daily schedule.

4 *Special Program*   This option is being used to only a limited extent at the present time. Nevertheless, it is a model that appears to be most appropriate for use at the secondary level. The program consists of multiple classes organized into an integrated unit to provide students with as near a normal type of program as possible. It is located within the regular school facility, allowing close proximity to regular classes, which facilitates integration of special students whenever possible. The special student may spend a majority of the day within the special program. Since the program consists of multiple classes, the student may change classes each period, allowing movement similar to that of the regular program. When used in the public school setting, this type of arrangement seems to best serve the moderate to mildly disordered student. It also works quite well with the adjudicated student. It does not segregate him or her from the student body or mark the student as different in the same way the self-contained class does, yet it provides an educational environment that offers an opportunity to be successful with learning.

Selection of a particular environmental arrangement for use in a secondary program may be determined by factors including the availability of space, program funds, and trained staff. A comprehensive approach to working with the emotionally or behaviorally disordered student at the secondary level would include all four options described. Such a continuum would provide services for all levels of severity.

Behavior Management

Behavior management is just as important at the secondary level as at any other level. The teacher's ability to manage the behavior of students determines the smoothness of flow through the daily schedule. The secondary teacher is in a somewhat different position than his or her elementary counterpart. The secondary teacher is not as naturally reinforcing, and teacher praise may work just the opposite from what is expected.

Peer reinforcement has a larger role among adolescents. Educators need to learn or develop effective ways of using the peer group to reinforce desired behaviors in students. One effective technique of behavior management with secondary students uses the Premack Principle in the form of contingency contracting (Homme, Csanyi, Gonzales, & Rechs, 1969). This procedure allows for student participation in selecting reinforcers and establishing procedures or criteria to be met before receiving reinforcement. Essentially, it is represented by a written agreement between student and teacher that spells out what the student is expected to do, what the teacher is expected to do, and the consequences for meeting the agreed upon expectations.

Long and Newman (1976), in their article on managing surface behavior, described several techniques that can be used to influence ongoing classroom behavior. These range from "planned ignoring" to physical restraint. Most of these techniques would be appropriate for use at the secondary level. Caution should be used with regard to physical restraint; most of us have found this technique to be an unsatisfactory alternative with secondary students. Most adolescents have sufficient language skills to allow the teacher to use words as a means of defusing conflict situations that have the potential of developing into physical aggression. A teacher should learn to talk with students and watch for clues of student frustration that might result in a conflict situation. One of the best skills a teacher can develop in regard to behavior management is the ability to plan ahead for behaviors that might occur and the resulting consequences for the individual student.

Sound behavior management is based on four major components:

1 Planning.
2 Arranging the classroom to be conducive to the desired activities.
3 Selecting appropriate educational tasks.
4 Selecting appropriate consequences to behavior.

If these four components are taken into consideration and the teacher remembers to place the major emphasis on positive behavior, a solid foundation will be established from which to manage the student's behavior in the classroom.

Curriculum

The curriculum serving the secondary level emotionally or behaviorally disordered student should be multifaceted to encompass needs identified at various degrees of severity. For a number of these students, adaptation of the traditional curriculum is sufficient. For others, the traditional curriculum has been inefficient in assisting them to gain basic skills. Remedial teaching based on a watered down version of this curriculum also has shown itself to be an ineffective technique. The time for traditional remediation has passed. Curriculum at the secondary level needs to be made relevant to the student. A curriculum should be allowed to evolve from functional life skills and organized in a manner that allows the student to utilize his or her life experiences. The curriculum must be relevant to the student's everyday needs. Basic concepts should be taught through the use of such topics as money management, job applications, bus schedules, obtaining a driver's license, home management, etc.

A teacher must be realistic in assessing the student's assets and deficits and understand that some of these students have been in special classes most of their school career. They probably have been exposed to many of the typical remedial techniques such as math programs that use the standard gimmicks of blocks, rods, chips, or money to teach number concepts. At this point, it may be more important that the student be taught to use a pocket calculator to carry out mathematical functions correctly. The teacher maybe should be more concerned with survival reading than with pleasure reading. A quick assessment should let the teacher know if the student can best use a phonetic approach to reading or a sight-say method. The format of any material used with adolescents should be geared to their age level. Reading and language skills might be approached by using newspapers, magazines, or high interest material like a driver's instructional manual.

Secondary curricula breaks out functionally into five general training areas: (1) Social Curriculum; (2) Academic Curriculum; (3) Vocational Curriculum; (4) Vocational Training; and (5) Workstudy Experiences. The social curriculum's purpose is to assist the student in developing the skills necessary for successful and appropriate interaction with others. A major component of this area is helping the student learn self-control. Many approaches are available to help the student achieve this, two of which will be mentioned here. The first is a program that should be on the market by early 1979. Goldstein (1974) has developed a social learning curriculum for use at the elementary level; the kit contains many helpful ideas and activities sequenced for the user. The secondary version, soon to be available, will provide the secondary teacher with an organized program for approaching the area of self-control. The second technique is the "Class Meeting," as described by Glasser (1969). The Class Meeting gives students an opportunity to learn problem solving skills through group interaction.

The academic curriculum may involve both the regular school curriculum and the special class curriculum. Students who are capable of handling the regular program should be encouraged to do so, and supported in their efforts. Students who are unable to function successfully with the regular curriculum should receive an individual educational plan, devised to incorporate methods and techniques of special education to present academic areas in which the student is capable of being successful.

The vocational curriculum includes pre-vocational training as well as assessment of vocational aptitudes. Its purpose is to provide the student with the basic skills necessary to function successfully in a vocational training program. The vocational curriculum must be modernized to reflect the changes in the job market if it is to provide a meaningful experience for the student. The vocational training area is concerned with developing competencies in a particular job area.

The workstudy area is a continuation of vocational training, with the student receiving on-the-job experience and, in most cases, receiving a salary for this work. While participating in the workstudy program, the student may return to the school for a portion of the day to complete additional training or to earn additional credits toward graduation.

Each of the five areas described above interacts with the others. They are mutually supportive as the student moves toward independence.

Parent Involvement

Parent participation in programs for the secondary level emotionally or behaviorally disordered student is a positive addition to the program. Too many parents of adolescent students have given up on trying to effect positive change in their child's behavior. They have tried every technique they know and some that others have suggested, with the hope of getting their child to behave in a manner acceptable to them. If these efforts have failed, by the time the child reaches high school they probably are ready to throw up their hands, and usually make some comment like, "He's yours now! I've tried everything I know and it hasn't helped a bit." Actions and remarks like these illustrate the frustrations parents feel in raising a child, particularly a child with behavior problems.

Kroth (1975) emphasizes the importance of establishing clear and direct lines of communication with parents. Such communication opens the door to a real team approach for working with behavior problems. Communication permits a sharing of ideas for working with behavior, as well as a support system for both the parent and the teacher. Parents who are knowledgeable about their child's program and who feel comfortable talking with the teacher tend to be supportive of the program. When questions arise, they feel free to contact the teacher and seek some type of resolution.

In-person conferences should be held between teacher and parents prior to a child's entering a special program. These initial meetings usually are of an informative nature. Regularly scheduled meetings, or even parent group meetings, should be established once the student has entered the program. These meetings serve to continue to provide information about the student's progress, to provide instruction on alternative techniques of working with the student, and to help in the problem solving process. Educators need to place more emphasis on developing new procedures for interacting with parents. Parents can be a formidable foe, but they also can be a strong ally. At this stage in the development of secondary programs, school personnel are well advised to seek parent support and find ways to maintain it.

PROPOSED PROGRAM ALTERNATIVE

Following is a brief description of one type of program alternative. It includes basic rationale, staff considerations, program objectives, and plans for implementation. It does not represent the only alternative but is a logical starting point based on the needs of secondary students in programs for the emotionally and behaviorally disordered.

Career and vocational education provide an alternative to the traditional (college preparatory) curriculum (Brolin, 1976). This alternative is logical when one considers that the major purpose of formal education is to prepare the student to become a productive member of society. Employability has become the primary factor by which this goal is measured. Then, our high schools have a responsibility to provide students with an appropriate program that assists in attaining skills necessary to successfully enter the job market.

Career and vocational programs for the regular student are not new (Brolin, 1976). Such programs to serve handicapped students within the public schools, however, are relatively new. Special education programs at the secondary level have given limited assistance in prevocational training and workstudy experiences. Although these programs have helped to revise existing curricula to make subject matter more usable and have introduced a broader use of individualized instruction, they have been limited in their ability to develop extensive training models for career and vocational education.

Program Description

This model, for vocational/occupational experiences for handicapped students, relies upon full cooperation of the school administration, the state department of education, and the parents of students participating in the program. All must agree that career and vocational education is a suitable and realistic alternative to the standard curriculum. Through joint agreement of these parties, successful completion of the program should result in High School graduation and a diploma. A solid commitment of facilities, personnel, equipment, and materials is a must. This commitment is necessary to guarantee continuation of the program and to protect the students participating in the program. Further, the model presented here is not meant to stand in isolation but is to be an integral part of the total educational program. It provides tasks and activities specific to the handicapped student and integrates where feasible with the regular program.

The vocational program model requires a minimum of three self-contained classroom areas in close proximity. These accommodations should be part of the regular physical plant to assist in integration of the special students into appropriate components of the regular program. Two of the classrooms are used for academic activities; one is identified as the *Math Room*, and the other is the *Language Arts Room*. The third classroom should be twice the size of a standard classroom; this room is used for vocational preparation activities.

Personnel for the program include a program director to administer the program, one math teacher, one language arts teacher, one industrial arts teacher, one home economics teacher, one workstudy coordinator, and two teacher aides. All teachers are to be certified in their identified area of speciality and in special education (preferably, in either behavioral disorders, learning disabilities, or mental retardation).

The program director's responsibilities include: (1) writing and evaluating objectives, (2) scheduling, (3) communications and coordination, (4) assisting the other teachers when necessary, (5) keeping records on student progress, (6) consulting with counselors, vocational teachers, regular staff, and appropriate district specialists, and (7) organizing and conducting inservice training. The program director is responsible to the building principal and the director of special education.

The math teachers and language arts teachers are responsible for their respective fields. The industrial arts teacher and the home economics teacher work together in the vocational preparation room and are assisted by two teacher aides. The workstudy coordinator is responsible to the program director. He or she works closely with the business community to arrange student job placements and to provide for supervision and evaluation of on-the-job performance.

The program's overall objective is to assist the student in attaining identified competencies which will provide a firm foundation for entering the world of work. The specific program objectives are:

1 To provide for social, vocational, and academic skill development that will aid students in formulating the basic competencies for employment and entrance into society.

2 To continually evaluate the students' skill performance and attitude, to determine the areas of skill strengths and weaknesses, and to provide occupational guidance based upon interest and areas of vocational strength.

3 To assist in the development and practice of good safety habits necessary in a working environment.

4 To assist students in developing positive feelings toward self and task performance.

5 To perform satisfactorily the assigned vocational tasks and to make related social attitude adjustments.

6 To present an occupational orientation related to relevant community employment.

7 To reduce the drop-out rate of handicapped students.

8 To develop an awareness of the responsibilities of being productive, self-supporting citizens.

Most of the above objectives are written as general statements and, as such, need to be broken into component parts and rewritten in behavioral terms to allow for clearer measurement and evaluation.

Prior to entering the program, the student and parents meet with the program director. A questionnaire designed around the vocational areas available in the program is completed by the student and parents with assistance by the program director. The purpose of this questionnaire is to identify hobbies, areas of interest, and aptitudes a student may have for given vocational areas. This information is used in assigning the student to a vocational task area. Students perform better when their initial experience in a new program involves a familiar task at which they can be successful. High interest, coupled with a task that is within the student's range of abilities, is a strong motivator.

The program itself is comprised of two phases. An entering student is placed in Phase 1, where he or she receives a general orientation to the program, and is administered a battery of interest and aptitude tests (Kolstoe & Frey, 1965). Test results are used in planning the areas of vocational concentration. Programs of study are individualized for the students; they are geared toward the student's areas of identified potential.

During Phase I, the student enters both the general education sequence and the vocational preparation area. The general education sequence contains the math program, the language arts program (reading, writing, and spelling) and the social economics program. The student's present level of functioning in each of these areas is determined by testing conducted by the teacher. The individual educational plan for each student begins at a level where there is a high probability of success (Vogel, 1974).

In the vocational preparation area, the student is assigned to one of the 25 available task work areas—an area identified as having a high success probability for the student. The vocational preparation area is located in the largest of the three rooms and is supervised by the two vocational teachers assisted by the two aides. The room is arranged so that each vocational task area is located in a work station. In addition, an open crafts area and a closed storage area are provided. Instructional units in the work stations include:

1 Tool Usage	**9** Leather Crafts
2 Soldering	**10** Book Binding
3 Lawnmower Repair	**11** Upholstery
4 Electrical Wiring	**12** Dexterity
5 Gear Assembly	**13** Bicycle Repair
6 Automotive	**14** Window Repair
7 Engraving	**15** Pipe Fitting
8 Jewelry	**16** Adding Machine

17 Cash Register	**22** Ironing
18 Filing	**23** Mail Sorting
19 Typing	**24** Telephone
20 Sewing	**25** Appliance Repair
21 Baby Care	

When the student enters the vocational preparation area, he or she goes to the assigned work station, located in a closed carrel which opens into a work area. The work station contains a programmed instruction manual pertaining to the assigned tasks, a cassette tape player, and a cassette tape which is a recording of the instruction manual. If a student should have difficulty reading the manual, the tape usually provides enough assistance so the student can continue the work. If more assistance is needed, the teachers and teacher aides are readily available.

The manual includes a list of materials and tools needed to complete the assigned task. The student must go to the closed storage area and check out the needed items. When the class period ends, the student must check the tools back in at the closed storage area; the project does not have to be dismantled. In a few areas such as electrical wiring and pipe fitting, where tampering or dismantling would be particularly detrimental, work stations are locked when not being used by the student. These stations rarely are assigned to more than one student at a time. Each assigned task at the work station must be performed with a certain degree of accuracy and approved by the teacher before the student is allowed to move on to the next task. Each student eventually will work in all of the twenty-five work stations.

A student enters Phase II when a predetermined level of proficiency has been reached in the academic areas (math, language arts, and social economics). At this time, he or she enters the "Related Education" sequence, meanwhile continuing to work in the vocational preparation area. The related education sequence consists of applied math and language arts. Math instruction is directed toward a specific vocational area, such as the math required for auto mechanics. The same is true for language arts. Spelling might relate to unique vocabulary of the upholstery field.

Upon satisfactory demonstration of certain competencies, the student may be mainstreamed into the regular education vocational program. He or she also may be placed in a work experience either on or off campus. By the senior year, the student should be working fulltime within the community, but with continued supervision from the work-study coordinator. The student earns credits for work experiences which are recognized by both the school and the state. The student accumulates these credits and, by the end of the senior year, should have the required number for graduation.

IMPLICATIONS

The immediate challenge to educators with regard to providing appropriate services for secondary level emotionally or behaviorally disordered students fo-

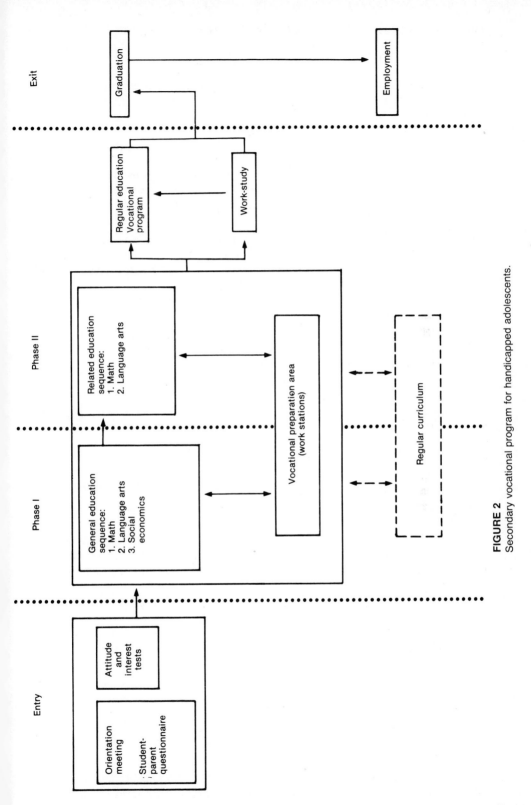

FIGURE 2
Secondary vocational program for handicapped adolescents.

215

cuses on four major concerns. Each requires creativity in thinking and planning, not only to re-assess the importance or value of present practices, but to design innovative programs to realistically meet the needs of students as they prepare to enter adult society.

1 Re-evaluate the purpose and goals of secondary education for the emotionally or behaviorally disordered student. The curriculum needs to be clarified and expanded to provide alternatives for reaching those goals.

2 Identify and evaluate community resources to determine the ways in which they may be utilized appropriately.

3 Develop an organized and systematic approach to train teachers for these secondary level programs. Most states already provide guidelines for certification, but specific training to work with disordered students at the secondary level is lacking. Decisions need to be made regarding the appropriateness of pre-service training, in-service training, and graduate training, as well as content to be included in the preferred model.

4 Identify or develop sources of funding sufficient for programs to operate in the manner in which they were designed. Funding also needs to be made available at the university level to support training programs.

The requirement for developing individualized education programs (IEPs) for students to meet the intent of an "appropriate education" dictates that regular education and special education work in close harmony. Service delivery systems for the emotionally or behaviorally disordered student must be designed and implemented, and also evaluated to determine their effectiveness in providing a relevant education. This is a task that cannot be assigned to tomorrow; it is one that should have been completed yesterday. Today is the time for action.

REFERENCES

Bower, E. M. *Early identification of emotionally handicapped children in school.* Springfield, IL: Charles C Thomas, 1960.

Brolin, D. E. *Vocational preparation of retarded citizens.* Columbus, OH: Charles E. Merrill, 1976.

Brown, G. D., & Palmer, D. J. A review of BEH funded personnel preparation programs in emotional disturbance. *Exceptional Children*, 1977, *44*(3), 168–174.

Glasser, W. *Schools without failure.* New York: Harper & Row, 1969.

Goldstein, H. *The social learning curriculum.* Columbus, OH: Charles E. Merrill, 1974.

Hewett, F. M. *The emotionally disturbed child in the classroom.* Boston: Allyn & Bacon, 1968.

Homme, L., Csanyi, A., Gonzales, M., & Rechs, J. *How to use contingency contracting in the classroom.* Champaign, IL: Research Press, 1969.

Kauffman, J. M. *Characteristics of children's behavior disorders.* Columbus, OH: Charles E. Merrill, 1977.

Kolstoe, O. P., & Frey, R. *A high school work-study program for mentally subnormal youth.* Carbondale, IL: Southern Illinois Press, 1965.

Kroth, R. L. *Communicating with parents of exceptional children*. Denver: Love Publishing Co., 1975.

Long, N. J., & Newman, R. G. Managing surface behavior of children in school. In N. J. Long, W. C. Morse, & R. G. Newman (Eds.), *Conflict in the classroom* (3rd ed.). Belmont, CA: Wadsworth Publishing Co., 1976, pp. 308–316.

McDowell, R. L. *An evaluation of a residential treatment program for adolescents as measured by post-hospital adjustment: A follow-up study*. Unpublished Dissertation, University of Kansas, Lawrence, 1969.

McDowell, R. L. *Program designs for teachers of the behaviorally disordered*. Santa Fe, NM: State Department of Education, Division of Special Education, 1975.

Nelson, C. M., & Kauffman, J. M. Educational programming for secondary school age delinquent and maladjusted pupils. *Behavior Disorders*, 1977, *2*(2), 102–113.

Pate, J. E. Emotionally disturbed and socially maladjusted children. In L. M. Dunn (Ed.), *Exceptional children in the schools*. New York: Holt, Rinehart & Winston, 1963.

Vogel, J. Learning and self-esteem: You can't have one without the other. *Learning*, *2* (7), 68–69.

ENABLING ACTIVITIES

To aid you to meet the objectives listed in the chapter study guide (page 177), the enabling activities listed below were designed to provide a variety of study directions and exploration activities ranging from the difficult and time-consuming to less complicated straightforward tasks. It is important that you understand that you do not have to do every enabler listed—choose only those that help you achieve a study guide objective or appeal to one of your specific interests in the chapter topic.

1 Summarize the federal and your state's legislative provisions for educating exceptional adolescents.

2 Visit a high school program for handicapped adolescents and compare what you observe with the description provided by Ramsey.

3 Prepare a "position paper" for or against the use of "process based" interventions with exceptional teenagers.

4 Interview high school special education teachers for their opinions as to "age" differences among exceptional students.

5 Organize and participate in a panel discussing the differences between secondary programs for EMR, LD, and ED students.

6 Interview several adolescents placed in special education programs and several in general education. Compare the responses of the two groups.

7 As a group project, locate as many graduates of a local special education secondary program as you can. Attempt to answer questions such as:

    a How many students are working and how are their jobs classified?

    b What is the range of leisure activity enjoyed by the graduates?

    c What is the salary range earned by the graduates?

    d What should the school have taught that it didn't?

SELF-TEST

True-False

1 Compulsory attendance laws caused adolescents with behavior and/or learning problems to be placed in classes for the educable mentally retarded.

2 Emotionally handicapped secondary students receive less special education services than elementary students.

3 According to the Evans, there has been an increase in professional literature about the handicapped adolescent.

4 Deviant behaviors and behaviors that occur during adolescence are clearly distinguishable.

5 The younger a student is, the easier it is to categorize her/his behaviors.

6 Colleges adequately prepare teachers of learning disabled students for their future role.

7 Students electing for work-study get paid for their services while they learn.

8 There are larger populations of severe learning disabled adolescents than elementary-aged.

9 How to learn is what is taught in the learning strategies model.

10 Initial assessment of an individual may be biased because past reports are given precedence to present difficulties.

11 Each area of exceptionality has its own unique curriculum designed to meet the needs of the learners.

12 There is still no agreement on the role secondary education plays for exceptional adolescents.

13 No empirical research is available on techniques that are successful with handicapped adolescents.

14 Inadequate funding is the greatest obstacle to achieving an appropriate curriculum for adolescents.

Multiple-Choice

15 Which of the following is not a prerequisite to healthy adolescence? The ability to:
(a) think out situations rationally
(b) prepare for future role expectations
(c) interact with male/female peers
(d) achieve independence

16 An individual who copes with adolescence by cutting classes is displaying a(n):
(a) academic-cognitive characteristic
(b) academic-emotional characteristic
(c) socioemotional characteristic
(d) socioacademic characteristic

17 A child that has reading deficits and severe hyperactivity would be classified as:
(a) learning disabled
(b) emotionally disturbed
(c) both of the above
(d) needs more data

18 Schmid, Algozzine, Wells, and Stoller reported that most teachers of learning disabled students:
(a) work part-time in resource rooms
(b) emphasize remediation of basic academic skills

    (c) are not certified to instruct LD adolescents
    (d) are males
19 The program option used in most schools was:
    (a) work-study
    (b) basic skills remediation
    (c) tutorial
    (d) functional curriculum
20 Secondary curriculum should be modified to consider:
    (a) inappropriate content emphasis
    (b) intervention strategies
    (c) the student's role as an adult
    (d) all of the above

7

TEACHERS, STRESS, AND BURNOUT

CHAPTER STUDY GUIDE

After reading the selections presented in this chapter and completing the enabling activities, the student should be able to:

1 Define and defend a definition of teacher burnout.
2 Differentiate between "environmental" and "personal" stressors.
3 Explain why special education teachers are more subject to burnout than regular education teachers.
4 Describe a model for coping with stress and burnout.
5 List 12 specific techniques for coping with stress.

Teachers, Stress, and Burnout

Gayle McBride

Most people observing Lynn Domenech with her learning disabled and emotionally handicapped students would have thought this 9-year veteran was a model special education teacher. Twice honored by her district as teacher of the year, she enjoyed the respect of her colleagues and the admiration of parents.

Behind the warm efficiency, however, things were not as smooth for Lynn as they seemed. "The challenge had disappeared. I would get up in the morning, go to school, face the same problems as last year and the year before. I felt like I was on a treadmill going nowhere," explained Lynn. "I knew I had mastered teaching and was facing a career crisis."

Lynn Domenech doesn't teach anymore. She started her own company, Teacher Support Software, to develop educational computer programs. The hours are long—longer than teaching, but her renewed enthusiasm and the daily challenges of building a successful business have restored the self-satisfaction missing in the latter years of her teaching.

Lynn is not unusual, nor is her success in switching careers unique. She is representative of "burnout"—that vaguely defined condition of national concern to both education and business.

WHAT IS BURNOUT?

Burnout appears to be a painful and often personally destructive response to excessive stress. Sometimes compared to "combat fatigue" or "combat neurosis," burnout is considered to be an occupational (Hendrickson, 1979) hazard in all the helping professions. It is frequently defined as complete physical, emotional, and attitudinal exhaustion (Freudenberger, 1980; Hendrickson, 1979; Pines & Maslach, 1978). It may simply be stress overload—an imbalance between demands and the capacity to meet them. The individual feels unable to cope with any more stress at that particular time.

THE CAUSE OF BURNOUT

The problems caused by stress, and the resultant stage called burnout, have been examined by researchers for the last 50 years. Recent studies indicate that the major cause of burnout is the inability to cope with stress (Shaw, Bensky, & Dixon, 1981).

Stress is produced by a variety of situations and experiences in one's personal or professional life. Personality factors, the general state of physical wellness, and the "normal" changes which occur in one's life all contribute to stress. These can be grouped into two general groups—"environmental" stressors, i.e., those things around us which cause stress, and "personal" stressors, or those behaviors or characteristics which are part of us, but also can cause stress. For teachers, specific job-related (environmental) stressors have also been identified.

Environmental Stressors

Dramatic shifts in American lifestyle, attitudes, beliefs, and values have occurred in the past century (Truch, 1980). These changes and the increasing complexity of society have resulted in stress for all of us. We may, in fact, be living in the "Age of Stress" (Truch).

TABLE 1
IDENTIFIED JOB-RELATED CAUSES OF STRESS FOR TEACHERS

Stressor	Frequency reported	Investigation											
		1	2	3	4	5	6	7	8	9	10	11	12
Excessive clerical work	(9)	X	X	X	X			X		X		X	
Troublesome students	(8)					X				X	X	X	X
Negative attitudes of students toward school	(6)			X	X	X					X	X	
Time pressures	(6)		X	X		X		X		X	X		
Classes overcrowded	(5)	X	X		X	X						X	
Additional duties (supervisory or extracurricular)	(4)		X		X	X							
Inadequate salary	(4)				X	X						X	
Daily interruptions	(4)		X			X				X			
Maintaining standards	(3)		X								X	X	
Individualized instruction	(3)						X				X		
Poor working conditions	(2)							X					
Involuntary transfers	(2)										X		
Parents	(2)											X	
Incompatible relationship with supervisor	(2)												
Lack of classroom materials	(1)							X					
Notification of unsatisfactory performance	(1)												
Violence and vandalism	(1)											X	
Lack of ability in students	(1)					X							
Lack of teaching skill	(1)												
Implementing Board of Education rules	(1)												
Promotion denied	(1)												
Reorganizing program or classroom	(1)												

Changes in one's life, especially in factors over which we have minimal control, are stress producing, some more than others. The death of a family member, divorce, or financial failure cause greater stress than vacations, Christmas, minor violations of the law, or changes in sleeping or eating habits. As change occurs in one's life, stress accumulates, building upon itself. Since it is not possible to live totally stress-free, reduction in the cumulative effects of stressors allows the individual to not only cope with unexpected stress, but be affected less by the usual stressors faced.

An important group of environmental stressors are those related to the job. Researchers have attempted to determine specific job-related stressors in teaching over the past half century through surveys and interviews. Stressors identified in these reports (in order of most to least often reported) are presented in Table 1.

The most often reported causes of job-related stress for teachers were excessive clerical work, troublesome students, negative attitudes toward school or school work, time pressures, and overcrowded classrooms. Additional supervisory duties, dissatisfaction with salary, interruptions during the school day, maintenance of standards, and the implementation of individualized instruction appear to cause lesser degrees of stress.

It is interesting to note that the teacher stressors reported in 1939 (National Educational Association, 1939) are not very different from those reported in current investigations. It would appear that educators have not been able to improve their situation much over the past four decades.

Personal Stressors

In addition to environmental elements, stress can develop from personal factors. An individual's personality, state of physical or mental well-being, and the coping techniques chosen may all contribute to or cause stress.

An individual's personality is an important factor in both coping with and causing stress. An example cited by Truch illustrates how personality affects or causes stress.

> In 1974, a casual comment from an upholsterer who worked in their office inspired two doctors to trace the behavior patterns of their coronary patients. The observation that the upholsterer made was that the edges of the seats the patients sat in got the most wear, as if these people were living examples of the expression, "sitting on the edge of your seat" (1980, p. 51).

Some people do seem to live "by sitting on the edge of their seats." These personalities (often intense, aggressive, competitive, and ambitious) deal with stress in a different manner than the easy-going, more relaxed person. The first type of person (Type A) seems to function under a need to race against the clock when getting things done. They are more prone to coronary disease, five times more likely to have a second heart attack, and have twice as many fatal heart attacks as the other person (Type B).

Another group of personal stressors is related to the individual's state of physical and mental well-being. Exercise, nutrition, use of relaxation techniques, sleep habits, as well as the use level of drugs, tobacco, alcohol, and caffeine products significantly affect how an individual responds to stress (Sparks & Hammond, 1981).

The third group of personal stressors is associated with how the individual copes with stress. The way in which one responds to stress may have been learned at an early age (Truch, 1980). Parents, peers, and others function as models for learning coping skills. Some ways prove to be effective, others are not. Short-term coping strategies, such as use of alcohol, daydreaming, cursing, or ignoring the problem generally are not as effective as more long-term strategies, such as talking with others about problems, developing alternative plans, or gaining additional information about the situation.

STRESS AND THE SPECIAL EDUCATOR

Teacher burnout exists at all levels in the educational system, and in all areas of curriculum. It has been suggested, however, that special educators are subject to additional stress due to the nature of the job and the problems associated with working with exceptional students. Mandates over which the individual teacher has no control (such as those required by PL 94-142) also increase stress. Unfortunately, limited research focusing on the special educator and burnout has been reported (Shaw, Bensky, & Dixon, 1981).

Causes of Stress for the Special Educator

While there is no evidence to suggest that the personal stressors of the special educator (personality, individual state of wellness, or coping styles) differ significantly from those of the general educator, the environmental stressors may be different (Weiscopf, 1980). Some of these have been identified in the literature (Bensky, Shaw, Gouse, Bates, Dixon, & Beane, 1980; DeShong, 1981; Shaw, Bensky, & Dixon, 1981; Weiscopf, 1980).

 1 Work overload. Special educators often perform many tasks in addition to providing instruction: planning and implementing the requirements mandated by PL 94-142, counseling with each child's parents, and working daily with individual learning and behavior problems are not uncommon duties.

 2 Lack of perceived success. While there may be some validity to the belief that special educators have an affinity for exceptional children, it has never been substantiated. Long teaching hours with little observable student progress will eventually take its toll. Lack of perceived success on the job affects a teacher's confidence, may lower self-esteem, and can contribute to burnout.

 3 Amount of direct contact with children. As with child care workers, special education teachers spend a great deal of time interacting with their students. Exceptional children often require constant adult supervision. Teachers

may have little time away from their students and limited interaction with colleagues. These conditions result in feelings of isolation.

4 Program structure. While many special education programs attempt to provide structure for the students, exceptional children vary in their ability to tolerate frustration. Unpredictable emotional outbursts may occur. A great deal of flexibility is required to meet these student needs, and the more flexible and less structured a program, the more demanding it has been found to be on the teacher.

5 Responsibility for others. Special educators often receive little emotional reinforcement from their students, students' parents, or colleagues. This can lead to emotional depletion for the teacher. Unless a teacher's ego is replenished, caring and concern for students diminishes and the probability of burnout increases.

6 Role clarification. The educator who has a clear perception of the job is significantly less likely to feel stress than the teacher who is unclear about job responsibilities. Role descriptions which are inappropriate, inefficient , or impossible to implement also increase the stress the teacher feels. Unfortunately, these situations often occur for the special educator. Definitions, criteria for placement, emphasis of programs, forms to use, as well as procedures to follow often change in special education, as state, federal, and district policies change.

BURNOUT PREVENTION

All individuals experience stress. Some cope—others burn out. The result of burnout in teachers is not only poor performance in the classroom by both teacher and students, but also high teacher absenteeism, high turnover rates, and increasing numbers of experienced teachers retiring early (Kyriacou & Sutcliffe, 1978; Dunham, 1976; Payne, 1974; Truch, 1980).

Coping effectively with stress requires one to assume an active role to program the necessary changes. The individual must be able to recognize personal stress symptoms and warning signals before burnout actually occurs. Although recovery from burnout is possible, prevention can decrease the potential misery to the individual, his or her family, and the students he or she teaches.

The management of stress and the prevention of burnout are tasks which may require the individual to make minor and/or major changes in lifestyle (Sparks & Hammond, 1981). New skills may need to be developed and confrontations may be required as sources of stress are reckoned with. No magic elixirs exist; stress management requires both patience and perseverance as well as support from family, friends, and colleagues.

To identify procedures for preventing teacher burnout, a literature review was conducted. The reports reviewed included survey and interview studies, professional opinions, and data-based group design studies. While a variety of control problems were noted (i.e., populations studied were different, instruments were nonstandardized), a recommended procedure evolved consisting of the series of steps presented in Figure 1.

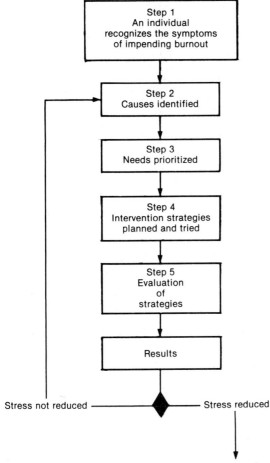

FIGURE 1
A procedure for preventing burnout.

Step 1: Recognition of Symptoms

Most people begin to exhibit behavior symptoms prior to reaching the point of "burning out" (Freudenberger, 1975). Usually, the drift toward burnout is gradual and unnoticed until a serious problem exists. It is critical that every teacher monitor personal behavior for signs of adverse reactions to stress. Some general indicators of impending burnout are consistently mentioned in the literature:

1 Feelings of fatigue, depression, boredom, apathy.
2 Changes in regular sleeping, eating, exercise habits.
3 Irritability, forgetfulness, inability to make decisions.
4 Chronic and unresolved problems with intimate relationships.
5 Increases in smoking, drinking, drug use.
6 Increase in blood pressure, heart and respiration rates.

7 Chest and back pains, headaches.

8 Ulcers.

9 Loss of sexual interest; sexual impotency.

10 Attempts to escape or run away from stress by calling in sick, daydreaming, not caring.

11 General lack of concern for others, feelings of isolation.

12 Lowering of self-esteem, self-confidence.

13 In the classroom, overindulgence or harsh punishment of students, students are more disruptive, and levels of achievement drop. Less-than-adequate teaching techniques are used.

14 Feelings of being owned by the clock. Undone things begin screaming to be completed. Everything is Priority 1.

15 The job becomes all-important. Sacrifices are made routinely "for the job." Feelings of being indispensable, afraid to take time off because no one can do your job.

16 No joy in work—everything is a problem.

Step 2: Identification of Causes

As discussed earlier, many factors cause stress. By assuming an active role in stress management, the individual can develop self-diagnostic skills which enable him or her to determine those factors causing the stress. Many indices, such as the Life Stress Scale II, Stress Profile for Teachers, "Hurry Sickness" Index, and the "Wellness Behavior" Test are available and may be helpful in the identification of stressors.

Step 3: Needs Prioritized

Once suspected causes of stress are identified, they must be ranked in some sort of order. It is not efficient (or possible) to resolve all of them at once. Those which appear to have the most serious effect should be remedied first. As a program of stress management is implemented, priorities may change as reassessment of needs occurs.

Step 4: Implementation of Intervention Strategies

Changes in behaviors may be necessary in order to cope with the stressors one faces daily. Some changes, such as development of ways to cope with certain individuals, to deal with ever-present paperwork, or to manage time efficiently may have obvious results. The results of other changes, such as improvement in physical and mental health, may be less obvious and less immediate. Some general strategies suggested in the literature for coping with stress and preventing burnout include:

1 Development of a support system. It is very important to have people who care about you and what you do. A close relationship with at least one other person is vitally important.

2 Take responsibility for what you do with your own body. Exercise regularly, eat properly, limit the use of tobacco, alcohol, and drugs.

3 Learn how to manage time effectively. Prioritize what needs to be done—do high-priority items first.

4 Know and respect your own limits, skills, energy, and level of commitment. Do those things which are your responsibility—learn to say no.

5 Spend time out of your usual role. Develop a hobby. Don't compete—just enjoy yourself.

6 Look upon life as a challenge. Take risks.

7 Take time off—"mental health" days, vacations, planning periods during the school day. Use relaxation techniques, self-hypnosis, or other ways to "escape" daily pressures for a few minutes every day.

8 Seek professional help—career or personal counseling may be appropriate.

9 Learn to cry "Uncle" when you need to. Realizing that stress is affecting you adversely is the first step in dealing with it.

10 Enjoy "strokes" when they occur. Get thanks, recognition, and validation from all available sources.

11 Stack the deck in your favor. Take on assignments, when possible, at which you will be successful.

12 Learn to laugh at yourself and the absurdities of life. Learn to live life with a sense of humor. Angels can fly because they take themselves lightly.

Perhaps because of the rate of burnout of individuals today, many approaches and programs are being offered. In addition to the professional literature (Gmelch, 1978; Moe, 1979; Styles & Cavanaugh, 1977), workshops, programs, and seminars are being provided nationwide through business organizations, corporations, wellness centers, and hospitals. For many, these programs can provide structure and professional guidance when learning to cope with stress.

Step 5: Evaluation

If the strategies attempted do not appear to be making a difference, reevaluation of the causes of stress, the priority levels assigned to the stressors, or the coping techniques being used is necessary. The stress level one can function under fluctuates, stressors change, and situations evolve. No one strategy can be guaranteed to reduce stress for everyone in all circumstances. Evaluating the results of your efforts and making necessary changes should be an ongoing process.

Burnout Prevention for the Special Educator

The general procedures already discussed are also appropriate for the special educator. First the symptoms of burnout must be recognized. Once they are, the causes of stress should be determined. Factors such as lack of administrative support, mislabeling of special children, problems with parents, paperwork problems, or even the potential for lawsuits are possible causes of stress for the special educator. It is also possible that the teacher is unable to identify specific causes of stress. Trial and error may be the only possible recourse.

The general suggestions offered earlier as intervention strategies are applicable for both the special and regular educator. Some additional suggestions specific to the field of special education include:

1 Special educators need to know in advance the type of emotional stress their particular job entails. Information such as the needs, academic levels, and social problems of their children should be made available in advance.

2 Realistic goals should be set. Planning for success on the job is necessary for both the teacher and students.

3 If possible, those tasks, such as paperwork and other nonteaching duties, should be delegated to others, providing more time as well as reducing the workload of the teacher.

4 Special educators often report feelings of isolation or state they are not considered part of the school. Efforts should be made to become involved with colleagues.

5 While on the job it is important that teachers break up the continuous direct contact they have with children. Team teaching, learning centers, and teacher time-outs can be used to reduce direct teacher-student time.

6 Staying mentally alert when away from the job significantly aids in burnout prevention. Continued learning through classes, workshops, conferences, or field trips also provides the educator with contact with other professionals. Sharing experiences and feelings through group participation activities also helps teachers decelerate the burnout process.

7 Life should be challenging, not boring. Repetition and routines are inherent in both regular and special education. Creativity is an important factor in burnout prevention. Newness and variety create excitement and interest for teachers and students.

CONCLUSION

Although stress is a part of everyone's life today, some individuals appear to be able to cope with it while others do not. Inability to cope with stress appears to be a major cause of the phenomenon called Teacher Burnout (Shaw, Bensky, & Dixon, 1981). Affecting both special and regular education teachers, burnout has become a major concern of those involved in education today. The cost of teacher burnout is high. Individual costs are difficult to determine, but high blood pressure, migraine headaches, ulcers, as well as many other physical ailments have been attributed to stress. Teachers suffering from burnout also report feelings of depression, isolation, apathy, and lack of confidence in their own abilities.

In the classroom, burned out or highly stressed teachers have been found to be less effective, less creative, and less concerned about their students (Fuller,

LIFE STRESS SCALE II
(Hough, Fairbank, and Garcia Adaptation)

Life event	Mean value	Life event	Mean value
1 Death of spouse	190	33 Frequent minor illnesses	53
2 Mental illness	142	34 Birth of second or later child	52
3 Divorce	137	35 Move over 1,000 miles	52
4 Racial intermarriage	116	36 Trouble with boss	52
5 Marital separation	115	37 Marriage	50
6 Death of close family member	111	38 Wife stops work	50
7 Fired at work	101	39 Begin school	48
8 Jail term	99	40 Wife begins work	46
9 Personal injury or illness	91	41 Engaged	46
10 Sex difficulties	90	42 Change in responsibilities at work	45
11 Pregnancy	89	43 End school	45
12 Marked decrease in income	88	44 Move out of city or area to within 1,000 miles	43
13 Lawsuit	85	45 Problems in school	42
14 Change in number of arguments with spouse	135	46 Trouble with friends	40
15 Marital reconciliation	85	47 Mortgage or loan less than $10,000	38
16 Foreclosure of mortgage or loan	83	48 Change in work hours or conditions	36
17 Failure at school or training school	82	49 Change in sleeping habits	36
18 Birth of first child	78	50 Change in social activities	35
19 Health of family member becomes worse	77	51 Marked increase in income	35
20 Death of close friend	77	52 Change in eating habits	33
21 Son or daughter leaving home	76	53 Minor violation of the law	32
22 Gain of new family member other than child	75	54 Outstanding personal achievement	31
23 Religious intermarriage	71	55 Change in residence to better neighborhood	31
24 Breakup with boyfriend		56 Christmas activities	26
25 Mortgage over $10,000	66	58 Change in number of family gatherings	24
26 Change in residence to worse neighborhood	66	59 Make move within city or area	23
27 Change in schools	66	60 Change in recreation	23
28 Retirement	62	61 Health of family member becomes better	21
29 Trouble with in-laws	60	62 Change in residence to same type of neighborhood	13
30 Business readjustment	55	63 Vacation	12
31 Change to different line of work	54		
32 Revision of personal habits	53		

Chance of Burning Out: High: 600+
Moderate: 400–599
Low: below 399

Truch, Stephen. *Teacher Burnout and What to Do about It*. Novato, CA: Academic Therapy Publications, 1979.

Name _____ Date _____

School _____ District _____

Stress Profile for Teachers

Instructions

The Wilson Stress Profile for Teachers is designed to help you more clearly define, on a self-scoring basis, the areas and frequency of your stress. As you read each item, evaluate the statement in terms of a period of time rather than a specific day you remember. Indicate how often the source of stress occurs by circling the number that corresponds to the frequency of occurrence. Do not read the stress profile scoring sheet until after you have completed items 1 through 32.

	Never	Seldom	Sometimes	Often	Very often
Student behavior					
1 I have difficulty controlling my class	1	2	3	4	5
2 I become impatient/angry when my students do not do what I ask them to do	1	2	3	4	5
3 Lack of student motivation to learn affects the progress of my students negatively	1	2	3	4	5
4 My students make my job stressful	1	2	3	4	5

Total items 1–4 _____

Employee/administrator relations					
5 I have difficulty in my working relationship with my administrator(s)	1	2	3	4	5
6 My administrator makes demands of me that I cannot meet	1	2	3	4	5
7 I feel I cannot be myself when I am interacting with my administrator	1	2	3	4	5
8 I feel my administrator does not approve of the job I do	1	2	3	4	5

Total items 5–8 _____

Teacher/teacher relations					
9 I feel isolated in my job (and its problems)	1	2	3	4	5
10 I feel my fellow teachers think I am not doing a good job	1	2	3	4	5
11 Disagreements with my fellow teachers are a problem for me	1	2	3	4	5
12 I get too little support from the teachers with whom I work	1	2	3	4	5

Total items 9–12 _____

Parent/teacher relations					
13 Parents of my students are a source of concern for me	1	2	3	4	5
14 Parents' disinterest in their child's performance at school concerns me	1	2	3	4	5

	Never	Seldom	Sometimes	Often	Very often

Parent/teacher relations (Continued)

	Never	Seldom	Sometimes	Often	Very often
15 I feel my students' parents think I am not doing a satisfactory job of teaching their children	1	2	3	4	5
16 The home environment of my students concerns me	1	2	3	4	5

Total items 13–16 _____

Time management

	Never	Seldom	Sometimes	Often	Very often
17 I have too much to do and not enough time to do it	1	2	3	4	5
18 I have to take work home to complete it	1	2	3	4	5
19 I am unable to keep up with correcting papers and other school work	1	2	3	4	5
20 I have difficulty organizing my time in order to complete tasks	1	2	3	4	5

Total items 17–20 _____

Intrapersonal conflicts

	Never	Seldom	Sometimes	Often	Very often
21 I put self-imposed demands on myself to meet scheduled deadlines	1	2	3	4	5
22 I think badly of myself for not meeting the demands of my job	1	2	3	4	5
23 I am unable to express my stress to those who place demands on me	1	2	3	4	5
24 Teaching is stressful for me	1	2	3	4	5

Total items 21–24 _____

Physical symptoms of stress

	Never	Seldom	Sometimes	Often	Very often
25 The frequency I experience one or more of these symptoms is: stomach aches, backaches, elevated blood pressure, stiff necks and shoulders	1	2	3	4	5
26 I find my job tires me out	1	2	3	4	5
27 I am tense by the end of the day	1	2	3	4	5
28 I experience headaches	1	2	3	4	5

Total items 24–28 _____

Psychological/emotional symptoms of stress

	Never	Seldom	Sometimes	Often	Very often
29 I find myself complaining to others	1	2	3	4	5
30 I am frustrated and/or feel angry	1	2	3	4	5
31 I worry about my job	1	2	3	4	5
32 I feel depressed about my job	1	2	3	4	5

Total items 29–32 _____

Scoring Sheet
Stress Profile for Teachers

Instructions for Scoring

1 After you have completed items 1–32, total the scores in each category and enter it in the corresponding box on this page.

2 Plot your score on the dotted line with an "X" and draw a line between your scoring "X's" so that a clear profile of your stress evaluation is visible.

3 Add up all your category scores and enter the number in the box after Total Overall Score. A score of 32–64 is low, 65–96 is moderate, and 97–160 is high.

4 Check your level on the same line as either low, moderate or high.

Stress Profile Scores

	Low	Moderate	High
	1 2 3 4 5 6 7 8	9 10 11 12 13 14 15	16 17 18 19 20
Student behavior	• • • • • • • •	• • • • • • •	• • • • •
Employee/admin. relations	• • • • • • • •	• • • • • •	• • • • •
Teacher/teacher relations	• • • • • • • •	• • • • • • •	• • • • •
Parent/teacher relations	• • • • • • • •	• • • • • • •	• • • • •
Time management	• • • • • • • •	• • • • • • •	• • • • •
Intrapersonal conflicts	• • • • • • • •	• • • • • • •	• • • • •
Physical symptoms of stress	• • • • • • • •	• • • • • • •	• • • • •
Psychological/emotional symptoms of stress	• • • • • • • •	• • • • • • •	• • • • •
Stress management techniques	• • • • • • • •	• • • • • • •	• • • • •

Total overall score   Low_____   Moderate _____   High _____

32–64   65–96   97–160

Truch, Stephen. *Teacher Burnout and What to Do about It*. Novato, CA: Academic Therapy Publications, 1979.

"HURRY SICKNESS" INDEX

Please indicate how often each of the following applies to you in daily life.

	Never	Rarely	Sometimes	Often	Always
1 Do you find yourself rushing your speech?	1	2	3	4	5
2 Do you hurry other people's speech by interrupting them with "umhm, umhm" or by completing their sentences for them?	1	2	3	4	5
3 Do you hate to wait in line?	1	2	3	4	5
4 Do you seem to be short of time to get everything done?	1	2	3	4	5
5 Do you detest wasting time?	1	2	3	4	5
6 Do you eat too fast?	1	2	3	4	5
7 Do you drive over the speed limit?	1	2	3	4	5
8 Do you try to do more than one thing at a time?	1	2	3	4	5
9 Do you become impatient if others do something too slowly?	1	2	3	4	5
10 Do you seem to have little time to relax and enjoy the time of day?	1	2	3	4	5
11 Do you find yourself overcommitted?	1	2	3	4	5
12 Do you jiggle your knees or tap your fingers?	1	2	3	4	5
13 Do you think about other things during conversations?	1	2	3	4	5
14 Do you walk fast?	1	2	3	4	5
15 Do you hate dawdling after a meal?	1	2	3	4	5
16 Do you become irritable after a meal?	1	2	3	4	5
17 Do you find yourself with clenched fists or tight neck or jaw muscles?					
18 Do you detest losing in sports or games?	1	2	3	4	5
19 Does your concentration sometimes wander while you think about what's coming up later?	1	2	3	4	5
20 Are you a competitive person?	1	2	3	4	5

Truch, Stephen. *Teacher Burnout and What to Do about It.* Novato, CA: Academic Therapy Publications, 1979.

THE "WELLNESS BEHAVIOR" TEST

This quiz will help you assess the behavior patterns that establish your own wellness. Use your judgment when answering. Total each section and the total test, giving you an overall test score as well as three section scores.

Relaxation

		Points
1 Do you take time to get completely away from work and other pressures to unwind?	Frequently	1
	Fairly often	2
	Sometimes	3
	Seldom	4
	I "just can't"	5
2 Do you sleep well? Fall asleep easily? Sleep through the night?	Very well	1
	Fairly well	2
	Not so well	3
	Have trouble	4
	"Certified Insomniac"	5
3 Do you take, or feel you need, aspirin, tranquilizers, sleeping pills, stomach medicines, or laxatives?	Seldom or never	1
	Occasionally	2
	Fairly often	3
	Quite often	4
	I'm hooked	5
4 Do you practice a form of deep relaxation (e.g. meditation, progressive relaxation, autogenic training, etc.) daily?	Nearly every day	1
	Often	2
	Occasionally	3
	Seldom	4
	What's deep relaxation?	5
	Relaxation Score:	

Exercise

1 Can you run a mile (at any speed) without becoming exhausted?	Easily	1
	Fairly well	2
	Can barely do it	3
	Can't do it	4
	Can't walk a mile	5
2 Can you play a fast game of tennis or other strenuous sport without becoming exhausted?	Easily	1
	Fairly well	2
	Get very tired	3
	Get exhausted	4
	Wouldn't try it	5
3 Do you jog or engage in some other very active exercise several times a week?	Usually	1
	Fairly often	2
	Occasionally	3
	Seldom	4
	Allergic to exercise	5
4 Are you fairly strong and physically able?	Very	1
	Moderately	2
	Adequate for my purposes	3
	Quite weak	4
	I can't stand up in a strong wind	5
	Exercise Score:	

THE "WELLNESS BEHAVIOR" TEST (CONTINUED)

Diet		
1 Are you overweight? (Just check to see how much surface fat is visible on your body.)	Not at all	1
	Mildly	2
	Moderate amount of flab	3
	Quite a paunch	4
	Butterball	5
2 Do you smoke?	Never	1
	2 or 3 a day	2
	Half-pack a day	3
	Pack or more a day	4
	Chain smoker	5
3 Do you drink liquor (including wine or beer)?	Rarely or never	1
	Socially and seldom	2
	One a day	3
	Several a day	4
	I'm an alkie	5
4 Do you drink coffee, tea, cola drinks, or other sources of caffeine and sugar?	Rarely or never	1
	1 or 2 a day	2
	Several a day	3
	Regularly, including with meals	4
	Can't do without it	5
	Diet Score:	

Relaxation Score: _____
Exercise Score: _____
Diet Score: _____

Total Test Score: _____

Albrecht, Karl. *Stress and the Manager: Making It Work for You.* Englewood Cliffs, NJ: Prentice-Hall, Inc., 1979.

1969; Youngs, 1978; Wilson, 1979). Extremes in responses to students have been reported, either overindulgence or use of harsh punishment. Student behavior and achievement are also adversely affected.

Learning to deal with stress, thereby preventing burnout, is possible. The steps involved in burnout prevention have been delineated. Beginning with the recognition of the symptoms of burnout through self-diagnosis, the individual determines the causes, then develops a plan to intervene with those stressors deemed most important first. Ongoing evaluation of the strategies tried and causes of stress is necessary.

Inherent in special education are many stressors that may not be found in general education. The procedures suggested for the general educator are also appropriate for the special educator. Perhaps through application of what we know about stress and burnout teachers will be able to better cope with the stress in their personal and professional lives.

REFERENCES

Bensky, J. M., Shaw, S. F., Gouse, A. S., Bates, H., Dixon, B., & Beane, W. E. Public Law 94-142 and stress: A problem for educators. *Exceptional Children*, 1980, *47*(1) 24–29.

DeShong, B. *The Special Educator: Stress and Survival*. Rockville, MD: Aspen Systems Corporation, 1981.

Dunham, J. Stress situations and responses. In National Association of Schoolmasters (Ed.), *Stress in Schools*. London: Hemmel Hemstead, 1976.

Freudenberger, H. *Burnout: The Cost of High Achievement*. New York: Anchor Press, 1980.

Fuller, F. F. Concerns of teachers: A developmental conceptualization. *American Educational Research Journal*, 1969, *6*, 207–226.

Gmelch, W. H. The principal's next challenge: The twentieth-century art of managing stress. *NASSP Bulletin*, February 1978, 5–9.

Hendrickson, B. Teacher burnout: How to recognize it; what to do about it. *Instructor*, 1979, *7*(5), 36–39.

Kyriacou, C., & Sutcliffe, J. Teacher stress: Prevalence, sources, and symptoms. *British Journal of Educational Psychology*, 1978, *48*, 159–167.

Lortie, D. *Schoolteacher: A Sociological Study*. Chicago, IL: University of Chicago Press, 1975.

McGuire, W. H. Teacher burnout. *Today's Education*, 1978, *68*, 5.

McLaughlin, J., & Shea, J. California teacher's job dissatisfactions. *California Journal of Educational Research*, 1960, *11*, 216–224.

Moe, D. A. A prescription. *Today's Education*, 1979, *64*, 35–36.

National Educational Association. The teacher looks at teacher load. *Research Bulletin*, 1939, *17*(5).

National Education Association. Teaching load in 1950. *Research Bulletin*, 1951, *29*(1), 3–50.

National Educational Association. Teacher's problems. *Research Bulletin*, 1967, *45*, 116–117.

Olander, H. T., & Farrell, M. E. Professional problems of elementary teachers. *Journal of Teacher Education*, 1970, *21*, 276–280.

Parsons, J. S., & Fuller, F. F. Concerns of teachers: Reliability, bipolarity, and relationship of teaching experience. Paper presented at the meeting of the American Educational Research Association, Chicago, 1972 (ERIC Document Reproduction Service No. 063-257).

Payne, L. W. *Educational Priority, Vol. 2: EPA Surveys and Statistics*. London: HMOS, 1974.

Pines, A., & Maslach, C. Characteristics of staff burnout in mental hospital settings. *Hospital and Community Psychiatry*, 1978, *29*(4), 233–237.

Rudd, W., & Wiseman, S. Sources of dissatisfaction among a group of teachers. *British Journal of Educational Psychology*, 1962, *32*, 275–291.

Scrivens, R. The bick click. *Today's Education*, November-December 1979, 34–35.

Shaw, S. F., Bensky, J. M., & Dixon, B. *Stress and Burnout: A Primer for Special Education and Special Services Personnel*, Reston, VA: CEC, 1981.

Sparks, D., & Hammond, T. Managing teacher stress and burnout. *ERIC Clearinghouse on Teacher Education*, ERIC SPO17376, February 1981.

Styles, K., & Cavanaugh, G. Stress in teaching and how to handle it. *English Journal*, January 1977, 76–79.

Truch, S. *Teacher Burnout and What to Do about It*. Novato, CA: Academic Therapy Publications, 1980.

Weiscopf, P. Burnout among teachers of exceptional children. *Exceptional Children*, 1980, *47*, 18–23.

Wilson, C. *Survey Conducted in San Diego County, San Diego, California:* Department of Education, 1979.

Youngs, B. B. Anxiety and stress: How they affect teachers's teaching. *NASSP Bulletin*, 1978, *62*, 78–83.

Slow Down: You Move Too Fast

Lee J. Gray

Setting: Any classroom U.S.A.

Time: 8:30 A.M.

Teacher: "There was a fight on the school bus?"

"Please sit down John!"

"No, I just can't come to the office right now."

"We'll find your snake in just a minute."

Every school day doesn't start like this, but many do. The pressure starts with the opening bell and frequently continues after the last. You're probably familiar with the most common results of dealing with stress ineffectively— fatigue, irritability and an inability to relax. Eventually you may have to pay some very serious dues, such as hypertension, heart disease, ulcers or insomnia.

As a school psychologist, I conduct many workshops for teachers on adult and child stress, and I counsel teachers on an individual basis. Based on my experiences I have developed an approach to coping with stress that I think most teachers can apply to their daily lives. The results can be far-reaching. When teachers learn to understand an effectively deal with the strains of their profession, they benefit not only themselves, but also their students.

In his book *Positive Addiction* (Harper and Row) William Glasser notes that we can become addicted to positive behaviors that make us better people, just as we become addicted to negative behaviors. In other words, we can make changes in our lives; we don't *have* to be victims to the ills of stress. This is a point I emphasize when I counsel teachers and an initial step in coping with stress. To bring this home, I ask teachers to examine their feelings of helplessness and frustration and to stop playing the "If-only" game: "If only it weren't for that principal, I could . . . "; "If only I had taken that other job . . . " Once

Gray, Lee J. Slow down: You move too fast. *Teacher*, 1979, *96*(8), 52–53. Reprinted by permission.

they accept the idea that they can control their responses to stress, it's easier to identify those negative behaviors and alter them.

Rushing, Dashing, Cramming

Teachers who fall in the stress danger zone suffer from what I call "rushism" or the "roadrunner syndrome." They are always dashing to or from something, even when they don't have to. They try to cram more activities into their classes than there is time for. They talk fast and allow little time for interaction with their students. For example, they cut short classroom dialog with such statements as "Uh huh, let's move on" and "Okay, that's good. Now as I was saying . . ."

Teachers who suffer from this malady are usually very impatient with others who do not rush around the way they do and equally annoyed with those who do. Grouchiness and a short temper are also common characteristics. "Roadrunners" rely very heavily on the use of sarcasm and find it difficult to accept a smooth-running situation. They become chronic fault-finders, often showing more concern for a small detail than the whole picture.

Another common characteristic of teachers who are under stress is constant looking at their watches or asking what time it is, even though they know a bell will signal their return to class. I watched one such teacher glance at his watch 13 times in nine minutes. When I asked him what time it was, he had to look again. After I called his frequent time checks to his attention, he said, "I really did that?" Within a few minutes he was doing it again.

Perhaps the most telling symptom of "rushism" is trying to do too many things at once. I have seen some "roadrunners" at lunchtime eat a sandwich with one hand, mark papers with the other, talk to someone (without seeming to hear what is said) and talk to themselves about the papers they are marking (usually about the faults they find) almost simultaneously.

If you have one or more of the above characteristics, consider the following specific steps to change matters. Try to be patient with yourself. It may take you a while to alter bad habits that you have developed over many years.

• If you haven't seen your doctor lately, make an appointment for a complete examination. Sometimes, "rushism" symptoms have a physical basis.

• Make a list of those "rushism" symptoms that you think you have. Show it to a friend to make sure you haven't missed something you're unaware of, such as eating too fast. Make a contract with yourself, in writing, to change specific behaviors.

• Concentrate on altering your daily routine. For example, get up a little earlier in the morning and relax with your morning beverage and a newspaper or book. Select a new route of driving to work, if possible. Leave just a little earlier and drive slowly. When you get home in the evening, try to discuss something positive that happened during the day, as opposed to the common habit of griping. Also, consider varying your dinner hour, which can be a relaxing way to "deregiment" your home life.

• Before entering school, pause and look at the sky. What kind of clouds do you see? Are there birds flying around? What does the wind sound like? Stopping to take in the pleasant aspects of your everyday environment can help you break a "rushism" pattern of behavior.

• Remove your watch if you have a bell system and try to pace your lessons without looking frequently at a wall clock.

• Allow your students time to answer you without rushing them.

• During breaks or lunch, avoid discussing school problems or highly charged topics, if possible. Read something light and do it slowly. (If you find yourself looking to see how many pages you have read, *stop*! You're only defeating your purpose.) Or, work on a long-term project, such as painting, writing or knitting.

• Try to find some place to relax or meditate whenever possible during the school day. Sit in a comfortable position and concentrate on breathing rhythmically, saying the number one as you exhale. This kind of exercise can give you relaxing benefits similar to those produced by reciting a mantra in transcendental meditation.

• Don't schedule more activities for any one day than you can comfortably accomplish.

• When you catch yourself displaying "rushism" behavior, such as interrupting conversation or fault-finding, make a mark on an index card and carry it in your pocket. Having a friend give you a cue or sign that you are unconsciously acting like a "roadrunner" will also help you monitor your behavior.

• Compose written reminders to yourself. For example, "I am going to slow down today and will feel better for it"; "Even if I hurry all day I won't finish everything"; "I am going to work on one lesson at a time—not the whole day." This last reminder, adapted from the code of Alcoholics Anonymous, leads me to want to start a "Roadrunners Anonymous."

Place the statements where you are likely to read them often during the day, such as on your desk or on a card tucked in your pocket. If you can't or won't remember to do this, associate reading the statements with something that you do daily, such as eating or sitting in the faculty room during breaks.

• Exercise regularly and moderately before or after school (or both) and learn to do some isometric exercises during the day. Some teachers have told me, "I just don't have time to exercise." I always respond with a comment I borrowed from Bob Hoffman, a weight trainer and former Olympic champion. He said, "If you got sick, you'd find time to be ill, wouldn't you?"

Of course, check with your doctor to make certain that you select the right form of exercise. Fit the exercise to you, not the reverse. Then, enjoy it and *relax*.

• For additional strategies on how to cope with stress I recommend the following books: *The Relaxation Response* by Herbert Benson (Morrow), *TM: Discovering Inner Energy and Overcoming Stress* by Harold H. Bloomfield, M. P. Cain and D. T. Jaffe with R. B. Cory (Dell) and *Stress* by Walter McQuade and Ann Aikman (Bantam).

Beep! Beep!

Learning healthy ways of dealing with stress isn't always easy. It takes time, effort and motivation. But I believe you won't regret making the decision to change. However, if you are a "roadrunner" and you decide not to do anything about your symptoms, please do me two favors. First, buy yourself a bicycle horn so that everybody else can get out of your way. Second, send me the address of your nearest hospital so that I can send you a get-well card.

Burnout: A Critical Issue for Educators

Robert H. Zabel
Mary Kay Zabel

Four weeks into the school year, a first year teacher in a class for behaviorally disordered junior high school students had quit, too physically and emotionally exhausted to continue. By all accounts, she was well prepared for her job, having completed teacher preparation programs in both regular and special education. She had been a good student in her classes, had had successful experiences in student teaching, and had worked as a teacher aide in a state hospital school during two previous summers. She was enthusiastic, appeared to have realistic expectations of what she was getting into, and wanted to teach behaviorally disordered children. In short, she showed considerable promise. Even so, she could not cope with the situation in which she found herself.

Tears came easily when she attempted to deal with the behavior of her students and when she talked to others about the problems she was having. She dreaded each new day and was so exhausted that she went to bed at 6:00 p.m. Finally, with feelings of confusion and frustration, mixed with anger toward the students, administrators, and most of all herself, she asked for a leave of absence. "It was hell," she said. "I've lost all of my self confidence and don't think I ever want to go back." She was apparently an extreme example of a syndrome that many special and regular teachers experience—burnout.

Teachers, administrators, and teacher trainers have long been aware of the "burnout syndrome," yet an examination of available literature reveals that little attention has been given to actually studying the condition with regard to teachers. Educators may, however, gain some insights from studies of burnout—what it is, how it develops, and how it may be prevented—with other health and social service professionals.

Zabel, Robert H., and Zabel, Mary Kay. Burnout: A critical issue for educators. *Education Unlimited*, 1980, 2(2), 23–25. Reprinted by permission.

WHAT IS BURNOUT?

Based upon studies involving day care center staff (Maslach & Pines, 1977), mental health professionals (Pines & Maslach, 1978), police officers (Maslach & Jackson, 1979), and others, Christina Maslach has identified a number of characteristics of burnout. These are (a) distancing or detachment from clients; (b) low morale regarding the job; (c) high job turnover. In addition, these characteristics were found positively correlated with physical and emotional exhaustion, psychosomatic conditions, alcohol and other drug abuses, mental illness, marital conflict, and even suicide. Maslach believes that these conditions are most likely to appear among health and social services professionals who are:

> Required to work intensely and intimately with people on a continuous basis. They learn about people's psychological, social and/or physical problems and are expected to provide aid or treatment of some kind. Some aspects of this job involve "dirty work" . . . tasks particularly upsetting or embarassing to perform. (Maslach & Pines, 1977, p. 100)

Certainly, many of the responsibilities of the special education teacher might be viewed as "dirty work," at least by society at large, since children are placed in special programs because they present special psychological, social, and/or physical problems. Examples of the dirty work that special educators engage in are many and varied. They include the teaching of basic self-care skills such as toilet training and eating to some physically and mentally handicapped children, and struggling with the irrational behavior of verbally and physically abusive children.

It is generally accepted that not everyone—not even every teacher—can deal successfully with these kinds of problems, which may demand some special skills and special personality traits as well. The need for special skills is addressed in certification requirements which typically involve considerable additional, or at least different, types of training than that required for regular classroom teaching. The issue of personality traits has been more difficult to address, since personality is an evasive construct, and it is not clear how it relates to coping skills.

Teachers who work with exceptional children must deal with emotions aroused by the nature of their work which may sometimes be painful, stressful, and even debilitating. If they do not develop ways of coping with these stresses, they will be unable to survive and persist in their educational efforts. A problem, however, is that the boundary between coping or positive defense mechanisms, enabling the teacher to more objectively protect against aroused emotions, and emotional detachment from students, resulting in low morale, absenteeism, and turnover, is not always distinct. It is related to the difference between empathy (or detached concern) and dehumanization. The former enables a teacher to deal objectively and effectively with students; the latter impairs those efforts.

Maslach has outlined some of the verbal and nonverbal coping techniques that are commonly employed in stressful, client-centered professions. Forms of these are also used by teachers of exceptional children, including:

• *Use of derogatory or abstract types of language*   Examples are use of such derogatory labels as "retards," "loonies," "gimps," or the use of more abstract, presumably precise, or scientific terms that intellectualize a behavior. For instance, the annoying behavior of a child may be termed "passive aggressive."

• *Compartmentalization between job and personal life*   The teacher who leaves his/her work at school, who resists thinking about or sharing his/her professional experiences at home attempts to reduce the boundaries of stressful experience by confining them to a smaller part of his/her life.

• *Withdrawal from interpersonal contact with students*   The teacher may attempt to spend as little time with students as possible by getting out of the room (e.g. withdrawing to the lounge or elsewhere), allowing less direct involvement by standing further away from student, and avoiding physical and eye contact.

• *Social techniques*   Some teachers may turn to others for advice, comfort, and tension reduction. Laughing at students' behavior or complaining about working conditions are additional coping techniques in this category.

Each of these forms of dealing with stressful job conditions may be personally helpful to a teacher's mental health up to a point. Beyond that, they become symptoms of detachment and dehumanization and are harmful to the teacher and students alike. Dehumanization of students is reflected in diminished efforts and poorer delivery of services. Additionally, the dehumanization process may lead to detachment from one's own emotions and motives, and ultimately result in burnout.

INSTITUTIONAL VARIABLES

There is evidence that, aside from possible personality factors, a number of institutional variables are related to the incidence of burnout in professions that have been studied. Included are such variables as ratio of clients to staff, length of working day, severity of clients' problems, quality of professional work relationships, and opportunities for time out. Generally, higher client to staff ratios, longer working hours (particularly in direct contact with clients), greater seriousness and chronicity of clients' problems, lack of opportunities for time out, and lack of professional work relationships are positively correlated with factors involved in burnout. Professionals who believe they are unable to adequately fulfill their duties become frustrated, and that frustration may take the form of anger directed outwardly at their clients and inwardly at themselves.

REDUCING BURNOUT

It would be desirable, in selecting individuals as teachers of exceptional children, to identify those persons who will be resilient and capable in stressful situations. Unfortunately, we are not at present able to do so reliably. Self selection exerts some influence, since many people recognize that they would have difficulty coping with exceptional children; others are screened out by teacher preparation programs, particularly during student teaching experiences. Yet these forms of prescreening do not ensure that teachers will be able to handle all the stressful situations they encounter. Even highly competent, successful teachers may experience burnout.

Since preservice screening is impractical and in fact, does not speak to the issue of burnout on the job, an alternate approach would be to reduce the job related conditions that encourage burnout. Based upon the established influence of institutional variables, a number of specific suggestions could be made. These include:

- *Reduction of student-teacher ratio*   The intent of state guidelines governing student-teacher ratios is to account for the extra "burdens" exceptional students may provide for teachers. There are no established best ratios, and what is appropriate or ideal depends upon a number of factors, including the nature and severity of handicaps, setting, delivery model, support services, and teacher characteristics. Nevertheless, there is some consensus of approximately what these ratios should be. When teachers become overwhelmed with unreasonable caseloads, they become frustrated in their efforts to provide appropriate programs for the students. The potential for abuse may be especially great with itinerant, resource, and consulting teachers whose caseloads are not so clearly defined. Regular classroom teachers who integrate exceptional students into their programs can be compensated with reduced enrollment in light of extra demands that are placed upon them.

- *Shorter work hours*   Many teachers report that their school-day work with students constitutes only part of their responsibilities and that the planning, involvement in IEPs, staffings, parent conferences, and the like involve considerable after school and weekend time. Recent federal and state requirements are frequently viewed as piling additional duties on top of an already overburdened schedule. Consequently, ways for compensating teachers for this extra time should be explored. Possibilities are provision of teacher aides and team teachers to allow opportunities for handling some of these jobs during the regular school day, additional inservice or work days, and even shortened instructional days or weeks. Rather than reducing instructional effectiveness, the benefits of planning time and acknowledgement of the administrative tasks should actually increase the quality of instruction.

- *Opportunities for time out*   It is not unusual for special teachers, particularly in self-contained public school programs, to have continuous and total responsibility for their students from the time they arrive at school until they leave. It is probably beneficial to get away occasionally and to break the routine of intense interactions. Again, the provision of aides and team teachers can provide this relief.

Time out does not have to be teacher lounge time, although this can be a legitimate activity. Time out may be used for attending staffings, contacting parents, and doing paper work. Other types of time out that should be considered are the provision of "mental health" days, when teachers may choose to stay away from school; sabbaticals for professional growth and training; and leaves of absence. Attendance at local and national professional meetings can not only facilitate professional development and growth, but can also provide opportunities for sharing, support, and time out from routines.

• *Sharing the student load*   Frequently, special education teachers "go it alone." Their classes may be physically isolated from programs similar to their own, and consequently, they may be without opportunities for sharing ideas, frustrations, and responsibilities. The team teaching mentioned earlier and the clustering of special programs in schools would allow for a greater flexibility for sharing responsibilities as well as for time out. An additional advantage of such programs for both students and teachers would be greater possibilities for interclass grouping, so that teachers could work with students with similar skills and behavior.

• *Training to deal with stress*   Not enough attention has been paid in either pre- or inservice education to dealing with the stresses of teaching exceptional children. Teachers may be well versed in characteristics of their students and methods for dealing with them, but not with the psychological and physical strain they themselves may experience. Consequently, teachers frequently feel that they are the only ones who face these problems, that they lack skills for coping, and that their problems are due to personal weaknesses. Teacher preparation programs should specifically address the conflicts that inevitably arise and the concomitant emotions and reactions that result.

• *Taking precautions as individuals*   Independent of institutional efforts to curb burnout, individual teachers must also develop awareness of stress-producing conditions in their work and become attuned to signs of impending burnout. This awareness may include acknowledging personal vulnerabilities and setting realistic standards of performance. It may also mean that special teachers, who devote so much time and effort to meeting the needs of others, must learn to attend to their own needs by cultivating a life away from the job, and displaying assertiveness in demanding institutional conditions that reduce burnout.

The issue of burnout is one of vital importance to all educators today. As more and more professionals are needed in this field, we cannot afford to waste the skills of competent, qualified teachers through institutional mishandling and lack of support. Teacher educators, school administrators, and teachers themselves must work together to create a climate that addresses the mental health needs of students and teachers alike.

REFERENCES

Maslach, C., & Jackson, S. E. Burned-out cops and their families. *Psychology Today*, 1979 (May), 59–62.

Maslach, C., & Pines, A. The burnout syndrome in a day care setting. *Child Care Quarterly*, 1977, *6*, 100-113.

Pines, A., & Maslach, C. Characteristics of staff burnout in mental health settings. *Hospital and Community Psychiatry*, 1978, *29*, 233–237.

Is Teaching Hazardous to Your Health?

Leanna Landsmann

Two years ago *Instructor*, a magazine for elementary school teachers, took this question to a number of governmental agencies, insurance companies, medical groups, university research facilities, and teachers' organizations. We got a startling answer. Ample health data were available on a number of other professional groups, but no one knew of studies on the effects of teaching on teachers.

To find at least some of the answers to our questions, *Instructor*, with the cooperation of the American School Health Association (ASHA), decided to ask the nearly 300,000 readers of the magazine some questions on teacher health by publishing a questionnaire in the September 1976 issue. More than 9,000 teachers responded.

The questionnaire contained both questions that could be answered with yes or no or some other simple word and questions that required a sentence or short paragraph for adequate response. Ninety-eight percent of the respondents took time to complete all questions. Many questionnaires were accompanied by a letter or extra notes.

Although this was a limited survey that did not use a scientific sample, nevertheless, the responses do give some indication of the condition of teacher health.

Let's begin by looking at the responses to the yes/no or single answer questions, then discuss them along with the information from the longer answers.

Sex? Female, 89%. Male, 11%. (Men were underrepresented among our respondents. About a third of all classroom teachers—and 17 percent of elementary teachers—are men.)

Is your school rural? 33%. Suburban? 38%. Urban? 27%.

Including preparation, how many hours do you work per day? 10.

How many hours of sleep do you average a night? 7½.

How many days were you absent last year because of illness? 4.5.

Were any of those days stress- or tension-related? No 25%, Yes 75%.

Do you ever call in sick for reasons of fatigue or nervous strain? No 65%, Yes 35%.

Landsmann, Leanna. Is teaching hazardous to your health? *Today's Education*, 1978, 67(2), 48–50. Reprinted by permission.

Have you been absent from school for an extended period (more than 10 days) in the last five years? No 82%, Yes 18%.

Did you have a cold last year? No 19%, Yes 81%. Flu? No 64%, Yes 36%.

Do you have a chronic health problem? No 73%, Yes 27%.

Have you ever been accidentally injured in school during the last five years? No 87%, Yes 13%.

Does the physical environment of your school negatively affect your health? No 65%, Yes 35%.

Do you currently take prescription drugs? No 60%, Yes 40%.

Have you ever had psychiatric treatment? No 93%, Yes 7%.

Has your view of teaching changed since you began? No 20%, Yes 80%.

Do you believe there are health hazards in teaching? No 16%, Yes 84%.

Does your principal take an active role in helping teachers stay physically and mentally healthy? No 61%, Yes 39%.

On a 1 (poor)-to-10 (excellent) scale how would you rate the following:

	Poor/Fair	Good/Excellent
Health during the school year	22%	78%
Health in the summer	4%	96%
Ability to cope with stress	23%	77%
Resistance to colds and flu	36%	64%
Attention to proper diet	33%	67%
Attention to exercise and keeping in shape	43%	57%

First, we note that 84 percent of teachers responding believe there are health hazards in teaching. The questions that elicited open-ended answers isolated three major areas of health concern—stress; weight, diet and exercise; and physical environment. We'll examine each area in some detail.

Stress   Over and over, teachers named stress (tension, pressure) as the major force affecting their health. The tension arose from predictable sources: large class sizes, lack of teaching materials, increase in discipline problems over the past few years, more public pressures on teachers, schedules that permit few breaks or none. In many localities, elementary teachers are still fighting for duty-free lunch. The schools of some large cities have a rule that primary children may not be left unattended. For teachers without aides, this often means that even bathroom breaks are a major problem.

Another source of stress teachers noted is the difficulty they have in accepting that there are limits to what schooling can achieve. A good teacher can't solve all a child's problems, but many equate acknowledging that with giving up. Many wish they could learn to leave the day's problems and frustrations at school. Several mentioned lack of general in-service education or of specific preparation for new programs, such as integrating the handicapped into the regular school program, as causes of undue stress. Others cited the trend to make the schools (thus the teachers) the major problem-solving agents of society.

A Syracuse, New York, teacher pointed out: "We're asked to assume broader roles, yet we are more and more criticized by the public. Areas once covered by the family and church (such as sex education and moral education) are now plopped on the teacher's lap. We're even administering breakfast programs. The same parents who are demanding that we go back to the basics (reading and math) also want us to teach their children discipline, to teach them right from wrong. It's no wonder more and more experienced teachers are leaving the profession. To do all these things without support is demoralizing."

Teachers recognize that too much stress and tension can lead to physical problems. Indeed, doctors acknowledge that many of the chronic problems teachers listed—headaches; allergies; colds; postnasal drip; hypertension; bladder, bowel, and kidney problems; colitis; "nervous stomach"; acne; and overweight—are often related to tension.

WEIGHT, DIET, AND EXERCISE

According to their responses, staying the right weight, achieving proper nutrition, and getting enough exercise are teachers' next most important health concerns. About 60 percent eat breakfast—typically, coffee, fruit juice, and toast. Forty percent have only coffee or no breakfast at all.

Lunch is a source of frustration. Only 25 percent buy lunch in the school cafeteria; the rest bring their own or skip lunch. A surprising number wish schools would provide a salad bar with fruit, vegetables, and high-protein sandwiches. Several want the junk-food machines in the teachers lounges removed.

Along with worry about weight comes concern for proper exercise. Many teachers suggest that an exercise period be set aside after school when they can use the gym and pool facilities.

Physical Environment   As the results show, more than one-third of the respondents feel that the physical environment of the school negatively affects their health. Most of the comments about environment had to do with temperature control in the classrooms. Many teachers mentioned lack of individually controlled thermostats in even new schools. Many old schools are drafty and poorly insulated. Some rooms in modern schools that have large expanses of glass for their outside walls become infernos when the sun strikes them or Arctic with uncontrolled air conditioning. During cold weather, teachers said, they are forced to teach with the drapes or blinds closed to retain heat.

Teachers also complained of poor lighting, flickering, fluorescent lights, or too much glare; poor acoustics or too much noise from the neighborhood; cold cement floors, dirty classrooms, and smoked-filled teachers lounges.

A surprising facet of the responses to the environmental question concerned injuries at school. Rather than falls, accidents closing windows, or the like, children caused most of the injuries cited. Children have bitten and scratched teachers, belted them when they were breaking up fights, and caused them both deliberate and accidental playground injuries.

After the questions about health concerns, we asked, "If you could do one thing to improve the health of you and your colleagues, what would that be?" The range of responses was surprisingly narrow. Noting that good health has to do with attitude and morale as well as disease, teachers strongly stated that principals could do much to improve teacher health in any school.

A subtabulation showed that the 39 percent of teachers responding *yes* to the question, "Does your principal take an active role in helping teachers stay mentally and physically healthy?" enjoy demonstrably better health than the 61 percent responding *no*.

Teachers are placing some responsibility for their health in principals' hands because principals can influence so many of the causes of health troubles. Principals can offer more positive reinforcement; help with curriculum decisions, especially controversial ones; act as buffers; and aid teachers in improving school/community relations. They can help reduce class size, foster more open communication among staff members, provide adequate in-service preparation for such programs as integrating the handicapped, sign the work orders to fix drafty windows, and enforce policies that keep sick children home until they are well.

Lillian Bernhagen, past president of the ASHA, who has observed teacher health for 24 years, agrees that the role of the principal is crucial. "You can't separate the mental and physical health problems in teaching. If teachers work in a school with a principal who creates a supportive environment, they will most likely feel positively reinforced and emotionally rewarded.

"But where a principal criticizes and never compliments, morale will drop and teacher absenteeism will increase. Teachers become emotionally exhausted and starved for positive reinforcement. Not long after comes some physical manifestation of frustration and stress."

In spite of teachers' numerous health problems, however, the outlook is bright. Teachers are taking their concerns into their own hands. Some groups are organizing after-school hobby and exercise programs. Several have written to say that either in teacher centers or in informal rap sessions they are beginning to share and solve the problems that plague them. From those sessions come not only the knowledge that "you're not alone," as one teacher put it, but shared joys and positive reinforcement as well.

In some localities, teachers are proposing the district-wide health provisions suggested by Stephen Jerrick of the ASHA:

- Annual physical examinations
- A district physician or medical consultant whom employees can contact for advice
- Access to counseling from a psychiatrist or psychologist
- A preventive medical program with screening and referral for hypertension, diabetes, obesity, alcoholism, and tuberculosis
- Smoking cessation programs
- A breast examination program

- In-service workshops on specific health problems such as proper nutrition, children's illnesses, and stress-release techniques.

What can an individual teacher do about his or her health? First, realize that health is a dynamic state—different for every individual, changing throughout a lifetime. Health is physical and mental well-being, not merely the absence of disease. To be a healthy teacher, suggests Vivian K. Harlin, M. D., director of health services for the Seattle Public Schools, form these habits:

- Have regular medical and dental examinations.
- Eat nutritious and well-balanced meals, and maintain your recommended weight.
- Exercise—20 minutes daily or, at least, 30 minutes three times a week.
- Get sufficient rest.
- Stand, sit, and walk with good posture—not only is it better for your body, but it projects an image of confidence.
- Maintain a positive attitude. Do not let personal problems carry over into the classroom. Talk them out with a spouse, confidant, or doctor.
- Do something every day to pamper yourself. You deserve it—if you aren't good to yourself, who will be? Make time for hobbies, friends, and special projects.
- Analyze your feelings about your job performance. If you're not happy, why aren't you? Maybe you need to find new approaches and methods, attend classes, change jobs, change subject areas, or observe other teachers or schools.

Strategies for Dealing with Burnout among Special Educators

Stan Shaw
Jeffrey M. Bensky
Benjamin Dixon
Rob Bonneau

Burnout can be defined as the end result of unsuccessful attempts to cope with a variety of negative stress conditions. The stresses identified by general education personnel focus on the students. These include vandalism, changing school populations, school violence, and class size (McGuire, 1979; Stevenson & Milt, 1975). The stressful conditions for special educators, on the other hand, seem to relate to the manner in which Public Law 94-142 has been

Shaw, Stan, Bensky, Jeffrey M., Dixon, Benjamin, and Bonneau, Rob. Strategies for dealing with burnout among special educators. *Education Unlimited*, 1980, 2(14), 21–23. Reprinted by permission.

implemented in the period 1975 to 1980 (Bensky, Shaw, Gouse, Bates, Dixon & Beane, 1980).

Stress may create a positive (heightened awareness, improved functioning) or negative (flight, fear, exhaustion) response. Current indications are that stress reactions of special educators are resulting in rapid staff turnover, interpersonal problems among professional groups (e.g., regular and special educators and administrators), and resistance to change (D'Alonzo & Wiseman, 1978; Morsink, Blackhurst, & Williams, 1979; Ryor, 1978). In addition, nonproductive approaches to dealing with stress used by special educators have been found to include providing less direct service to children, lowering expectations for students, taking drugs (liquor, pills) as well as resigning (Dixon, Shaw & Bensky, 1980). It is clear that these nonproductive approaches to dealing with stress result in a reduction in the quantity and quality of services provided to handicapped students. They are also testimony to the physical, psychological, and spiritual exhaustion of increasing numbers of special educators.

STRESSORS

In an attempt to evaluate whether Public Law 94-142 is related to burnout, data were collected from educators in Connecticut (Bensky, Shaw, Gouse, Bates, Dixon & Beane, 1980). The data indicated that the best predictors of perceived stress for special educators were "clear-role expectations and discrepancy between teacher's perception of the role vs. other's expectations of the teacher's role." Therefore, the better the special educator understood the job expectations, the more perceived stress was decreased. On the other hand, the perception of job-related stress was increased by a discrepancy between special educators' expectations and others' expectations for their educational roles. It is important to note that the two role clarity variables had more impact on stress than did all the task-specific stressors.

The task factors creating stress for special educators included job related work after hours, writing IEPs, due process paperwork, working with parents, pupil load, diagnosis, and dealing with other teachers.

It is important for supervisors and administrators to know that the variability of the data indicated that stressful factors will differentially affect staff members. Individuals certainly have varied capacities to deal with stress and different roles. Special class and resource room teachers have varying kinds and degrees of stress. It is necessary to assess both individual and organizational stress (Dixon, Shaw, & Bensky, 1980).

DEALING WITH THE PROBLEM

There is a growing body of literature (Gmelch, 1978; Moe, 1979; Sparks, 1979; Styles & Cavanaugh, 1977) describing approaches for persons in the helping professions to use in dealing with the problem of burnout. Recommendations generally include proper diet, physical fitness, relaxation training, and developing outside interests. We will attempt, however, to focus on particular approaches leadership personnel could consider to manage stress and prevent burnout among special educators. The approaches focus on personnel and organizational management.

The general assessment strategies recommended by Dixon, Shaw, & Bensky (1980) can be used to identify the specific groups of individuals or elements of the organization which require support. Approaches are suggested for evaluating the success of interventions which have been tried.

PERSONNEL MANAGEMENT

• Provide a professional and accountable means to specify the role and student load for special educators. This could be done after the individualized education programs are written for each student in the school. The special educator can then meet with the supervisor to negotiate a job description for the year. In addition to direct service (teaching contact hours with handicapped children), responsibilities for diagnosis, placement or team meetings, due process paperwork, consulting, and so on can be specified. This provides for clarification and negotiation of all role priorities/needs in a noncrisis situation. The all too typical alternative to this approach is a "battle of wills" between the administrator and special educator regarding placing another child in an overloaded program.

• Ensure that all other school personnel know and understand the agreed upon role and responsibilities for special educators. In addition, make sure that all necessary assistance is provided. Is there help available for regular classroom teachers with mainstreamed children? Are personnel available to do a thorough educational evaluation on referrals?

• When hiring new staff, provide a complete job description. Try to determine that the persons considered for the job have the ability and willingness to fulfill all the specified responsibilities. In addition, interview procedures should seek to identify persons who seem to have the personal mental health, flexibility, and willingness to learn new procedures, as required of special educators since the enactment of PL 94-142.

• New staff members should receive ongoing support during that first critical year of adjustment. A buddy system and periodic mental health meetings might be appropriate. It would be helpful to provide training in communication and small group processes as a first step.

• Provide support for staff so they may productively handle the responsibilities assigned them. Hire an aide or substitute teacher for staff required to attend placement team meetings. If a resource teacher is expected to do consulting during the school day, provide an extra aide who is prepared to teach students in the resource room. Hire extra secretarial help so that the school psychologist doesn't spend time writing reports which could be dictated, or handling other clerical responsibilities.

Although these suggestions seem to require "extra" money in these times of tight budgets and taxpayer revolts, it is our contention that they are cost efficient and effective. Using Public Law 94-142 funds for support personnel should provide for greater productivity of current staff and may lessen the need to hire new professional staff members.

• Administrators need to encourage or at least be more open to role modifications, changes, and transfers. We have noted that after 3 to 5 years, many special educators need a change in environment (it may be from resource room to special class or vice versa). In other cases, the special educators may find one particular aspect of the job (e.g., consulting or diagnosis) to be causing stress; a transfer to another building might alleviate stress caused by problems associated with certain students, colleagues, or administrators. Such changes cost no money and may increase staff productivity.

• Schools need to be positive places to both learn and work. To paraphrase a familiar behavioral cliche, "catch a teacher being good." When a teacher develops a new curriculum material, organizes a special instructional unit, teaches a good lesson, succeeds with a particularly difficult child, let that teacher know. The teacher who gives 100 percent effort each day should be told that someone cares.

Administrators can encourage parents, students, and other teachers to provide positive feedback to one another. Administrators can seek ways for staff members to be recognized for outstanding efforts or achievements and have special opportunities to learn and grow (e.g., attend conferences or workshops at school expense; plan and carry out inservice training programs for extra pay).

• Support systems must be available to educators coping with the problem of burnout in each school system. This can be formally or informally provided in a number of ways. A school system can include free, confidential counseling to staff members for job related stress as part of the fringe benefit package. One creative central office administrator with limited fiscal resources made it known that one particularly competent school psychologist was available for staff counseling as part of the job description. Another approach is to provide a comprehensive support system to deal with the total problem—physical, mental, and emotional—which might include one day seminars, extensive workshops or ongoing programs on mental health topics and treatment alternatives. (For more information, contact the Department of Health Promotion, St. Louis University Medical Center.)

Providing a total program that attends to the well being of the entire individual may be initially a costly venture. However, data are substantiating the long range benefits: a decrease in health care costs; an increase in job productivity and performance; better use of professional and personal resources. The fact that the business sector is providing this kind of training for its personnel should indicate the attendant benefits.

Programs that go beyond simple stress management techniques are necessary and essential. A program that promotes the entire well being of the individual is one positive alternative. Well being is a state that would include intervention concepts such as: habit control, physical fitness, positive living, stress management, and job burnout prevention.

ORGANIZATIONAL MANAGEMENT

• Develop or modify special education policies and procedures so they efficiently fulfill the requirements of Public Law 94-142, particularly those relating to the placement team process, IEPs, and least restrictive alternative. Most schools are not theoretically in "compliance" with the law; the current need is for increased efficiency to better meet the needs of handicapped students and professional staff.

• Provide time, money and staff involvement in the modification of policies as well as in the revision and streamlining of forms and routines used to carry out Public Law 94-142. Deal with concerns such as: Is a 15 page IEP necessary? Do we need all the due process forms we're currently using? Are we "overinterpreting" the mandates of the law and therefore following procedures which are neither required nor helpful?

• Encourage understanding (knowledge) and support (attitude) for those policies and procedures throughout the school system, beginning with the board of education.

To be successful, virtually all of the approaches described in this article require an inservice training component. The program should provide the necessary knowledge, attitude, and skills for all school constituencies, including the board of education, superintendents, principals, regular and special educators, and parents (for more information, see Shaw & Bensky, 1980). Also, teachers' sense of ownership of the inservice goals, objectives, and activities have been demonstrated to increase participant motivation, generalizability of information, and actual implementation of new skills, knowledge, and positive attitudes. Having the inservice participants involved in this planning may be a stress reducing activity in itself.

Various sources of support are available including Public Law 94-142, Teacher Centers, state funds (through state education agency inservice funds or competitive state grants), and federal grants (particularly the inservice training grants available through the Bureau of Education for the Handicapped).

As schools attempt to maintain effective programming for handicapped children during this time of fiscal constraint, runaway inflation, and family/societal disintegration, burnout will surely escalate. It is, therefore, important that ongoing assessment of the problem and the success of interventions aimed at dealing with it continue. The goal for leadership personnel during the 1980s will be assuring an appropriate education for each handicapped student while providing a productive and fulfilling career for regular and special educators.

REFERENCES

Bensky, J. M., Shaw, S. F., Gouse, A. S., Bates, H., Dixon, B., & Beane, W. P.L. 94-142 and stress: A problem for educators. *Exceptional Children*, 1980, *47*, 24–29.

D'Alonzo, B. J., & Wiseman, D. E. Actual and desired roles of the high school learning disability resource teacher. *Journal of Learning Disabilities*, 1978, *11*, 390–397.

Dixon, B., Shaw, S. F., & Bensky, J. M. The administrator's role in fostering the mental health of special services personnel. *Exceptional Children*, 1980, *47*, 30–36.

Gmelch, W. H. The principal's next challenge. The twentieth-century art of managing stress. *NASSP Bulletin*, 1978, *59*, 5–12.

McGuire, W. H. Teacher burnout. *Todays Education*, 1974, *64*, 5.

Moe, D. A. prescription. *Todays Education*, 1979, *64*, 35–36.

Morsink, C. V., Blackhurst, A. E., & Williams, S. SOS: Follow-up support to beginning learning disabilities teachers. *Journal of Learning Disabilities*, 1979, *12*, 150–154.

Pointer, Teachers under stress: Survival techniques. Winter, 1980, 24(2).

Ryor, J. 94-142: The perspective of regular education. *Learning Disability Quarterly*, 1978, *1*, 6–14.

Shaw, S. F., & Bensky, J. M. Making inservice training work: A model personnel development program. *Education Unlimited*, 1980, 2(2), 5–9.

Sparks, D. A teacher center tackles the issue. *Todays Education*, 1979, *64*, 37–39.

Stevenson, G. S., & Milt, H. Ten tips to reduce teacher tension. *Todays Education*, 1975, *64*, 52–54.

Styles, K., & Cavanaugh, G. Stress in teaching and how to handle it. *English Journal*, 1977, *66*, 76–79.

ENABLING ACTIVITIES

To aid you to meet the objectives listed in the chapter study guide (page 221), the enabling activities listed below were designed to provide a variety of study directions and exploration activities ranging from the difficult and time-consuming to less complicated straightforward tasks. It is important that you understand that you do not have to do every enabler listed—choose only those that help you achieve a study guide objective or appeal to one of your specific interests in the chapter topic.

1 Develop a list of the most common stress-producing conditions for teachers.

2 Interview five teachers on conditions that produce stress for them.

3 Prepare a 20-minute oral presentation that lists and describes techniques for coping with stress.

4 Examine yourself for factors that produce stress.

5 Go to your library and identify stressful conditions in professions other than teaching.

6 Prepare a paper for special education students identifying coping strategies for coping with stress.

7 Develop a checklist identifying the existence of stress in individuals.

8 Go to your library and look up all the references dealing with stress.

SELF-TEST

True-False

1 Excessive stress and physical/emotional exhaustion could lead to an inability of the individual to cope, contributing to burnout.

2 Deviant student behavior is the major cause of burnout in educators.

3 Teachers of the 1930s identified stressors that are similar to those faced by present-day educators.

4 A Type B person can eliminate the chances of a heart attack by slowing down their lifestyle.

5 Short-term coping skills are generally more beneficial because stress will not accumulate.

6 Special educators are preoccupied with personal stressors more than regular educators.

7 An environmental stressor that is unique to special educators is lack of support from regular education and other special educators.

8 Perceived job expectations is related to accompanying stress; the more realistic the perceptions, the less stress.

9 Indices, such as those in this chapter, help a person to rank her/his priorities.

10 Laughter is sometimes the best medicine for tension.

11 "Playing hooky" may not always be a bad idea when things start piling up.

12 Once a coping strategy works successfully, you can return to it when a similar situation arises again.

13 Children can be affected negatively by a burned-out teacher.

14 Prevention is the best way to deal with burnout.

Multiple-Choice

15 An environmental stressor least reported by teachers is:
   (a) time pressures
   (b) violence and vandalism
   (c) parents
   (d) daily interruptions

16 A personal factor that does not influence coping strategies is:
   (a) racial background
   (b) personality
   (c) physical/mental well-being
   (d) all of the above

17 Which of the following is an example of a personal stressor?
   (a) death of a family pet
   (b) your birthday
   (c) going on a diet
   (d) clock-watching

18 An example of stress experienced by special educators would be:
   (a) trying to schedule time for IEP meetings
   (b) unpredictable outbursts by students
   (c) constant supervision of students
   (d) all of the above

19 Which of the following is not a symptom warning you of a potential burnout?
  (a) sleeping late
  (b) apathy
  (c) eating less
  (d) ulcers

20 Which of the following would not reduce stress for the special educator?
  (a) an aide to do nonteaching duties
  (b) more interaction with colleagues
  (c) high expectations for student's growth
  (d) less contact with students

ANSWERS
TO CHAPTER SELF-TESTS

One

1. F
2. F
3. T
4. T
5. F
6. F
7. F
8. T
9. F
10. F
11. F
12. A
13. D
14. A
15. C
16. B

Two

1. F
2. F
3. T
4. T

5. F
6. F
7. F
8. A
9. D
10. C
11. D
12. B
13. C
14. B
15. D

Three

1. T
2. F
3. T
4. F
5. T
6. T
7. T
8. T
9. F
10. T

11. T
12. F
13. F
14. F
15. T

Four

1. T
2. F
3. F
4. F
5. T
6. F
7. F
8. F
9. T
10. T
11. F
12. T
13. C
14. D
15. C

16. A
17. C
18. B
19. B
20. A

Five

1. T
2. F
3. T
4. F
5. F
6. F
7. F
8. T
9. F
10. F
11. F
12. T
13. T

14. T
15. F

Six

1. F
2. T
3. T
4. F
5. T
6. T
7. F
8. F
9. T
10. T
11. F
12. T
13. T
14. F
15. A
16. C
17. D
18. B

19. B
20. D

Seven

1. T
2. F
3. T
4. F
5. F
6. F
7. T
8. T
9. F
10. T
11. T
12. F
13. T
14. T
15. B
16. A
17. D
18. D
19. A
20. C

INDEX

Italic letters next to page numbers indicate that the reference is to be found in an illustration *(i)* or a table *(t)*.

Date Due